EARNED VALUE MANAGEMENT

Using Microsoft® Office Project

A Guide for Managing Any Size Project Effectively

Sham Dayal, PMP

J.ROSS PUBLISHING

ISBN-10: 1-932159-98-1
ISBN-13: 978-1-932159-98-1

Printed and bound in the U.S.A. Printed on acid-free paper
10 9 8 7 6 5 4 3 2

Library of Congress Cataloging-in-Publication Data

Dayal, Sham, 1972-
    Earned value management using Microsoft Office Project : a guide for
managing any size project effectively / by Sham Dayal.
        p. cm.
    Includes index.
    ISBN 978-1-932159-98-1 (pbk. : alk. paper)
    1. Microsoft Project. 2. Project management--Computer programs. I.
Title.
    HD69.P75D395 2008
    658.4'04028553--dc22   2008017551

Phone: (954) 727-9333
Fax: (561) 892-0700
Web: www.jrosspub.com

To my wife, Shailaja, and my daughter, Jyothsna,

who gave me support while I spent endless hours, day after day, writing.

To all of the people who encouraged me to write this book. The writing journey

was exciting.

May project managers across the world benefit from this book and the tool.

CONTENTS

PREFACE

In the life cycle of a project, achieving effective schedule and cost management is essential. Yet, many projects fail because of ineffective management of these two essential components—even with the widespread use of Microsoft® Office Project (MPP) and earned value management (EVM) techniques.

MPP is the most commonly used tool for schedule management and EVM is the most commonly used technique for cost management. EVM is mandated for most government projects in the United States, and expectations are that other countries will soon follow suit. Unfortunately, a popular myth exists among some project managers that EVM can be (or should be) used only for large projects—and that EVM will *only* be effective if a project is *large enough*.

This book will dispel the myth about EVM and project management and show readers how EVM can be effectively applied to any type of project—whether small or large—with the same rigor as that used for a large, critically important project. Budding or experienced project managers at all levels will find this book useful because it facilitates gaining a greater understanding of the total concept of schedule and cost management through the use of EVM. The book contains practical discussions and is a guide for complete end-to-end schedule and cost management using MPP and the EVM reporting tools. Numerous new tips are also included which enhance the use of MPP and the EVM reporting tools.

One of the many important features of this book is the tool that comes with it. This tool will help project managers to more effectively manage their projects and enable them to take necessary corrective and/or preventive action *before* a project fails. Readers receive a CD containing a full version of *EVM Report Template for Projects*, which is licensed for 6 months. *EVM Report Template for Projects* is a tool to track and report the status and progress of projects using EVM techniques (a $99.50 value). (Note: Purchasers of this book who are interested in obtaining a fully licensed version of this tool may purchase it at a 50% discount from www.connoizor.com by keying in a discount code of BOOKDISCOUNT. Customer support is provided by the Connoizor staff for both the full version which is licensed for 6 months and the fully licensed version of the software. All inquiries or difficulties encountered that are related to the 6-month trial version or the fully licensed version of the software should be directed to support@connoizor.com.)

A feature that may be important to many readers is that this book is aligned with the *Practice Standard for Earned Value Management* (published by Project Management Institute, Newtown Square, PA, U.S.), which is now the accepted EVM standard for ANSI (The American National Standards Institute, Washington, DC, U.S.).

Earned Value Management Using Microsoft® Office Project: A Guide for Managing Any Size Project Effectively has been written with the intent that readers will benefit significantly from its contents in their day-to-day project management activities. If I have achieved this objective, please spread the word about the benefits of using EVM for any type of project to help ensure a successful outcome.

—**Sham Dayal, PMP**

ACKNOWLEDGMENTS

I greatly appreciate the increased knowledge and perspective that I have received from Project Management Institute (PMI) and the Project Management Professional (PMP) credential process. I have been able to apply this knowledge and perspective to my personal project management activities successfully. The ideas presented in this book are largely a result of lessons learned and from reading PMI® publications.

I am also indebted to my organization, MphasiS, *An EDS Company*, which provided guidance to enable me to achieve the PMP credential as well as a platform in which I could apply the techniques described in this book in project management activities. I also appreciate the encouragement received to improve my project management skills.

ABOUT THE AUTHOR

Sham Dayal is a certified Project Management Professional (PMP), a postgraduate in Applied Statistics, and a graduate in Computer Science who has over 13 years of practical experience in the information technology industry. He currently holds a program management position with MphasiS BFL Limited, a leading application, business process outsourcing, and infrastructure technology outsourcing services company with over 25,000 employees. MphasiS BFL is an Electronic Data Systems (EDS) company which is based in Bangalore, India, with operations in the United States, Europe, Asia Pacific, Japan, and the Middle East. Sham is also co-founder of Connoizor Software Pvt. Ltd., a company specializing in software tools and templates, project execution, and product development.

During the course of his career as a practitioner, Mr. Dayal has executed numerous successful IT projects. At MphasiS, he was the first to successfully implement earned value management for project tracking (progress, status, and forecasting). He was also instrumental in creating a unique technique for tracking the progress of production support projects. This new technique, which is based on the EVM concept, won a Quality Knowledge Excellence Award from MphasiS. Mr. Dayal has spoken and written articles about EVM pertaining to more effective project life cycle management which have been recognized and published in leading journals and in the Project Management Institute's *PMI ISSIG Review*. He is an active member of Project Management Institute and the Bangalore PMI chapter.

Mr. Dayal has been managing projects with EVM and Microsoft® Office Project using innovative techniques for quite some time, with significantly improved execution results. It is the author's hope that this book and the EVM tool included with it will help other project management practitioners to achieve similar results.

AN INTRODUCTION TO THE CHAPTERS

Chapter 1, **EVM in Project Management**, is an introduction to the purpose and goals of the book. It discusses common problems faced by project managers in executing projects around the world and across different domains and provides an overview of the solutions that can be implemented to overcome these problems. In addition, a summary of the EVM report template, included with this book as a CD-ROM, and its various features are presented. This invaluable tool can help you forecast future project performance based on current period status using the EVM technique and data about your project from Microsoft® Office Project plan (MPP).

Chapter 2, **Schedule Management**, is an introduction to a schedule and the basic elements involved in creating and implementing it, including work breakdown structure (WBS), estimates, resources, resource costs, and task dependencies. Each of these elements is comprehensibly defined and the methods and techniques involved in compiling these elements from various sources of project information are discussed. Chapter 2 also explains the steps involved in creating a WBS, the methods and techniques used to arrive at the estimates for a schedule, the work involved in estimating the number of resources needed for a project, and the details of assigning resource costs and task dependencies.

Chapter 3, **What Is EVM?**, starts with an overview of the EVM technique used for monitoring projects and then proceeds to the calculations of the different EVM performance measures. It details the entire set of performance measures used in the EVM technique (these measures are aligned with PMI's *Standards for Earned Value Management*, which is also the standard for ANSI). Using a case study that runs throughout the chapter, it details the basic elements of the EVM technique: earned value (EV), planned value (PV), and actual cost (AC). Other performance measures, such as budget at completion (time) and to-complete cost performance index, are also explained using their calculation formulas and practical examples of the calculations. After reading chapter 3, you will understand the entire EVM technique and be able to relate the performance measures to practical problems faced in your projects.

Chapter 4, **Why EVM?**, discusses why the EVM technique should be used to monitor a project and report its status. It outlines the various advantages that are derived from using the EVM technique alongside MPP to improve the management of a project. Interesting benefits unique to this book, which will provide a fresh perspective about how the techniques can be used, are explained. Chapter 4 presents how a project manager can save time in monitoring the progress of a project, using the weekly status report to forecast future project status and reduce variance, and how to take total control of a project status to enable continuous improvement.

Chapter 5, **Creating a Schedule**, illustrates how to create a schedule using MPP in a concise, step-by-step, logical approach. It describes the various options in MPP and how they can be used efficiently to create a schedule. MPP has numerous capabilities that are not sufficiently understood and therefore not used by project managers. Chapter 5 addresses this issue and shows how to create an effective schedule quickly by using the suggested advice and tips that will benefit both the new and experienced project managers. After presenting the information for the various aspects of schedule setup, the steps are then bulleted at the end of each section for quick reference. By the end of the chapter, you will know how to create a highly functional schedule using MPP.

Chapter 6, **Setting Up the EVM Report Template**, presents how to set up the EVM report template using the CD-ROM included with the book. It provides essential information about correctly building the template to suit the needs of each project so that tracking and monitoring the project are effective and, at the same time, the status of the project can be easily reported to project stakeholders. At the end of this chapter, you will be able to construct the EVM report template using your project's details and data, configure it for use based on the project's requirements, and start tracking and forecasting the schedule with MPP.

Chapter 7, **Tracking Progress in the Schedule**, explores the most important aspect of schedule management—tracking project progress. Tracking progress is actually more important than creating a schedule because only by tracking progress can a project be effectively managed and the necessary corrective and/or preventive actions be taken. Chapter 7 walks you through the various techniques of tracking schedule progress and, by the end of this chapter, you will be able to choose an appropriate tracking method for your project. It includes a discussion about translating project progress into the EVM report template so that the EVM technique can be used for tracking and reporting the status of a project. You will be equipped with the knowledge required to successfully track schedule progress and to recognize and manage the various nuances likely to be encountered during tracking.

Chapter 8, **Monitoring the Schedule**, describes how progress in a schedule can be easily monitored using MPP and the EVM report template. It provides an understanding of the performance measures that need to be checked in a schedule and how to read the various graphs that can be drawn using the EVM performance measures. Each graph depicts different information about the project. Chapter 8 discusses how to interpret the graphs so that the necessary action can be taken. It also shows how to record the findings for each period and then store the data internally in the EVM report template for use later—during the next stage in a project or at the end of the project to derive lessons learned. At the end of chapter 8, you will be acquainted with all of the graphs in the EVM report template and the methods for monitoring a schedule.

Chapter 9, **Additional Schedule Management Techniques**, explains additional techniques which are beneficial in a schedule management endeavor. For example, it shows how to quickly switch from a macro-level of management to a micro-level using MPP and the EVM report template to reveal the resources that are affecting the schedule in both a positive or negative manner. The EVM report template provides a macro-level perspective of a project; however, at times, when a project is in trouble, a project manager will need to switch to a micro-level perspective to address the problem. Chapter 9 describes how to select an underperforming performance measure (e.g., the schedule) and drill down to see which tasks are affecting the current status of this underperforming performance measure using MPP. Having this ability enables a project manager to take a closer look at the problem and then make the informed, appropriate decision needed to bring the project back on track.

Appendix A, **EVM for Production Support**, explains a methodology for using EVM techniques to measure and monitor team performance on production support issues.

Appendix B, **Schedule Management—An End-to-End Example**, provides an example of complete end-to-end tracking of a project using MPP and the EVM report template supplied with this book.

Appendix C, **EVM Template Quick Guide**, provides you with a quick reference that may be used after reading the text. It briefly covers five key processes of the software that is supplied with this book and indicates the chapters which contain in-depth coverage of each process. These five key processes are steps for the setup of the: EVM report template;

MPP prerequisites; EVM data sheet update; periodic updating of the EVM report template; and periodic status/progress review.

 Web Added Value™

Free value-added materials available from
the Download Resource Center at www.jrosspub.com

At J. Ross Publishing we are committed to providing today's professional with practical, hands-on tools that enhance the learning experience and give readers an opportunity to apply what they have learned. That is why we offer free ancillary materials available for download on this book and all participating Web Added Value™ publications. These online resources may include interactive versions of material that appears in the book or supplemental templates, worksheets, models, plans, case studies, proposals, spreadsheets, and assessment tools, among other things. Whenever you see the WAV™ symbol in any of our publications, it means bonus materials accompany the book and are available from the Web Added Value™ Download Resource Center at www.jrosspub.com.

Downloads available for *Earned Value Management Using Microsoft® Office Project: A Guide for Managing Any Size Project Effectively* consist of an EVM report template user manual for the software included with the book, a project schedule created using Microsoft Office Project and the techniques explained within the book, an EVM PowerPoint presentation, and valuable Excel tables with defined formulas for each of the EVM calculations demonstrated in the book. These downloads are available from the Web Added Value™ Download Resource Center at www.jrosspub.com.

1

EVM IN PROJECT MANAGEMENT

Project managers worldwide face numerous project management hurdles. Apart from routine project management issues, a project manager is often faced with the challenge of a project that is incurring cost and schedule overruns. More often than not, cost and schedule overruns are not realized until after a project has ended or has been terminated because of these problems. Although both the client and the vendor have roles in cost and schedule overruns, project managers often do not have objective evidence of the exact causes.

Project managers spend significant time and energy in preparing, updating, and showing the status of a project at any point in time. Some tasks might go on hold many times before they are completed due to dependencies with the client, suppliers, and other external agencies, but project managers have no effective mechanism to account for these delays and/or to report actual schedule or cost overruns.

The earned value management (EVM) technique coupled with thorough planning and effective use of Microsoft® Office Project plan (MPP) will eliminate this problem and enable reporting of actual schedule and cost overrun parameters at any given point in time with ease. (Note: For simplicity, throughout this book Microsoft® Office Project plan will be referred to as MPP.) To facilitate this effort, the author has created a tool which will enable any project manager to apply the EVM technique in managing projects of any size. The EVM tool which is included with this book provides an effective mechanism to track project status and progress and allows a project manager to forecast the future state of a project based on the current status.

COMMON PROJECT MANAGEMENT ISSUES

Most project managers can easily relate to the following list of commonly encountered project management problems:

- A schedule or effort overrun which was not reported until after project deliverables were delivered to a client
- An overall project schedule or effort overrun which was unknown until a project was at the end of completion
- A schedule or effort overrun for a project (generally calculated as an average of the schedule overrun of tasks) which gave a wrong impression
- Lack of available information about schedule and effort parameters at a given point in time
- Calculated schedule overruns which had no way of excluding a hold period on a task, resulting in a huge schedule overrun that should not have been attributed to the project
- Resource/task links using the **Predecessor** field in MPP which became a very time-consuming activity
- Updates to MPP which required almost half of the project manager's time
- Project plan monitoring which became a tedious job using the filters in MPP and the need to deal with dates for calculations

THE SOLUTION

The common project management issues from the list above would obviously benefit from a solution which would enable a project manager to overcome these issues and thereby ensure a smooth delivery of projects. A solution is now available which includes the following:

- EVM
- Deliverables oriented WBS
- Use of the **Priority** field for sequencing tasks in MPP
- Automatic resource leveling in MPP based on priority and standard leveling heuristics

THE EVM REPORTING TOOL

The EVM report template included on a CD-ROM with this book can be used to report project status and project progress and also to forecast future project performance based on current period performance. The reporting period for the EVM report template can be customized to any reporting period, e.g., weekly, fortnightly, monthly, or bimonthly.

Most of the information needed for the EVM report template comes from MPP. However, MPP must be prepared in a specific way to enable data collection to update the EVM report template. For the EVM report template tool to operate correctly, there are two *mandatory* prerequisites:

1. A clear WBS (work breakdown structure) must be prepared with the top-level activity being the project and the second-level activities being phases of the project (or some other type of task as required by the project).

2. The schedule should be tracked using the **Duration** column. Effort should be tracked using the **Work** column. (Note: Using the **Work** and **Duration** columns is discussed in greater depth in Chapter 5.)

The EVM report template contains the following sheets/screens:

Project details. The project details sheet is used for configuring information such as company name, project name, and project start and end dates. The project details sheet is also used as a main menu sheet. All sheets can be accessed from the project details sheet, and all subsequent sheets have a link back to this sheet.

Configuration. The configuration sheet is used once—for setting up the EVM report template at the beginning of a project. The configuration sheet specifies the reporting period, additional periods, other indexes, and the method of calculating the estimate at completion (EAC). Once these values are entered, clicking on the **Setup** button will create the sheet. If a mistake is made, use the **Clear Setup** button to clear the setup and start over.

Data entry. The data entry sheet is used to enter periodic data into the EVM report template for every reporting period. Required details to be entered are percent (%) complete, earned value, actual cost, etc. This data needs to come from MPP. (Note: Details of how to obtain this data from MPP can be found in Chapter 7.)

Summary. The summary sheet contains various measures and their respective data for a current period, e.g., schedule variance, cost variance, schedule performance indicator (SPI), cost performance indicator (CPI), etc., and provides a summary of project performance for the current period. To get details for a particular status date, enter the period date in the status date field and click on **Update Status Date**. This sheet allows the recording of a performance measure, the reasons for having the performance measure, and the corrective action planned. Additionally, the history of a performance period can be stored by clicking on the **Update History** button. Reviewing the history of performance periods can be very useful when constructing the lessons learned at the end of a project.

Help on abbreviations. This sheet contains information about abbreviations used in the summary sheet.

EVM data. The EVM **Data Sheet** is the main sheet. It contains the data used for EVM calculations. Data such as percent (%) complete, planned value, earned value, and actual costs are updated automatically from the data entry sheet. If necessary, changes to these values are allowed. However, only columns in white allow editing; the rest of the sheet cannot be edited.

Performance history. The performance history sheet is used for storing the history of periodic performance data from each reporting period. This sheet keeps a record of all performance measures and the corrective and/or preventive actions taken for each reporting period. The performance history sheet can be very useful for reviewing the past history of a project at any given point in time and for providing a record from which the lessons learned may be created at the end of a project.

Earned value graph. The earned value graph is not displayed until the EVM report template has been set up using the configuration sheet. An earned value graph shows earned value based on planned value and actual cost.

Forecast ($). The forecast ($) graph is not displayed until the EVM report template has been set up using the configuration sheet. A forecast ($) graph displays the estimate at completion based on the budget at completion (also known as an S-curve graph).

Forecast (time). The forecast (time) graph is not displayed until the EVM report template has been set up using the configuration sheet. A forecast (time) graph shows the estimate at completion in weeks/months, depending on the period chosen based on the total weeks/months initially budgeted.

Forecast (index). The forecast (index) is not displayed until the EVM report template has been set up using the configuration sheet. A forecast (index) graph shows the to-complete cost performance and schedule performance indexes. The to-complete cost performance and schedule performance indexes indicate what the schedule and performance need to be going forward in the project.

Variances ($). The variances ($) graph is not displayed until the EVM report template has been set up using the configuration sheet. A variances ($) graph shows schedule variance and cost variance as measured by efforts/cost. A variances ($) graph is generally in hours/dollars, depending on the variance measured. (Note: Schedule variance measured by efforts/cost is a poor measure to use because efforts/cost drop to zero at the end of a project regardless of whether the project is on schedule or not. It is included here because this method of calculating schedule variance is the standard used in the industry.)

Variance (time). The variance (time) graph is not displayed until the EVM report template has been set up using the configuration sheet. A variance (time) graph shows schedule variance as measured in time periods, e.g., weeks, fortnights, or months.

Schedule and cost indexes. Schedule and cost indexes are not displayed until the EVM report template has been set up using the configuration sheet. A schedule and cost indexes graph shows the schedule performance indicator and the cost performance indicator for a project as of the current period. A value of 1 for these indexes indicates that schedule and cost performance are on target.

Other indexes. The other indexes graph is not displayed until the EVM report template has been set up using the configuration sheet. The other indexes graph shows additional performance measures.

Important System Requirements: The following system requirements are necessary to operate the *EVM Report Template for Projects* software tool:

Windows NT/2000/XP/2003 Server/Vista, Microsoft Excel 2003/Word 2003

READ ME FIRST INSTRUCTIONS

Setting up the EVM report template is purposely not covered until Chapter 6 of this book because of the knowledge that you will need to gain before you are ready to begin the process. However, to register and correctly enable the tool for future setup and use, you must follow several *Read Me First Instructions.* (**Important:** To register the tool, an Internet connection is required.)

Introduction. Before getting into the steps for registering and enabling the tool, it is important to understand that the CD included with this book is for installing the tool to your local PC. You will be saving the tool to your local PC for later use during the installation process. After installing the software, store the CD in a safe place in the event that you need to reinstall it. The steps for installing the tool to your local PC are as follows:

Load the CD. Load the CD included with this book into your computer. The EVM report template will appear. Double click on the template to open it. If your Excel security is currently set at **Medium** or **Low**, you will immediately receive an Excel prompt to **Enable Macros**. (Note: A setting of **Medium** is sufficient for most users.) Because the EVM template tool uses Excel macros, you must enable these macros in order to use the tool. If your Excel security is currently set at **High**, an Excel prompt will inform you that the security level needs to be changed to **Medium** or **Low**; click **OK**. To enable the macros if your security is currently set at **High**, go to Excel **Tools** > **Macro** > **Security** and set security to **Medium** or **Low** and click **OK**.

Install the tool. The next step is to install the tool to your local PC desktop. The security level changes that you have made will take effect upon saving the tool and then reopening it. To save the tool, go to Excel **File** and click on **Save As**. Save the tool to your desktop and then close the original file completely. From this point forward, you will be accessing the copy of the tool that has been saved to your desktop.

Enable macros. Now, go to the copy of the tool which has been saved to your desktop and double click on it to open the tool. You will immediately see a prompt asking if you want to enable macros. Click on **Enable Macros**. (Note: Each time you close the tool, the macros will automatically be disabled; therefore, *each time* you open the tool you will need to click on the **Enable Macros** button to use the tool.)

Install add-ins. The EVM template tool also uses two Excel **Add-ins**. You must install these add-ins to be able to use the tool. To install the add-ins, go to Excel **Tools** > **Add-ins** and select the **Analysis-Toolpak** and **Analysis-Toolpak VBA** and then click **OK**. These options are the first two listed. (Note: Although a rare occurrence, depending on how you initially installed Excel to your computer, having your Excel installation CD may be necessary in order to install the two add-ins.)

Register the tool. Upon completion of the add-ins process, click on the **Go to the Main Page** button on the cover page of the software. On the main page, click on each field and enter the information that is requested: your company name (**Company** field), then your name in both the **Company Contact** and the **Project Manager** fields, and your e-mail address. For registration purposes, the company contact name and the project manager name should be the same. After completing this process, click on the **Register for Trial** button. Remember that an Internet connection is required to register the tool. When the registration process has been completed, the tool will be enabled for use. At this point, only a limited number of screens will be accessible because most of the screens are driven by the parameters of the project which you will set up later. (Note: For readers who want to preview all of the various screens, how to create a mock setup using fictitious data will be explained after additional important user notes are given.)

Important User Notes: The cells which are enabled for data entry are color coded in white with a border. The other cells are protected elements of the tool that you are not permitted to change. If you try to enter data into any of these cells, Excel will give an error message saying that the tool is protected. Additionally, the EVM template tool is completely protected. Therefore, you are not permitted to change or add new sheets (or anything else) to the tool, but you are permitted to change the formatting of data. If desired you may create a PDF version of the report that is generated by the tool using any PDF converter tool available in the marketplace. To create a PDF version of the report generated by the tool, install the PDF converter as a printer and print to the PDF converter.

MOCK SETUP PROCESS

Before beginning this mock setup, it is *imperative* to understand the need to *clear this setup* and *delete* the data from *each and every* screen that is part of this mock setup *before* closing the tool to avoid the risk of corrupting the tool beyond repair. Instructions for this process are provided immediately after the steps for setup and viewing of the various screens.

To create a mock setup, click on **Go to the Main Page** and enter a fictitious project start date, project end date, and budgeted cost. Next go to **Configuration** and click on **Setup**. The tool will perform a limited setup to allow access to all of the various screens. The setup field will let you know when the setup is complete. Although few screens will contain any data, the screens will be available for preview.

To preview the various screens, click on **Go Back to Main Page**. On the main page you will see a number of buttons to click on to view the various screens. You will only be able to view one screen at a time. After viewing one screen, you will need to click on **Go Back to Main Page** to click on and view another screen.

When you have completed previewing the various screens, remember that it is *imperative* that you clear all of the fictitious information before closing the tool. To do this, from the main page, click on **Configuration** and then click on the **Clear Setup** button. Next, click on each and every **Delete** prompt that pops up to clear all of the screens. When this part of the process is complete, the **Setup Status** field will read **Setup Not Done !!!**. Next, click on **Go Back to Main Page** and delete the fictitious project start date, project end date, and budgeted cost from each field. The tool is now safe to close. Go to the Excel file and click on **Close**. A prompt will appear asking if you want to save the changes made to the tool. Click on **No** and finish closing the tool for future use. *Warning: Do not forget to clear setup and to delete the information from every screen prompted before closing the tool to avoid the risk of corrupting a screen or the tool, as a whole, beyond repair.*

For convenience, the *Read Me First Instructions* are also available in the software and in the free downloadable *EVM Report Template User Manual* which is available from the Web Added Value™ Download Resource Center at www.jrosspub.com.

CUSTOMER SUPPORT

For any difficulties encountered when using the EVM template tool or for queries related to the EVM template tool or MPP or any other software-related concerns, contact Connoizor Customer Support at the following e-mail address: support@connoizor.com. Do not contact J. Ross Publishing, Inc., publisher of this book. J. Ross Publishing does not provide assistance for software developed and produced by another firm or party.

2

SCHEDULE MANAGEMENT

Microsoft® Office Project plan (MPP), which has evolved over time through various releases, is a tool used worldwide by project managers for schedule management. Typically project managers spend 30 to 50% of their time creating, updating, and tracking schedules using MPP. In terms of the functionality provided, it is extensive, but all of the features are seldom used in schedule management. Instead, MPP is most commonly used to keep track of the dates of the tasks to be performed in a project. As a result, the focus is always on dates and time lines, even though MPP offers a complete end-to-end solution for managing the triple constraints of scope, cost, and time. (Note: Although other schedule management tools are available in the marketplace, the techniques presented in this book are very specific to MPP; yet they can also be applied when using the other available tools.)

Before beginning a discussion of schedule management, the project management processes are introduced and, how these processes are tied to schedule management are explained.

BASIC PROJECT MANAGEMENT PROCESSES

A typical project has five phases—planning, executing, monitoring, controlling, and closing out. Connected to these phases is a five-step project management process—plan, execute, monitor, control, and closeout when a project reaches an end. Note that the first four steps in this project management process are cyclical in nature and do not have a specified frequency (Figure 2.1). Schedule management plays an important role in the five-step management process.

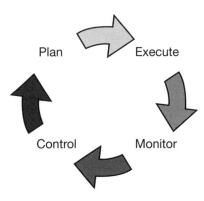

Figure 2.1. The first four steps of a five-step project management cycle.

BASIC SCHEDULE ELEMENTS

A schedule is a deliverable which is prepared during the planning phase. The schedule is then executed during the executing phase; monitored during the monitoring phase; controlled and revised during the controlling phase; and completed when the project enters the closing out phase.

A typical schedule encompasses the scope of the project, the costs involved in finishing the project, and the time required to finish the project. Scope, cost, and time are the *triple constraints* of every project. Managing the triple constraints well will almost certainly ensure project success. A schedule is comprised of the following basic elements:

- Work breakdown structure
- Effort estimates
- Resources
- Resource costs
- Task dependencies

Work Breakdown Structure

A work breakdown structure (WBS) is a hierarchical grouping of the tasks and activities to be performed in a project to produce the deliverables of the project. A WBS generally has the project at the top level, the phases in the next level, the deliverables in the third level, and the activities to produce the deliverables in the last or lowest level. A well-structured WBS is almost a necessity for all projects. Therefore, a project manager must focus on creating a well-structured WBS (Figure 2.2).

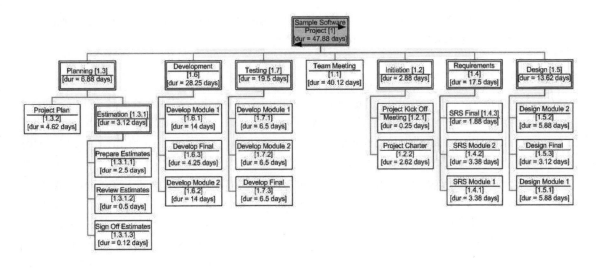

Figure 2.2. A well-structured work breakdown structure.

A WBS is produced from the scope statement (or the statement of work) and should encompass all deliverables in a project and all activities to be performed in the project. *Important:* A WBS must include all of the activities to ensure that the entire scope of the project has been covered and that nothing has been left out.

Also important is that a WBS is as granular as possible—which makes life a little tough at the beginning of the project, but is beneficial in the long run. A highly granular WBS reduces the risk of under- or overestimating the activities. In estimating, a good rule is that the smaller the activities, the more accurate the estimates will be for those activities. Yet, the 8- to 80-hour rule, which says that the tasks in a project should be within the 8- to 80-hour effort limit, must be kept in mind. Anything outside this range is considered to be unmanageable.

Many project managers tend to leave trivial activities, such as team meetings, out of a WBS. Yet if trivial activities are omitted, the expense associated with these activities, which entails a significant amount of effort, will not be tracked even though funds from the project's budget are being spent on them. Almost certainly, if trivial activities are not tracked, the project manager will have a tough time answering questions about project overruns.

WBS templates are available for different types of projects and companies. Using a company-provided WBS template is a good practice because doing so ensures that all projects done by a company have a standard WBS. A company-provided WBS template also aids consolidation of project metrics up to the company level. Additionally, a company-provided standard WBS template assists a project manager by ensuring that all activities, which might otherwise be overlooked due to human error, are covered by the WBS. A standard WBS template also evolves over time; therefore many lessons learned have already been addressed.

Effort Estimates

Estimates are the second element of a schedule. Once the WBS is ready, estimates now need to be assigned to each of the lowest-level tasks and to be rolled up to the summary level tasks and finally to the project level. Estimates must be effort estimates in units of hours or days depending on project size.

Becoming confused by effort estimates and duration estimates is not uncommon; therefore, a brief explanation of the basic difference between these two estimates will be helpful. Effort estimates are the *number of man hours/days/weeks* required to complete a task, whereas duration is the *calendar time* required to complete a task. For example, if a task requires 16 hours of effort for completion, the duration required to complete this task will be 2 calendar days, assuming that the task is completed by a single resource who has an 8-hour workday. Suppose this task is undertaken by two resources who have an 8-hour work day. Then the duration for this task would be 1 day.

In the software development industry, different mathematical models are used to arrive at estimates for a project, e.g., PERT estimation (the **p**roject **e**valuation and **r**eview **t**echnique), function point analysis, the COCOMO model (**co**nstructive **co**st **mo**del), object point estimation, etc. Likewise, other models are available for other types of industries.

One estimation technique, however, known as *bottom-up estimation*, applies to almost all projects worldwide and across different industry verticals. The prerequisite in bottom-up estimation is to have a well-structured WBS. The lowest-level activities are then assigned estimates with the help of experts in each specific area. This technique is known as bottom-up because first the work is broken down into the lowest-level activities and then estimates are assigned to the lowest-level activities and rolled up to the summary activities. Bottom-up estimates are known to be more accurate than any other form or technique of estimation.

In PERT estimation, a three-point estimate is derived: *pessimistic*, *most likely*, and *optimistic*. To eliminate some degree of human error, obtain these three estimates from three different people. The PERT formula is then applied to the three estimates to arrive at a final estimate. If the PERT estimate is applied to the bottom-up technique, the formula would be:

$$PERT\ estimate = \sum_{i=1}^{n} \left(\frac{optimistic_i + 4 \times most\,likely_i + pessimistic_i}{6} \right)$$

where n is the task number.

Resources

Resources are the third element to be included in a project schedule. Resources can be human, material, or machinery. Usually project resources are estimated from the effort estimates, duration constraints, and cost constraints. Adding additional resources to a project does not necessarily mean that the project's schedule will be shortened, but adding resources will, in fact, increase the cost of the project. Therefore, the optimal number of resources must be assigned to (or brought into) a project so that the schedule and costs are not significantly affected.

Resources are first divided into groups—human resources, material resources, and machinery. The resources are further divided into subgroups, e.g., the skills required for human resources, the types of material for material resources, and the types of machinery for machinery resources. Then these groups and subgroups of resources are applied to the WBS tasks and the effort required for each resource group is calculated. Based on the total effort for each group, the number of resources needed can be calculated.

For example, if E is the total effort needed for a subgroup of resources, h is the hours per day that the type of resource can work, and n is the number of calendar days when one resource performs the tasks after enforcing the dependencies, then N, the number of resources needed, can be estimated by using the following formula:

$$N = \frac{E}{n \times h}$$

This calculation assumes that no task will be performed by multiple persons. N is the maximum number of resources that can be assigned for a subgroup on the project—beyond this amount, adding more resources would be meaningless. However, depending on time and other constraints, N can be reduced to optimally use the resources.

Next, resource leveling and optimization are performed to arrive at the optimum resource levels in the project by duration. (Note: Performing resource leveling and optimization using MPP will be discussed in Chapter 5.) In any project, for optimal use of resources, resources must be brought in and moved out. The number of project resources

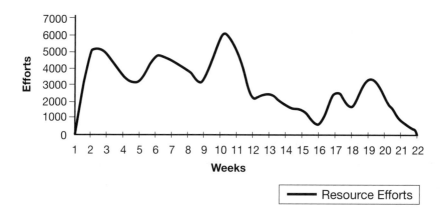

Figure 2.3. Resource efforts on a software project.

reaches a peak during the middle of a project and then declines during the end stages (Figure 2.3).

Resource Costs

Resource costs are the fourth element required in a schedule. Resource costs are an important element—they are required to obtain an accurate picture when applying the EVM technique in tracking a project. (Note: Effort instead of cost can be used when applying the EVM technique. Although using effort will not give the most accurate picture, the EVM technique can still be applied effectively using effort.)

Resource costs include the cost of human resources, materials, and machinery. In MPP, these costs must be specified in terms of rate per hour (rate/hr). If a rate/hr value for resources is not available, but instead a fixed price for a month is available, the rate/hr can be calculated by applying a formula.

For example, if R is the fixed cost per month, n is the number of working days in a month for the resource, and h is the number of working hours per day, the formula for calculating the cost per hour (cost/hr) is as follows:

$$Cost/hr = \frac{R}{n \times h}$$

When considering costs, factor in all costs in the rate/hr. The major costs will be due to the wages and salaries of the human resources. Additionally, other costs must be included to get a correct picture of the EVM metrics. For example, suppose the fixed overhead cost per seat per month for human resources is known. (For this purpose, the fixed overhead cost per seat per month is obtained from the finance department in a company.) Then cost/hr

Table 2.1. Effect of Resource Cost on Variance

Resource	Task	Rate/hr	Original Effort	Actual Effort	Variance	Cost Variance
A	1	$20	100	110	10	$200
B	2	$50	100	110	10	$500

can be calculated and added to the resources' rate/hr to obtain the final cost of the resources.

For example, if *F* is fixed monthly overhead cost per resource, *n* is the number of working days per month, and *h* is the number of working hours per day, the following formula may be used to calculate overhead cost/hr:

$$Overhead\ cost/hr = \frac{F}{n \times h}$$

When using costs, the final rate/hr to be applied is as follows:

$$Rate/hr = cost/hr + overhead\ cost/hr$$

When price is used, all calculations become simple because price has already been factored in with all other costs plus a margin. The price per hour of each type of resource is then taken and applied.

In situations in which the costs are not available for application in EVM, effort can be used instead of cost. When effort is used instead of cost, $1 is used as the cost for all resources, which will enable MPP to calculate effort instead of cost.

Important: Remember an important fact when using actual cost and effort—no two resources on a project will have the same cost to the company. For example, a junior resource working on a task has a lesser cost to a project than a senior resource. Therefore, if a junior resource takes more time to complete a task, the project might not be affected as significantly as when a senior resource uses more time to complete a task simply because the additional cost incurred for the junior resource is less than that of the senior resource.

A simple example demonstrates this situation. Resource A is a junior resource who has been assigned to Task 1 with an effort of 100 hours; Resource B is a senior resource who has been assigned to Task 2 with an effort of 100 hours. Costs for Resource A are assigned to the project at $20 per hour; costs for Resource B are assigned to the project at $50 per hour. Both resources take an extra 10 hours to finish their tasks. As can be seen in Table 2.1, compared to Resource A, Resource B's extra time has a higher cost to the project. This increased cost will impact calculation of the EVM parameters when it is rolled up.

Target audience for reports. When applying resource costs, the target audience for EVM reports is an important consideration. The target audience can vary depending on project type. For example, if a project is an internal initiative, then *resource costs* are the concern of the target audience (internal senior management). If a project is being executed for a customer, and the target audience of reports is customer executives, then the *price* being charged to the customer is the concern of the target audience. Additionally, if a project is being executed for a customer, two different types of audiences must be addressed—the customer and internal senior management. For the customer, *price* is the concern; for internal senior management, *cost* is the concern. Therefore, two different EVM reports must be produced—one for the customer with a price for resource costs and the other for internal senior management with the cost of resources.

Task Dependencies

Every project has tasks that are grouped into phases and subphases. These tasks are dependent on one another in some way. Some tasks must be performed after completion of another task; other tasks must be performed after a group of tasks is completed. Task dependencies are very important for a schedule to be complete and for the schedule to calculate the project end date correctly.

Task dependencies are further divided into soft and hard dependencies. Hard dependency is a form of dependency between tasks in a schedule that is fixed, i.e., a specific order of completion must be followed. Soft dependencies generally arise due to resource loading (how resources are assigned to a project, usually by activity). Soft dependencies also follow a specific order, but sometimes their completion date can be manipulated by using another resource for the task. Soft dependencies are generally determined by resource availability.

A simple example demonstrates hard and soft dependency. Consider a house construction project with the tasks of laying pillars and laying a concrete roof slab. In this situation, obviously the task of laying the pillars must be completed before the roof slab can be laid. This dependency is considered to be a *hard* dependency—the second task cannot be started until the first task is completed. A hard dependency is based on tasks. Now consider the tasks of making doors and windows. In this situation, both of these tasks are done by carpenters. The carpenters need 10 days to finish the doors and 10 days to finish the windows. The plan is to complete the doors first and then start work on the windows, but because the order in which the work is done can always be changed—have the carpenters make the windows first and the doors later—this situation is known as *soft* dependency. A soft dependency is based on resources.

MPP allows the specification that both hard and soft dependencies are taken into consideration when resource assignment and leveling are performed. Some of the hard dependencies allowed in MPP include:

- Finish-to-Start
- Start-to-Finish
- Start-to-Start
- Finish-to-Finish

Finish-to-start is the default hard dependency and the most commonly used dependency. However, at times, the other dependencies must be used. (Note: Each of the dependencies is described in greater detail in Chapter 5.)

This book has free material available for download from the
Web Added Value™ resource center at *www.jrosspub.com*

3

WHAT IS EVM?

Earned value management (EVM) is a technique used to track the progress and status of a project and to forecast its future performance. The EVM technique integrates the triple constraints of scope, time, and cost. It was originally devised by the U.S. Department of Defense to keep track of defense projects and is currently the most preferred project management technique worldwide. Increasingly, for better control and management, customers request that their projects be tracked with EVM.

Good planning coupled with effective use of the EVM technique will reduce the impact of a significant number of project issues which are due to schedule and cost overruns. Use of the EVM technique also aids negotiations with end customers about scope increase. Because cost and schedule increases nearly always occur due to scope creep, this effect will be quite evident to project stakeholders.

The EVM technique also provides answers to many project stakeholder questions that are related to the project's performance. By using statistical methods, the EVM technique can show past performance, current performance, and the predicted future performance of a project.

BASIC ELEMENTS OF EVM

Planned value (PV), earned value (EV), and actual cost (AC) are the three basic elements of the EVM technique. These terms are also referred to as budgeted cost of work scheduled (BCWS), budgeted cost of work performed (BCWP), and actual cost of work performed (ACWP), respectively. In EVM, these three elements are captured on a regular basis based on the reporting date chosen.

Table 3.1. Planned Value Calculation (Effort)

Task ID	Tasks	Effort Hours	Duration in Days	Start Day	End Day	Resource
1	Task 1	24	3	1	3	R1
2	Task 2	32	6	4	9	R2
3	Task 3	48	8	4	11	R3
4	Task 4	64	12	4	15	R1
5	Task 5	16	2	16	17	R1
6	Task 6	32	6	10	15	R2
7	Task 7	24	5	12	16	R3
8	Task 8	40	7	4	10	R4
9	Task 9	48	8	4	11	R5
10	Task 10	64	12	4	15	R6

Task ID	DEP	Day 1	Day 2	Day 3	Day 4	Day 5	Day 6	Day 7	Day 8	Day 9	Day 10	Day 11	Day 12	Day 13	Day 14	Day 15	Day 16	Day 17
1		8	8	8														
2	1				8	8			8	8								
3	1				8	8			8	8	8							
4					8	8			8	8	8	8	8			8		
5	4																8	8
6	1										8	8	8			8		
7	1												8			8	8	
8	1				8	8			8	8	8							
9	1				8	8			8	8	8	8						
10	1				8	8			8	8	8	8	8			8		
Total		8	8	8	48	48	0	0	48	48	48	32	32	0	0	32	16	8
PV		8	16	24	72	120	120	120	168	216	264	296	328	328	328	360	376	384

DEP: dependency.

Recently, two more parameters have been added to facilitate calculating schedule variance at the end of a project. These new parameters are planned time (PT) and elapsed time (ET).

Note: In the examples throughout this chapter, a simple 17-day project will be used to demonstrate the various calculations of EVM performance measures. Using the same project will enable readers to relate to the different views quickly and to easily understand the calculations involved.

Planned Value

Planned value (PV) (or budgeted cost of work scheduled, BCWS) is the cost of the work scheduled/planned as of a particular date. The PV element represents the work that was supposed to have been completed as of a particular date (or simply the work planned as of a certain date). Table 3.1 illustrates an example of the calculation of PV.

Table 3.2. Planned Value Calculation (Cost)

Task ID	Tasks	Effort Hours	Duration in Days	Start Day	End Day	Resource Rate	Resource
1	Task 1	24	3	1	3	$2.00	R1
2	Task 2	32	6	4	9	$3.00	R2
3	Task 3	48	8	4	11	$4.00	R3
4	Task 4	64	12	4	15	$2.00	R1
5	Task 5	16	2	16	17	$2.00	R1
6	Task 6	32	6	10	15	$3.00	R2
7	Task 7	24	5	12	16	$4.00	R3
8	Task 8	40	7	4	10	$2.50	R4
9	Task 9	48	8	4	11	$2.50	R5
10	Task 10	64	12	4	15	$2.50	R6

Task ID	DEP	Day 1	Day 2	Day 3	Day 4	Day 5	Day 6	Day 7	Day 8	Day 9	Day 10	Day 11	Day 12	Day 13	Day 14	Day 15	Day 16	Day 17
1		$16	$16	$16														
2	1				$24	$24			$24	$24								
3	1				$32	$32			$32	$32	$32							
4					$16	$16			$16	$16	$16	$16	$16			$16		
5	4																$16	$16
6	1										$24	$24	$24			$24		
7	1												$32			$32	$32	
8	1				$20	$20			$20	$20	$20							
9	1				$20	$20			$20	$20	$20	$20						
10	1				$20	$20			$20	$20	$20	$20	$20			$20		
	Total	$16	$16	$16	$132	$132	$ —	$ —	$132	$132	$132	$80	$92	$ —	$ —	$92	$48	$16
	PV	$16	$32	$48	$180	$312	$312	$312	$444	$576	$708	$788	$880	$880	$880	$972	$1,020	$1,036

DEP: dependency.

In Table 3.1, ten tasks with dependencies among themselves are shown. Days 6, 7, 13, and 14 (in shaded columns) are weekends and are considered to be nonworking days. Therefore, no work is planned for any resource on these days. The planned value as of any given day in the project is shown in the total column. Planned value as a cumulative value of the total hours expended per day to date is shown in the last row of each column. For example, the planned value status as of Day 10 of the project is 264 hours.

If resource rates are applied to the planned value numbers, a dollar value of planned value will be obtained. As Table 3.2 shows, the dollar value of planned value for Day 10 is $708. The dollar value is obtained by multiplying the effort in hours by the rate/hr to get the cost in dollars. For example, for Day 1 only one task is in progress, and working hours per day are 8 hours; therefore, the cost of work for Day 1 is $16 (8 hours × $2, with $2 being the rate/hr for resource R1).

Earned Value

Earned value (EV) (or budgeted cost of work performed, BCWP) represents the cost of work that has actually been completed as of a particular date (or simply the earned value of work completed to date). In other words, earned value represents the value created or earned in a project by the project team as of a particular date. At times, earned value is compared to the total payments made to date to a vendor by a customer. This gives the customer complete transparency in understanding whether (or not) payments made to the vendor to date have been utilized properly on the project and if the customer has gained value for the payments made so far.

Earned value is an important element in EVM from both a customer and a vendor point of view. In the case of an internal project, earned value is important from a management and project team point of view. If an IT department is executing a project for a business group inside the company, earned value is important from the business group and the IT department point of view.

For a vendor, project team, or department, earned value gives an indication as to whether (or not) the invoicing to the customer is in line with the value created by the project to date. If necessary, invoices can be adjusted accordingly to avoid overbilling (which could become a problem at a later stage in the project).

Earned value can be more or less than planned value (or budgeted cost of work scheduled, BCWS). Earned value that is less than planned value indicates a schedule overrun; earned value that is more than planned value indicates that a project is ahead of schedule. When earned value is equal to planned value, the project is on schedule.

Similarly, earned value can be more or less than actual cost (or actual cost of work performed, ACWP). Earned value that is less than actual cost indicates a cost or effort overrun (if effort is used instead of cost); earned value that is more than the actual cost indicates that the project is under budget or under effort.

The important parameter in calculating earned value is the percent (%) complete of all tasks. The % complete multiplied by effort and then multiplied by the rate/hr will give earned value. If rate/hr is not used, earned value is indicated in terms of effort.

When discussing % complete, no hard and fast rule exists for updating the % complete—% complete is left to the discretion of the project manager and his team. No two individuals will come up with the same % complete on a particular task because determining % complete is very subjective in nature. A task which is said to be 50% complete by one person might be considered to be only 45% complete by another. However, there are some basic rules about updating the % complete.

Remaining effort. The % complete must be updated keeping in mind the remaining effort to be completed on a task. Suppose a task has a total effort of 40 hours and a team member has spent 10 hours on the task. Using basic mathematics, one could immediately say that the task is 25% complete because 10 hours ÷ 40 hours × 100% is 25%. Yet this calculation might not be correct because the remaining effort required to complete the task has not been considered. Instead an assumption has been made—that planned effort will be used exactly as planned to finish the task. This situation is not always the case—sometimes a task can be completed with less effort, but at times more effort is required. Once a task is underway, a resource can more easily provide a closer estimate of the effort needed to complete the task. Continuing with the example above, once the task is underway and the resource has provided the remaining hours needed to complete the task, then this *new amount* of effort can be used in calculating the percentage complete, which will give a more accurate picture. For example, suppose the resource says that he needs 20 more hours to complete the task. This means that he will need to spend less effort on the task; the new percentage complete therefore will be 33.33% rather than 25%. To obtain the value of 33.33%, take the effort used to date (10 hours), add this to the remaining effort (20 hours), and divide effort used to date (10 hours) by the total expected effort (10 + 20 = 30). So 10 hours × 100% ÷ 30 hours) = 33.33%. Using this new % complete, the picture of earned value is quite different. In this case, earned value is higher than planned value, meaning the project is ahead of schedule and also under budget. Similarly, a reverse scenario would highlight a possible schedule, effort, or cost overrun and enable quick decisions to be made to try to bring the project back on track. This explanation illustrates the importance of obtaining the correct % complete on all tasks to enable having an accurate picture of the project.

Project earned value. Another consideration is that in every project some tasks will take more effort/cost than planned, while others might take less effort/cost. Therefore, when managing a project consider the *overall* project earned value rather than the *individual task* earned value. Looking at the individual task earned value might result in micromanaging which could become counterproductive. Instead, begin by looking at the overall project-level picture and then try to balance out overruns and underruns at an individual task level (this might be all that is needed). Having said this, certain situations require micromanagement. Therefore, for each project, a decision must be made about whether the project needs macro- or micromanagement of earned value.

50/50 assignment. Another method of assigning the % complete to tasks is known as 50/50 assignment. In the 50/50 method, as soon as a task is started, it is assigned a value of 50% complete; therefore, the earned value would be 50% of total project cost. (Note: Using this method is not recommended because it does not give a heads-up about the variances of

Table 3.3. Earned Value Calculation

Task ID	Tasks	Effort Hours	Duration in Days	Start Day	End Day	% Complete	Resource	Resource Rate	DEP	Day 10 PV	Day 10 EV
1	Task 1	24	3	1	3	100%	R1	$2.00		$48.00	$48.00
2	Task 2	32	6	4	9	75%	R2	$3.00	1	$96.00	$72.00
3	Task 3	48	8	4	11	60%	R3	$4.00	1	$160.00	$115.20
4	Task 4	64	12	4	15	100%	R1	$2.00		$80.00	$128.00
5	Task 5	16	2	16	17		R1	$2.00	4	$ —	$ —
6	Task 6	32	6	10	15	50%	R2	$3.00	1	$24.00	$48.00
7	Task 7	24	5	12	16		R3	$4.00	1	$ —	$ —
8	Task 8	40	7	4	10	100%	R4	$2.50	1	$100.00	$100.00
9	Task 9	48	8	4	11	100%	R5	$2.50	1	$100.00	$120.00
10	Task 10	64	12	4	15	50%	R6	$2.50	1	$100.00	$80.00
									Total	$708.00	$711.20

Legend: **Red** (black) **Green** (gray)

DEP: dependency.

individual tasks. Once variances are discovered, it might be too late to recover from the variances of some tasks.)

Continuing with the example we used to calculate planned value, let's see how earned value is calculated. In Table 3.3, Tasks 2, 3, and 10 are behind schedule (in Red; see legend), whereas Tasks 1, 4, 6, 8, and 9 (in Green) are on schedule or ahead of schedule). So, overall, at the project level, the schedule is still ahead. Now based on this situation, and considering the remaining effort required for the tasks which are behind schedule, a calculated decision can be made and appropriate measures can be taken to bring these tasks back on track or to leave them "as is." Earned value provides a good picture of where action needs to be taken and where improvising is required to bring a project back on track.

Actual Cost

The actual cost (AC) (or the actual cost of work performed, ACWP) element represents the actual costs incurred on a project as of a particular date (or simply the actual money spent to date on a project). Actual cost represents the value in dollars spent by a project team on a project. Actual cost is not related to payments made by a customer. Payment by the customer is generally made after completion of a milestone or as an advance for a milestone. Actual cost serves as a good indication to a vendor and a customer of the amount of money remaining in a project or the amount of money needed to be received for a project.

Because actual cost represents funds already spent on a project, actual cost cannot be changed. The money has been spent. A vendor or a customer cannot get this money back (unless the customer files a lawsuit to recover the money from the vendor).

Table 3.4. Actual Cost Calculation

Task ID	Tasks	Effort Hours	Duration in Days	Start Day	End Day	% Complete	Resource	Resource Rate	DEP	Day 10 PV	Day 10 AC	Day 10 EV
1	Task 1	24	3	1	3	100%	R1	$2.00		$48.00	$60.00	$48.00
2	Task 2	32	6	4	9	75%	R2	$3.00	1	$96.00	$96.00	$72.00
3	Task 3	48	8	4	11	60%	R3	$4.00	1	$160.00	$110.00	$115.20
4	Task 4	64	12	4	15	100%	R1	$2.00		$ 80.00	$100.00	$128.00
5	Task 5	16	2	16	17		R1	$2.00	4	$ —	$ —	$ —
6	Task 6	32	6	10	15	50%	R2	$3.00	1	$24.00	$30.00	$48.00
7	Task 7	24	5	12	16		R3	$4.00	1	$ —	$ —	$ —
8	Task 8	40	7	4	10	100%	R4	$2.50	1	$100.00	$100.00	$100.00
9	Task 9	48	8	4	11	100%	R5	$2.50	1	$100.00	$130.00	$120.00
10	Task 10	64	12	4	15	50%	R6	$2.50	1	$100.00	$100.00	$80.00
									Total	$708.00	$726.00	$711.20

Legend: █ Red ▓ Green

DEP: dependency.

Actual cost is another important element that requires close monitoring by a customer and a vendor. Close monitoring is required to gain an understanding of whether (or not) spending on a project is in line with the value being created by the project team. A comparison between actual cost and earned value will indicate whether value (or worth) has been created (or not) for the money already spent on the project.

Actual cost can be greater than or less than earned value. When actual cost is greater than earned value, the situation indicates a cost overrun; when actual cost is less than earned value, an under-budget situation is indicated. When actual cost is equal to earned value, the project is on budget (very rare).

Actual cost is simply the effort spent by resources on a project multiplied by the resource rate for the project. Suppose the effort spent to date on a project by Resource 1 is 20 hours and the resource rate for Resource 1 is $20 per hour. Then the actual cost to date of Resource 1 on the project would be 20 hours × $20 = $400.

Continuing with the same example we used for planned value and earned value, let's see the results of using actual cost. Table 3.4 shows that the tasks now indicated by "red" and "green" (see figure legend) are different than the tasks in Table 3.3 (which was the earned value calculation in which earned value was compared with planned value). In Table 3.4, earned value is compared with the actual cost for the cost variances. Note: A task which has a schedule overrun might not always have a cost overrun because a schedule considers calendar days used and cost considers actual *effort* spent on a task.

Table 3.4 shows that the planned value for Task 1 is $48 and that actual cost is $60. The explanation is that the elapsed time for Task 1 in the project is 6 days, assuming an 8-hour work day. Instead, Resource 1 has spent more than 8 hours per day to complete this task; therefore the actual cost is $60, which is higher than the planned value and also higher than the earned value. In this situation, although there is no schedule variance, there is definitely a cost variance of $12. Also notice that Task 3 in this scenario has a schedule variance, but is still under budget.

Planned Time

Planned time (PT) is earned value measured in units of time (also known as earned time). Planned time is calculated in a similar way to earned value. Calculation of planned time uses the % complete and indicates how much time to date has been used efficiently. Therefore, if planned time is 8 days on Day 10, then 8 days of the 10 days have been utilized effectively and efficiently.

Planned time is always compared with elapsed time (ET) to determine variances in time. Planned time compared to elapsed time gives a clear indication as to whether a project is ahead or behind the time planned. This gives us an exact picture of the time part of a schedule. Planned time is calculated using the formula:

$$PT = P \times Pc$$

where P is the total number of reporting periods on a project in days and Pc is the % complete on the project. (Note: All of the nuances of % complete that are discussed in the earned value section apply.)

Using our example, let's apply planned time and calculate the other elements of EVM. Table 3.5 shows that planned time is calculated using total duration and % complete—these two values are multiplied to derive planned time.

In Table 3.5, days are used as the reporting period because the project is very small. Notice on Day 10, that planned time is 7 days, yet the elapsed time is 10 days. Clearly the project is behind schedule—in this case it is 3 days behind schedule. With this information, a project manager has a better idea of what he needs to do to bring the project schedule back on track. For example, to compensate for the current 3-day schedule overrun, he might consider having resources work longer hours during the remaining days of the project. (Note: For larger projects, reporting periods might be in weeks or months; therefore, the variance would be in the units of the reporting period used. For example, if the project in Table 3.5 had a reporting period of weeks, then the project would have a 3-week schedule overrun instead of a 3-day overrun.)

Notice in our example in Table 3.5 that the project was on schedule for the first 3 days; then it started slipping. If the project manager had calculated planned time on the fourth

Table 3.5. Planned Time Calculation

Task ID	Tasks	Effort Hours	Duration in Days	Start Day	End Day	Resource	Resource Rate
1	Task 1	24	3	1	3	R1	$2.00
2	Task 2	32	6	4	9	R2	$3.00
3	Task 3	48	8	4	11	R3	$4.00
4	Task 4	64	12	4	15	R1	$2.00
5	Task 5	16	2	16	17	R1	$2.00
6	Task 6	32	6	10	15	R2	$3.00
7	Task 7	24	5	12	16	R3	$4.00
8	Task 8	40	7	4	10	R4	$2.50
9	Task 9	48	8	4	11	R5	$2.50
10	Task 10	64	12	4	15	R6	$2.50

Task ID	DEP	Day 1	Day 2	Day 3	Day 4	Day 5	Day 6	Day 7	Day 8	Day 9	Day 10
1		$16	$16	$16							
2	1				$24	$24			$24	$24	
3	1				$32	$32			$32	$32	$32
4					$16	$16			$16	$16	$16
5	4										
6	1										$24
7	1										
8	1				$20	$20			$20	$20	$20
9	1				$20	$20			$20	$20	$20
10	1				$20	$20			$20	$20	$20
	Total Duration	17	17	17	17	17	17	17	17	17	17
	% Complete	5%	10%	15%	20%	25%	25%	25%	30%	35%	40%
	PT	1	2	3	3	4	4	4	5	6	7

DEP: dependency.

day (rather than waiting until Day 10), he would have realized that a slippage was occurring and could have immediately taken corrective action to change the course of the project.

Elapsed Time

Elapsed time is simply time that has passed in a project. The elapsed time element is calculated in the units of the reporting period (days, weeks, etc.). For example, if the reporting period for a project is weeks, then elapsed time is the number of weeks that have elapsed.

Elapsed time is a very simple calculation. Important to note, however, is that elapsed time has already occurred; nothing can be done to get it back. Therefore, to maintain the schedule, remaining work must be completed in the remaining time allotted to the project (or the available time).

CALCULATION OF EARNED VALUE PERFORMANCE MEASURES

The three basic elements of planned value, earned value, and actual cost (PV, EV, and AC) can be derived from the work breakdown structure (WBS) by associating costs to each task (or, as mentioned earlier, by using effort instead). Manual calculation of the elements is tedious, especially for a project with many tasks, but calculations are easily obtained using scheduling software such as MPP. (Note: The author recommends using scheduling software to obtain project details.) Because a comprehensive description of the theory of how these elements are obtained is beyond the scope of this book, please refer to the following sources for explanations: *The PMI Practice Standard for EVM* (www.pmi.org) and *Wikipedia* (http://en.wikipedia.org/wiki/Earned_value_management).

Although using MPP eliminates the need for manual calculations, this chapter demonstrates how the calculations are made for purposes of illustration. (Using MPP to obtain values will be explained in Chapter 7.) Numerous performance measures are used in these calculations. The following table provides a quick view of the performance measures used:

EVM Performance Measures

BAC_t	Budget at completion (time)	How much time is budgeted for the entire project?
SV_t	Schedule variance (time)	How much is the project ahead/behind schedule?
SPI_t	Schedule performance index (time)	How efficiently is time utilized in the project?
EAC_t	Estimate at completion (time)	When are we likely to finish the project?
CV	Cost variance	How much over/under budget is the project?
CPI	Cost performance index	How effectively are resources being used?
TCPI	To-complete cost performance index	How efficiently must remaining resources be used?
TSPI	To-complete schedule performance index	How efficiently must remaining time be used?
BAC	Budget at completion	How much cost/effort is budgeted for the entire project?
EAC	Estimate at completion	What is the estimated cost/effort at completion of the project?
VAC	Variance at completion	What will the variance in cost/effort be at the end of the project?
ETC	Estimate to complete	How much cost/effort is estimated for completion of remaining work?

Source: Adapted from *Project Management Practice Standard for Earned Value Management.* Project Management Institute, Inc., 2005. Copyright and all rights reserved. Material from this publication has been reproduced with the permission of PMI.

Table 3.6. Schedule Variance Calculation

Task ID	Tasks	Effort Hours	Duration in Days	Start Day	End Day	% Complete	Resource	Resource Rate	DEP	Day 10 PV	Day 10 AC	Day 10 EV	Day 10 SV
1	Task 1	24	3	1	3	100%	R1	$2.00		$48.00	$60.00	$48.00	
2	Task 2	32	6	4	9	75%	R2	$3.00	1	$96.00	$96.00	$72.00	$(24.00)
3	Task 3	48	8	4	11	60%	R3	$4.00	1	$160.00	$110.00	$115.20	$(44.80)
4	Task 4	64	12	4	15	100%	R1	$2.00		$80.00	$100.00	$128.00	$48.00
5	Task 5	16	2	16	17		R1	$2.00	4	$ –	$ –	$ –	$ –
6	Task 6	32	6	10	15	50%	R2	$3.00	1	$24.00	$30.00	$48.00	$24.00
7	Task 7	24	5	12	16		R3	$4.00	1	$ –	$ –	$ –	$ –
8	Task 8	40	7	4	10	100%	R4	$2.50	1	$100.00	$100.00	$100.00	$ –
9	Task 9	48	8	4	11	100%	R5	$2.50	1	$100.00	$130.00	$120.00	$20.00
10	Task 10	64	12	4	15	50%	R6	$2.50	1	$100.00	$100.00	$80.00	$(20.00)
									Total	$708.00	$726.00	$711.20	$3.20

Legend: **Red** | Green

DEP: dependency.

Schedule Variance

Schedule variance (SV) is the variance between earned value and planned value. It shows the amount of work that has either exceeded planned value or is lower than planned value. SV value is shown in terms of dollars when cost is used and in hours when effort is used. It also indicates how much ahead or behind schedule a project is.

A formula can be used to give variance in terms of cost, which indicates how much *cost of work* is yet to be completed according to the schedule or how much cost of work has been completed over and above the scheduled cost. Positive variance indicates that a project is ahead of schedule; negative variance indicates that the project is behind schedule. Schedule variance can be calculated using the formula:

Schedule variance (SV) = earned value (EV) – planned value (PV)

or

Schedule variance (SV) = BCWP – BCWS

Using our example, let's see how schedule variance is reflected in the status of individual tasks and in the overall schedule. In Table 3.6, schedule variance is shown on Day 10 in the last column. Task 2 has a negative schedule variance (shown in parentheses and indicated by "Red"; see legend), meaning the task is behind schedule. Task 2 is behind schedule by $24. So what does "behind schedule by $24" mean? It simply means that as of Day

10, $24 worth of work associated with this task has not been completed; therefore Task 2 is behind schedule by $24.

Notice that three tasks are behind schedule (Tasks 2, 3, and 10), but also that other tasks are ahead of schedule. Overall, then, the project is actually ahead of schedule by $3.20.

At this point, it is at the discretion of the project manager to determine if he should focus on the tasks which are behind schedule and work with the resources associated with them to see if these tasks can be brought back on track. If the project manager finds that he cannot do much with the tasks that are already behind schedule, another option is to work with resources who have tasks which are ahead of schedule to find out why these tasks are ahead. Perhaps he can take advantage of the reasons given by the resources to get these tasks completed even further ahead of schedule to compensate for the time lost on the other tasks. The project manager can also work with tasks which have not yet started, trying to find ways to improve the schedule variance for those tasks.

This calculation method of schedule variance, however, has a flaw. The flaw is that schedule variance calculated by this method yields a $0 value at the end of a project simply because at the end of a project, earned value and planned value become *equal* even if the project is *behind schedule* by say 10 days. This flaw, however, has been recognized and corrected—by introducing the time factor, a new parameter which will be discussed in the sections that follow.

Schedule Variance Percent

Schedule variance percent (*SV%*) indicates how much ahead or behind schedule a project is in terms of the percent of work completed. A formula will give the variance in terms of a percent which indicates what percent of work has slipped with respect to the planned duration or what percent of work has been completed over and above the planned schedule as of a given day/period. Positive variance % indicates the percent ahead of the planned schedule; negative variance % indicates the percent behind the planned schedule. Schedule variance % can be calculated using the formula:

$$SV\% = schedule\ variance\ (SV) \div planned\ value\ (PV)$$

or

$$SV\% = SV \div BCWS$$

Using our example, let's consider schedule variance %. In schedule variance (SV) calculations, we see the dollar value by which a schedule is ahead or behind. In schedule variance

Table 3.7. Schedule Variance Percent Calculation

Task ID	Tasks	Effort Hours	Duration in Days	Start Day	End Day	% Complete	Resource	Resource Rate
1	Task 1	24	3	1	3	100%	R1	$2.00
2	Task 2	32	6	4	9	75%	R2	$3.00
3	Task 3	48	8	4	11	60%	R3	$4.00
4	Task 4	64	12	4	15	100%	R1	$2.00
5	Task 5	16	2	16	17		R1	$2.00
6	Task 6	32	6	10	15	50%	R2	$3.00
7	Task 7	24	5	12	16		R3	$4.00
8	Task 8	40	7	4	10	100%	R4	$2.50
9	Task 9	48	8	4	11	100%	R5	$2.50
10	Task 10	64	12	4	15	50%	R6	$2.50

Task ID	DEP	Day 10 PV	Day 10 AC	Day 10 EV	Day 10 SV	Day 10 SV%
1		$48.00	$60.00	$48.00		0%
2	1	$96.00	$96.00	$72.00	$(24.00)	–25%
3	1	$160.00	$110.00	$115.20	$(44.80)	–28%
4		$80.00	$100.00	$128.00	$48.00	60%
5	4	$ —	$ —	$ —	$ —	0%
6	1	$24.00	$30.00	$48.00	$24.00	100%
7	1	$ —	$ —	$ —	$ —	0%
8	1	$100.00	$100.00	$100.00	$ —	0%
9	1	$100.00	$130.00	$120.00	$20.00	20%
10	1	$100.00	$100.00	$80.00	$(20.00)	–20%
	Total	$708.00	$726.00	$711.20	$3.20	0%

Legend: Red   Green

DEP: dependency.

%, however, we see the amount in percent by which a schedule is ahead or behind. Schedule variance % provides a clearer perspective by showing the percentage of the work that is behind schedule.

In the example shown in Table 3.7, Tasks 2, 3, and 10 are behind schedule by 25, 28, and 20%, respectively. Because other tasks are ahead of schedule, however, overall the schedule variance % for the project is 0%, meaning the project is more or less on schedule when the entire project is considered.

By knowing the percentage value of schedule variance, a project manager can see where he should take corrective action to bring the project back on schedule. As discussed in the schedule variance calculation, measures can be taken to bring affected tasks back on track, attention can be given to tasks which are ahead of schedule to try to maximize the potential of being ahead of schedule, or work can be done on tasks not yet started to compensate for the schedule overruns in some tasks.

In the formula, notice that schedule variance is compared with planned value to arrive at schedule variance %, i.e., it is based on the work planned as of a particular date, not for the overall schedule. However, if the schedule is compared with the budget at completion (BAC), schedule variance % is with respect to the overall schedule. Variance calculated with this method assumes that the remaining work in the project will be done exactly as planned with no negative deviations.

Because schedule variance % is calculated using schedule variance and planned value as of a particular date, a large schedule variance % at the beginning of a project is quite manageable; however, as a project progresses, bringing a project which has a huge schedule variance back on track becomes more and more difficult.

Schedule Performance Indicator

Note: When preparing a schedule an assumption is made that all resources in a project will perform at the same level and at a 100% efficiency level. However, this is rarely true for any type of project.

The schedule performance indicator (SPI) is an index which shows the efficiency of time utilized on a project from the aspect of schedule. The schedule variance formula below gives the efficiency of the project team in utilizing the time allocated for the project. A schedule performance indicator value above 1 indicates that a project team is very efficiently using the time allocated to a project. Conversely, a schedule performance indicator value below 1 indicates that a project team is using time allocated to a project less efficiently. The schedule performance indicator can be calculated using the formula:

$$SPI = \frac{earned\ value\ (EV)}{planned\ value\ (PV)}$$

or

$$SPI = \frac{budgeted\ cost\ of\ work\ performed\ (BCWP)}{budgeted\ cost\ work\ scheduled\ (BCWS)}$$

Let's see how the schedule performance indicator figures into the example that we have been using to explain the different performance measures. Remember that Table 3.6 illustrated the *dollar value* of schedule variance, and Table 3.7 illustrated the *percentage value*

Table 3.8. Schedule Performance Indicator Calculation

Task ID	Tasks	Effort Hours	Duration in Days	Start Day	End Day	% Complete	Resource	Resource Rate
1	Task 1	24	3	1	3	100%	R1	$2.00
2	Task 2	32	6	4	9	75%	R2	$3.00
3	Task 3	48	8	4	11	60%	R3	$4.00
4	Task 4	64	12	4	15	100%	R1	$2.00
5	Task 5	16	2	16	17		R1	$2.00
6	Task 6	32	6	10	15	50%	R2	$3.00
7	Task 7	24	5	12	16		R3	$4.00
8	Task 8	40	7	4	10	100%	R4	$2.50
9	Task 9	48	8	4	11	100%	R5	$2.50
10	Task 10	64	12	4	15	50%	R6	$2.50

Task ID	DEP	Day 10 PV	Day 10 AC	Day 10 EV	Day 10 SV	Day 10 SPI
1		$48.00	$60.00	$48.00	$ —	1.00
2	1	$96.00	$96.00	$72.00	$(24.00)	0.75
3	1	$160.00	$110.00	$115.20	$(44.80)	0.72
4		$80.00	$100.00	$128.00	$48.00	1.60
5	4	$ —	$ —	$ —	$ —	1.00
6	1	$24.00	$30.00	$48.00	$24.00	2.00
7	1	$ —	$ —	$ —	$ —	1.00
8	1	$100.00	$100.00	$100.00	$ —	1.00
9	1	$100.00	$130.00	$120.00	$20.00	1.20
10	1	$100.00	$100.00	$80.00	$(20.00)	0.80
	Total	$708.00	$726.00	$711.20	$3.20	1.00

Legend: **Red**   Green

DEP: dependency.

of schedule variance. Table 3.8 illustrates the *schedule performance indicator* which is another view of schedule performance. Notice in Table 3.8 that at Day 10 the index hovers around a value of 1 (remember that anything below 1 is considered to be behind schedule and anything above 1 is considered to be ahead of schedule, with 1 indicating that a project is on schedule). Table 3.8 clearly shows that overall, the project is on schedule. However, some individual tasks are ahead or behind schedule.

The efficiency of a project team, as derived from the schedule performance indicator, can also be looked at as a percentage. Looking at Task 2, the schedule performance indicator is 0.75, meaning that the efficiency of the project team is at the 75% level compared to the optimum level of 100% or more. This value of 0.75 also means that the project team is performing inefficiently by 25%.

Even if the overall efficiency of a project team is 100%, some resources perform inefficiently. Therefore, the current efficiency of a project team can be used by a project manager to see if team efficiency can be improved going forward—from the aspect of the schedule in this case. Corrective actions can be taken by a project manager to bring the project team back on track by trying to maximize the performance of highly efficient resources and to minimize the performance setbacks of resources who are less efficient.

Each schedule performance measure indicates a different value. Knowing each of these three values allows a project manager to make guided judgments in a decision-making process.

To-Complete Schedule Performance Indicator

The to-complete schedule performance indicator (TSPI) is an index showing the efficiency at which the remaining time on a project should be utilized. The formula below gives the efficiency at which the project team should utilize the remaining time allocated for the project. A to-complete schedule performance indicator value below 1 indicates a project team can be a bit lenient in utilizing the remaining time allocated to the project, while a value above 1 indicates a project team needs to work harder to utilize the remaining time efficiently. The to-complete schedule performance indicator can be calculated using the formula:

$$TSPI = \frac{(total\,budget - EV)}{(total\,budget - PV)}$$

or

$$TSPI = \frac{(total\,budget - BCWP)}{(total\,budget - BCWS)}$$

Continuing with our example, Table 3.9 shows the calculation of the to-complete schedule performance indicator. The last column in Table 3.9 has the to-complete schedule performance indicators (TSPI) for the same tasks in Table 3.8 that had schedule performance indicators (SPI) indicating that they were behind schedule. Because the TSPI forecasts the *future* performance required by a project team to bring the tasks behind schedule back on track (indicated by "Red"; see figure legend), if the TSPI for a particular

Table 3.9. To-Complete Schedule Performance Indicator Calculation

Task ID	Tasks	Effort Hours	Duration in Days	Start Day	End Day	% Complete	Resource	Resource Rate
1	Task 1	24	3	1	3	100%	R1	$2.00
2	Task 2	32	6	4	9	75%	R2	$3.00
3	Task 3	48	8	4	11	60%	R3	$4.00
4	Task 4	64	12	4	15	100%	R1	$2.00
5	Task 5	16	2	16	17		R1	$2.00
6	Task 6	32	6	10	15	50%	R2	$3.00
7	Task 7	24	5	12	16		R3	$4.00
8	Task 8	40	7	4	10	100%	R4	$2.50
9	Task 9	48	8	4	11	100%	R5	$2.50
10	Task 10	64	12	4	15	50%	R6	$2.50

Task ID	DEP	Day 10 PV	Day 10 AC	Day 10 EV	Day 10 SV	Day 10 SPI	Day 10 TSPI
1		$48.00	$60.00	$48.00	$ —	1.00	0.00
2	1	$96.00	$96.00	$72.00	$(24.00)	0.75	N/A
3	1	$160.00	$110.00	$115.20	$(44.80)	0.72	2.40
4		$80.00	$100.00	$128.00	$48.00	1.60	0.00
5	4	$ —	$ —	$ —	$ —	1.00	1.00
6	1	$24.00	$30.00	$48.00	$24.00	2.00	0.67
7	1	$ —	$ —	$ —	$ —	1.00	1.00
8	1	$100.00	$100.00	$100.00	$ —	1.00	0.00
9	1	$100.00	$130.00	$120.00	$20.00	1.20	0.00
10	1	$100.00	$100.00	$80.00	$(20.00)	0.80	1.33
	Total	$708.00	$726.00	$711.20	$3.20	1.00	0.99

Legend: Red   Green

DEP: dependency.

task or an entire project is 1.25, then the task or the entire project needs to be performed at 125% efficiency to bring it back on track.

The to-complete schedule performance indicator can be interpreted in several ways. One interpretation is that the project team or a particular resource needs to work at 25% higher efficiency than the normal 100%. So how does this translate into the work that must be done by the project team or by an individual resource? If a resource works 8 hours a day and he must perform at 125% efficiency, then this resource needs to perform work that has a worth of 10 hours in an 8-hour workday—10 hours is derived by 8 hours × 1.25 (125%).

Yet we must understand that if we increase the hours per workday, we will also increase cost. An ideal solution for this situation would be for the resource to perform 10 hours of work in 8 hours by using some tool or technique which will reduce the time required to do the work.

For example, notice Task 2 in our example. Task 2 has a to-complete schedule performance indicator of "N/A" ("not applicable") because the task has gone over its schedule and nothing can be done to bring it back on schedule. Because the to-complete schedule performance indicator is a forecast of the performance needed to bring a task or project back on schedule, if a schedule is past its end date, we cannot forecast the performance needed to bring the task back on track. The performance now needed is the best possible performance to *minimize* the schedule variance.

Similarly, notice Task 3 in our example. Task 3 has a to-complete schedule performance indicator of 2.40, meaning the resource must perform at 240% efficiency to bring the task back on schedule. The size of this percent clearly indicates that achieving this performance level will be quite difficult. In this scenario, the project manager must focus on keeping the variance of Task 3 as small as possible going forward. The project manager should focus on compensating for this situation in the other tasks.

So far we have examined the various schedule performance measures. Each one provides a different view of the same schedule, which allows a project manager and project stakeholders to have clear and concise information that will enable them to take appropriate actions to control a project schedule. We have calculated these performance measures using cost, not the time factor. If we only use cost in calculating performance measures, we do not have a "picture" of time. At the end of a project, even if a project is behind schedule, the performance measures will indicate that the project is on schedule—because earned value and planned value, the two elements used in the calculation of these measures, have become equal. We will continue our discussion using the time factor.

Schedule Variance (Time)

Schedule variance time (SV_t) is schedule variance shown in terms of time rather than a dollar value or effort as shown by schedule variance (SV). SV_t is the difference between planned time (PT) and elapsed time (ET). When SV_t is positive, indications are that a project is ahead of schedule; when it is negative, indications are that the project is behind schedule. SV_t is exactly the same as SV, which uses cost or effort, except that SV_t shows actual values in terms of time. Suppose the SV_t is –2 and the reporting period for the project is in weeks; then the project is behind schedule by two reporting periods or 2 weeks. The formula is used to calculate the schedule variance (time):

$$SV_t = PT - ET$$

Table 3.10. Schedule Variance Time Calculation

Task ID	Tasks	Effort Hours	Duration in Days	Start Day	End Day	Resource	% Complete	Wgtd Avg %	DEP	Day 10 PT	Day 10 ET	Day 10 SV$_t$
1	Task 1	24	3	1	3	R1	100%	6%		3.00	10.00	0.00
2	Task 2	32	6	4	9	R2	75%	6%	1	4.50	7.00	−2.50
3	Task 3	48	8	4	11	R3	60%	7%	1	4.80	7.00	−2.20
4	Task 4	64	12	4	15	R1	100%	16%		12.00	7.00	5.00
5	Task 5	16	2	16	17	R1		0%	4	0.00	0.00	0.00
6	Task 6	32	6	10	15	R2	50%	4%	1	3.00	1.00	2.00
7	Task 7	24	5	12	16	R3		0%	1	0.00	0.00	0.00
8	Task 8	40	7	4	10	R4	100%	10%	1	7.00	7.00	0.00
9	Task 9	48	8	4	11	R5	100%	12%	1	8.00	7.00	1.00
10	Task 10	64	12	4	15	R6	50%	8%	1	6.00	7.00	−1.00
		392		1	17			71%		12.00	10.00	2.00

Legend: **Red** Green

Wgtd Avg: weighted average
DEP: dependency

Continuing with our example, let's examine the schedule variance (time) performance measure. In Table 3.10, schedule variance is calculated using the time factor and is shown in terms of time. The reporting period used is days. Therefore, for a schedule variance time of −2.50, the particular task or project being considered has a delay of 2.5 days.

Table 3.10 clearly shows that some tasks are behind schedule and some are ahead of schedule, but overall the project is ahead of schedule by 2.00. Important to note is that delays in individual tasks will not roll up to the project level because the project is measured by the total duration available for the project and the weighted average of the percentage complete (wherein the weighted averages are derived using the efforts on that task). Yet by looking at individual tasks in the project separately, schedule variances are accurate at that level.

Another consideration is that the elapsed time for each task is different because elapsed time is dependent on the task start day and the current day. Therefore, if a task starts Day 1, and the status is taken as of Day 10, then the elapsed time for that task would be 10 days. If the task starts on Day 4, and the status is taken as of Day 10, then the elapsed time for that task would be 7 days (10 − 4 + 1). This type of calculation is done because each task is considered to be a separate project when calculating elapsed time.

In Table 3.10, Tasks 2, 3, and 10 are behind schedule; Tasks 4, 6, and 9 are ahead of schedule. The schedule variance time values shown for these tasks are the actual number of days a task is ahead or behind schedule. At the project level, the schedule variance (time) value shows the number of days the project is ahead or behind schedule; in this case the project is ahead of schedule by 2.00 days.

Let's now look at the calculations involved in determining schedule variance time. The two important elements in determining schedule variance time are planned time (PT, or earned time) and elapsed time (ET). At the individual task level, take the % complete and multiply it by the duration of the task to determine the planned time. Elapsed time is determined using the formula: status day – task or project start day + 1. When calculating the schedule variance time for an entire project, take the project % complete, which is derived using the weighted average of % complete of each individual task:

$$Project\ \%\ complete = \sum_{i=i}^{n} \%\ complete_i \times \frac{task\ effort_i}{total\ effort}$$

where i is the task number. This formula is to be applied separately for each summary task; then, using the summary tasks, apply the formula to the project.

Schedule Variance Percent (Time)

Schedule variance percent (time) ($SV_t\%$) is calculated similarly to schedule variance percent (SV%); however, $SV_t\%$ shows the percentage of schedule variance with respect to the time factor. A positive $SV_t\%$ indicates that a project is ahead of schedule; a negative $SV_t\%$ indicates that a project is behind schedule. It is similar to schedule variance percent (SV%, which is related to the percent of work that was planned in the schedule). Therefore, when $SV_t\%$ is 10% and the overall duration of a project is 100 days, then deriving the actual number of days that the project is behind schedule is easy: 100 days × 10% = 10 days. Schedule variance % (time) is calculated using the formula:

$$Sv_t\% = \frac{planned\ time\,(PT)}{elapsed\ time\,(ET)}$$

Continuing with our example, let's see how $SV_t\%$ is reflected in the project's status. In Table 3.11, its values are shown in the last column for individual tasks and also at the project level. Notice that some tasks appear to be significantly over schedule. Similarly, some tasks appear to be far ahead of schedule. This situation occurs because the individual tasks are being viewed at task level rather than at project level. However, at the project level, the schedule has a positive variance, meaning that the project is actually ahead of schedule. Notice also that Task 3 has a negative variance of 46%, which translates into the 2.20-day

Table 3.11. Schedule Variance % (Time) Calculation

Task ID	Tasks	Effort Hours	Duration in Days	Start Day	End Day	Resource	% Complete	Wgtd Avg %	DEP	Day 10 PT	Day 10 ET	Day 10 SV$_t$	Day 10 SV%$_t$
1	Task 1	24	3	1	3	R1	100%	6%		3.00	10.00	0.00	0%
2	Task 2	32	6	4	9	R2	75%	6%	1	4.50	7.00	–2.50	–56%
3	Task 3	48	8	4	11	R3	60%	7%	1	4.80	7.00	–2.20	–46%
4	Task 4	64	12	4	15	R1	100%	16%		12.00	7.00	5.00	42%
5	Task 5	16	2	16	17	R1		0%	4	0.00	0.00	0.00	0%
6	Task 6	32	6	10	15	R2	50%	4%	1	3.00	1.00	2.00	67%
7	Task 7	24	5	12	16	R3		0%	1	0.00	0.00	0.00	0%
8	Task 8	40	7	4	10	R4	100%	10%	1	7.00	7.00	0.00	0%
9	Task 9	48	8	4	11	R5	100%	12%	1	8.00	7.00	1.00	13%
10	Task 10	64	12	4	15	R6	50%	8%	1	6.00	7.00	–1.00	–17%
		392		1	17			71%		12.00	10.00	2.00	17%

Legend: ▉ Red ▨ Green

Wgtd Avg: weighted average
DEP: dependency

delay (shown in the SV$_t$ performance measure column). (Note: Expect to have similar figures when applying this formula to live projects. As a word of caution, look at the overall project schedule variance % (time) to obtain an accurate picture.)

One might raise the question: why do we need to use schedule variance % (time) when instead we could use the schedule variance (time) performance measure? The explanation is that most companies have projects of varying sizes within their companies. Therefore, benchmarking against a specific duration to identify all projects at risk is not possible. For example, for a 5-year project, a company could benchmark 20 days of schedule variance as an acceptable level; yet using a benchmark of 20 days for a 3-month project is not feasible. Setting a benchmark in days is almost impossible. However, setting the benchmark parameter as a percentage is acceptable, e.g., 0 to 10% of the schedule variance % (time). Beyond the 10% parameter, a project would be considered at risk and require involvement of senior management. (Note: Some companies benchmark the schedule performance indicator as well.)

Schedule Performance Indicator (Time)

Schedule performance indicator (time) (SPI$_t$) is an index showing the efficiency of time utilized on a project. The formula below gives the efficiency of the project team in utilizing the time allocated for the project. A SPI$_t$ value above 1 indicates a project team is very

Table 3.12. Schedule Performance Indicator (Time) Calculation

Task ID	Tasks	Effort Hours	Duration in Days	Start Day	End Day	Resource	% Complete	Wgtd Avg %
1	Task 1	24	3	1	3	R1	100%	6%
2	Task 2	32	6	4	9	R2	75%	6%
3	Task 3	48	8	4	11	R3	60%	7%
4	Task 4	64	12	4	15	R1	100%	16%
5	Task 5	16	2	16	17	R1		0%
6	Task 6	32	6	10	15	R2	50%	4%
7	Task 7	24	5	12	16	R3		0%
8	Task 8	40	7	4	10	R4	100%	10%
9	Task 9	48	8	4	11	R5	100%	12%
10	Task 10	64	12	4	15	R6	50%	8%
		392		1	17			71%

Task ID	DEP	Day 10 PT	Day 10 ET	Day 10 SV_t	Day 10 $SV\%_t$	Day 10 SPI_t
1		3.00	10.00	0.00	0%	1.00
2	1	4.50	7.00	-2.50	-56%	0.64
3	1	4.80	7.00	-2.20	-46%	0.69
4		12.00	7.00	5.00	42%	1.71
5	4	0.00	0.00	0.00	0%	1.00
6	1	3.00	1.00	2.00	67%	3.00
7	1	0.00	0.00	0.00	0%	1.00
8	1	7.00	7.00	0.00	0%	1.00
9	1	8.00	7.00	1.00	13%	1.14
10	1	6.00	7.00	-1.00	-17%	0.86
		12.00	10.00	2.00	17%	1.20

Legend: ■ Red   ▨ Green

Wgtd Avg: weighted average
DEP: dependency

efficient in utilizing time allocated to the project, whereas a SPI_t value below 1 indicates a project team is less efficient in utilizing time allocated to the project. Schedule performance indicator (time) can be calculated using the formula:

$$SPI_t = \frac{planned\ time(PT)}{elapsed\ time(ET)}$$

Continuing with our example, let's consider SPI_t. In Table 3.12, notice that SPI_t values are in the last column. These SPI_t values reflect the same type of picture as shown earlier for the other schedule (time) performance measures. The only difference is that SPI_t gives the efficiency of the project team in utilizing time allotted for the project. A SPI_t below 1 is not good—it indicates that a task or the project is behind schedule; a SPI_t above 1 indicates that a project team has been very efficient in utilizing time for a task or project; therefore, the task or project is ahead of schedule.

SPI_t also shows the current performance of a team as of a particular date (which is considered to be the current status of the project). Notice that Task 2 has a SPI_t value of 0.64, meaning the resource on this task is utilizing time at 64% efficiency. Because this efficiency is lower than the planned efficiency of 100%, Task 2 is behind schedule. Similarly, other tasks are ahead or behind schedule. Yet notice that at the project level, indicated at the bottom of the Table 3.12, the SPI_t value is 1.20, meaning that as a team the project team has been very efficient because the time utilized on the project has been at 120% efficiency. Therefore, the overall project is ahead of schedule even though individual tasks might have a different status. However, by looking at a drill-down view of tasks and at the overall project, a project manager can quickly move between macro and micro project management to aid decision making.

So what does 120% efficiency mean at the project level? It simply means that on Day 10 the project is ahead by 2 days—derived from the following calculation: $(1.20 \times 10) - 10$ days = 2 days. In this case the result is in days because a reporting period of days has been chosen; if the reporting period is weeks, then the result would be in weeks. Always keep the reporting period in mind when reporting status based on EVM values.

We have examined the different schedule performance measures from the perspective of time. Clearly the difference in reporting is that from the time aspect, performance measures are reported in units of time (rather than in the units of cost). Keep in mind that the individual task level schedule performance indicator (time) (SPI_t) will not roll up to overall project SPI_t because individual tasks are considered as separate projects when calculating SPI_t.

To-Complete Schedule Performance Indicator (Time)

The to-complete schedule performance indicator (time) ($TSPI_t$) is a forecast of schedule performance needed going forward, keeping the current status (as reflected by $TSPI_t$) in mind. A $TSPI_t$ forecast shows the efficiency with which a project team must utilize the remaining time in a project. A $TSPI_t$ value above 1 indicates that a project is currently behind schedule and that the project team needs to work at a higher efficiency level to bring the project back on track. A $TSPI_t$ value below 1, however, indicates that the project

Table 3.13. To-Complete Schedule Performance Indicator (Time) Calculation

Task ID	Tasks	Effort Hours	Duration in Days	Start Day	End Day	Resource	% Complete	Wgtd Avg %	DEP	Day 10 PT	Day 10 ET	Day 10 SPI$_t$	Day 10 TSPI$_t$
1	Task 1	24	3	1	3	R1	100%	6%		3.00	10.00	1.00	0.00
2	Task 2	32	6	4	9	R2	75%	6%	1	4.50	7.00	0.64	1.25
3	Task 3	48	8	4	11	R3	60%	7%	1	4.80	7.00	0.69	1.22
4	Task 4	64	12	4	15	R1	100%	16%		12.00	7.00	1.71	0.00
5	Task 5	16	2	16	17	R1		0%	4	0.00	0.00	1.00	1.00
6	Task 6	32	6	10	15	R2	50%	4%	1	3.00	1.00	3.00	0.88
7	Task 7	24	5	12	16	R3		0%	1	0.00	0.00	1.00	1.00
8	Task 8	40	7	4	10	R4	100%	10%	1	7.00	7.00	1.00	0.00
9	Task 9	48	8	4	11	R5	100%	12%	1	8.00	7.00	1.14	0.00
10	Task 10	64	12	4	15	R6	50%	8%	1	6.00	7.00	0.86	1.10
		392		1	17		71%			12.00	10.00	1.20	0.71

Legend: ☐ Red ☐ Green

Wgtd Avg: weighted average
DEP: dependency

is currently ahead of schedule and that the project team can work at a lower efficiency level to keep the project on schedule. TSPI$_t$ is calculated using the formula:

$$TSPI_t = \frac{(total\ periods - PT)}{(total\ periods - ET)}$$

In this formula, notice that we are using *total periods,* which is actually the total reporting periods—or budget at completion (time), BAC$_t$, which indicates the total reporting periods. Using our example, the value for total periods would be 17 days because the reporting periods are in days and the total days for the project are 17.

Remembering that a to-complete schedule performance indicator (time) value is shown in units of the reporting period used, in our example the TSPI$_t$ value obtained will be in days. (Another project might have weeks chosen as the reporting period; in this case, the TSPI$_t$ value would be in weeks.)

Using our example, let's see how TSPI$_t$ is reflected in the project's status. Table 3.13 adds TSPI$_t$ to our picture of SPI$_t$ and the other schedule performance measures. Each measure gives a different message because the meaning derived from each performance measure is different. Like the to-complete schedule performance indicator (TSPI), the to-complete schedule performance indicator (time) (TSPI$_t$) is a forecast of the future performance needed on the schedule (or the time aspect of the project) to keep it on track.

In Table 3.13, the TSPI$_t$ is 1.25 for Task 2, meaning that the future efficiency of the resource on Task 2 needs to be at the 125% level rather than at the 100% level. As seen using the other measures, although some tasks are behind schedule and some are ahead of schedule, overall, at the project level, the project is doing well.

At this point, the question might be why is TSPI$_t$ 0.71 (71%) and not 0.80 (80%), which can be derived from the 1.20 (120%) value of the SPI$_t$? The reason is that we are not at the halfway point in the project—we are past the halfway mark. If we were exactly at the halfway point in the project in terms of duration, then we could derive TSPI$_t$ from SPI$_t$ just by using the formula (SPI$_t$ − 2).

Cost/Effort Variance

Cost/effort variance (*CV*) as opposed to schedule variance is the measure of the variance between earned value of the project and actual costs incurred in the project. By using the cost/effort variance performance measure, a project manager can easily tell if a project is over or under budget as of a particular day or reporting period. (Note: As mentioned earlier, instead of using actual costs in dollars, effort in hours can also be used to compute cost variance. If effort is used, the result is called the effort variance.)

The terms over budget and under budget describe how much cost or effort has been saved or overspent on a project as of a particular reporting period. The following formula gives variance in terms of cost or effort which will indicate how much less/more cost or effort has been used to complete work to date. A positive variance indicates an under-budget situation; a negative variance indicates an over-budget situation. Cost variance can be calculated using the formula:

$$Cost\ variance\ (CV) = earned\ value\ (EV) - actual\ cost\ (AC)$$

or

$$Cost\ variance\ (CV) = BCWP - ACWP$$

Continuing with our example, let's examine cost variance in our project. In Table 3.14, as of Day 10, Tasks 1, 2, 9, and 10 are over budget and Tasks 3, 4, and 6 are under budget. At the overall project level, the project is over budget. Task 2 is over budget by $24, meaning $24 more has been spent than the planned budget ($72) for work completed so far in the project. A task/project can go over budget in many ways. Most often an over-budget situation is due to a schedule overrun; however, a task can be on schedule, yet be over budget as in Task 1. In Task 1, the over-budget situation could be because some resources worked extra hours per day.

Table 3.14. Cost Variance Calculation

Task ID	Tasks	Effort Hours	Duration in Days	Start Day	End Day	% Complete	Resource	Resource Rate	DEP	Day 10 PV	Day 10 AC	Day 10 EV	Day 10 CV
1	Task 1	24	3	1	3	100%	R1	$2.00		$48.00	$60.00	$48.00	$(12.00)
2	Task 2	32	6	4	9	75%	R2	$3.00	1	$96.00	$96.00	$72.00	$(24.00)
3	Task 3	48	8	4	11	60%	R3	$4.00	1	$160.00	$110.00	$115.20	$5.20
4	Task 4	64	12	4	15	100%	R1	$2.00		$80.00	$100.00	$128.00	$28.00
5	Task 5	16	2	16	17		R1	$2.00	4	$ —	$ —	$ —	$ —
6	Task 6	32	6	10	15	50%	R2	$3.00	1	$24.00	$30.00	$48.00	$18.00
7	Task 7	24	5	12	16		R3	$4.00	1	$ —	$ —	$ —	$ —
8	Task 8	40	7	4	10	100%	R4	$2.50	1	$100.00	$100.00	$100.00	$ —
9	Task 9	48	8	4	11	100%	R5	$2.50	1	$100.00	$130.00	$120.00	$(10.00)
10	Task 10	64	12	4	15	50%	R6	$2.50	1	$100.00	$100.00	$80.00	$(20.00)
										$726.00	$711.20		$(14.80)

Legend: Red Yellow Green

DEP: dependency.

Using cost variance, we have the same situation of some tasks being over or under budget and the overall project being over or under budget. Cost variance provides another view at individual task level and at overall project level to facilitate moving between macro- and micromanagement of the project.

For cost variance, a project manager should maximize tasks which are under budget and minimize the effect of tasks which are already over budget. Tasks that are already completed cannot be corrected; therefore, a project manager should concentrate on tasks that are currently underway or are planned for the future.

Cost Variance Percent

Cost variance percent (CV% or cost variance %) indicates how much a project is over or under budget in terms of percent. A formula can be used to derive the variance of money spent (how much less or how much more) to complete the work as planned. A positive variance percent indicates the percent under budget; a negative variance percent indicates the percent over budget. Cost variance % can be calculated using the formula:

Cost variance percent (CV%) = cost variance (CV)/earned value (EV)

or

$$CV\% = CV/BCWP$$

Using our example, let's see how cost variance % is shown and what can be deduced from the values (Table 3.15). Notice that cost variance percent column has been added to

Table 3.15. Cost Variance Percent Calculation

Task ID	Tasks	Effort Hours	Duration in Days	Start Day	End Day	% Complete	Resource	Resource Rate
1	Task 1	24	3	1	3	100%	R1	$2.00
2	Task 2	32	6	4	9	75%	R2	$3.00
3	Task 3	48	8	4	11	60%	R3	$4.00
4	Task 4	64	12	4	15	100%	R1	$2.00
5	Task 5	16	2	16	17		R1	$2.00
6	Task 6	32	6	10	15	50%	R2	$3.00
7	Task 7	24	5	12	16		R3	$4.00
8	Task 8	40	7	4	10	100%	R4	$2.50
9	Task 9	48	8	4	11	100%	R5	$2.50
10	Task 10	64	12	4	15	50%	R6	$2.50

Task ID	DEP	Day 10 PV	Day 10 AC	Day 10 EV	Day 10 CV	Day 10 CV%
1		$48.00	$60.00	$48.00	$(12.00)	–25%
2	1	$96.00	$96.00	$72.00	$(24.00)	–33%
3	1	$160.00	$110.00	$115.20	$5.20	5%
4		$80.00	$100.00	$128.00	$28.00	22%
5	4	$ –	$ –	$ –	$ –	0%
6	1	$24.00	$30.00	$48.00	$18.00	38%
7	1	$ –	$ –	$ –	$ –	0%
8	1	$100.00	$100.00	$100.00	$ –	0%
9	1	$100.00	$130.00	$120.00	$(10.00)	–8%
10	1	$100.00	$100.00	$80.00	$(20.00)	–25%
		$726.00	$711.20	$(14.80)		–2%

Legend: **Red** **Yellow** **Green**

DEP: dependency.

this table. Cost variance percent provides the same picture as cost variance (from Table 3.14), except cost variance percent is a view of the same picture from a different angle—it gives the percent of variance from the aspect of cost/effort.

Notice that Task 1 has a negative 25% variance, meaning the project team has utilized 25% more cost/effort to finish Task 1 than was originally planned for Task 1. As in earlier examples, some tasks are under budget and some are over budget; overall the project is over budget by 2%.

When the cost variance percent at the overall project level is 2%, then for every $100 of planned work, the project team is spending $102 to complete the work. Generally, all companies have red/yellow/green indicators with thresholds for each color which are clearly defined. Commonly (and this is used for Tables 3.14 – 3.17), red is used for values below (<) –10%; yellow is used for values below (<) 0% but greater than or equal to (≥) –10%; and green is used for values that are 0% or above. Using these indicators provides a quick "snapshot" of a performance measure and indicates the severity of the situation, allowing a project manager to take the necessary action.

All tasks/projects might not necessarily have a schedule and a cost variance; yet they can have either or both. Often, however, a schedule variance leads to a cost variance. When a task/project is put on hold, and no work is done, a *schedule* overrun occurs, but because no effort is being used for the tasks/project, no cost overrun occurs.

Remember that effort may be used instead of cost. In this case, the performance measure is known as effort variance rather than cost variance. To use effort, apply a resource rate of $1 to arrive at effort variance.

Cost Performance Indicator

The cost performance indicator (CPI) is an index showing the efficiency of resource utilization in a project. A formula can be used to determine the efficiency of resource utilization allocated to a project. A cost performance indicator value above 1 indicates that the efficiency of resource utilization for resources allocated to the project is good; a cost performance indicator value below 1 indicates that the efficiency of resource utilization of resources allocated to the project is poor. The cost performance indicator can be calculated using the formula:

Cost performance indicator (CPI) = earned value (EV)/actual cost (AC)

or

$$CPI = BCWP/ACWP$$

Using our example, let's see how the cost performance indicator value is shown (Table 3.16). Remember that the cost performance indicator measures the efficiency of resources being used in a project or the efficiency of a project team in utilizing money in the project. In the last column of Table 3.16, the cost performance indicator provides the same type of picture as the other two performance measures which are also related to cost. However, the cost performance indicator measure shows efficiency (which can be converted into a percent). By default, in every schedule, resources are expected to perform at 100% efficiency to achieve the required schedule on time and on budget. Usually there will be differing efficiency levels among the resources because no two resources are the same; some perform better, while others perform at lower efficiency levels. Overall, how efficiently

Table 3.16. Cost Performance Indicator Calculation

Task ID	Tasks	Effort Hours	Duration in Days	Start Day	End Day	% Complete	Resource	Resource Rate
1	Task 1	24	3	1	3	100%	R1	$2.00
2	Task 2	32	6	4	9	75%	R2	$3.00
3	Task 3	48	8	4	11	60%	R3	$4.00
4	Task 4	64	12	4	15	100%	R1	$2.00
5	Task 5	16	2	16	17		R1	$2.00
6	Task 6	32	6	10	15	50%	R2	$3.00
7	Task 7	24	5	12	16		R3	$4.00
8	Task 8	40	7	4	10	100%	R4	$2.50
9	Task 9	48	8	4	11	100%	R5	$2.50
10	Task 10	64	12	4	15	50%	R6	$2.50

Task ID	DEP	Day 10 PV	Day 10 AC	Day 10 EV	Day 10 CV	Day 10 CV%	Day 10 CPI
1		$48.00	$60.00	$48.00	$(12.00)	–25%	0.80
2	1	$96.00	$96.00	$72.00	$(24.00)	–33%	0.75
3	1	$160.00	$110.00	$115.20	$5.20	5%	1.05
4		$80.00	$100.00	$128.00	$28.00	22%	1.08
5	4	$ –	$ –	$ –	$ –	0%	1.00
6	1	$24.00	$30.00	$48.00	$18.00	38%	1.60
7	1	$ –	$ –	$ –	$ –	0%	1.00
8	1	$100.00	$100.00	$100.00	$ –	0%	1.00
9	1	$100.00	$130.00	$120.00	$(10.00)	–8%	0.92
10	1	$100.00	$100.00	$80.00	$(20.00)	–25%	0.80
		$726.00	$711.20	$(14.80)	–2%	0.98

Legend: | Red | Yellow | Green |

DEP: dependency.

resources perform as a project team determines if a project is under budget, over budget, or on budget.

In Table 3.16, Task 2 has a cost performance indicator of 0.75, meaning that the resource(s) working on this task is/are being utilized at a 75% efficiency level compared to the optimum level of 100%—which is the reason the task is over budget. For example, if a task has been budgeted at $75, and it is being completed at a 75% level, then this task is being completed at an actual cost of $100.

Similarly, the cost performance indicator also shows that some tasks are over budget and some are under budget, but that overall the project might have a different outcome (in this case, the project is slightly over budget overall). Therefore, the project manager has to first look at the cost performance indicator at the project level and then drill down to the individual task level to take the necessary action.

In Table 3.16, the cost performance indicator at project level is 0.98, meaning that project resources are being utilized at a 98% efficiency level. Using red/yellow/green categorization, this situation might fall into the yellow category, meaning that although the project is over budget, it is still manageable and no senior management intervention is needed. However, the project manager needs to work toward bringing the cost performance indicator value up to 1 or above.

To-Complete Cost Performance Indicator

The to-complete cost performance indicator (TCPI) is an index showing the efficiency at which project resources should be utilized for the remainder of a project. The formula below gives the efficiency at which the project team should be utilized for the remainder of the project. A to-complete cost performance indicator value below 1 indicates resource utilization by the project team for the remainder of the project can be lenient, whereas a value above 1 indicates resource utilization for the remainder of the project should be stringent. The to-complete cost performance indicator can be calculated using the formula:

To-complete cost performance indicator (TCPI) = (total budget – EV)/(total budget – AC)

or

$$TCPI = (BAC - BCWP)/(BAC - ACWP)$$

Let's see how the to-complete cost performance indicator calculation is reflected in the status of our example (Table 3.17). Remember that the to-complete cost performance indicator forecasts the future performance needed to keep the project on track. Therefore, the TCPI value of 1.03 for Task 2 in the last column indicates that the future efficiency of resource utilization on the task must be at 103% compared to the 100% level. The resource on Task 2 must perform at a higher efficiency level because the current state of the task is over budget. In other words, when we say that the future efficiency of project resources utilization must be at the 103% level, $100 worth of work must be completed by spending $97.

All of the forecasting performance measures—to-complete schedule performance indicator, to-complete schedule performance indicator (time), and to-complete cost performance indicator—are to provide forecasts of what needs to be done to bring a project back on schedule or back on budget. Corrective measures may be taken only up to a cer-

Table 3.17. To-Complete Performance Indicator Calculation

Task ID	Tasks	Effort Hours	Duration in Days	Start Day	End Day	% Complete	Resource	Resource Rate
1	Task 1	24	3	1	3	100%	R1	$2.00
2	Task 2	32	6	4	9	75%	R2	$3.00
3	Task 3	48	8	4	11	60%	R3	$4.00
4	Task 4	64	12	4	15	100%	R1	$2.00
5	Task 5	16	2	16	17		R1	$2.00
6	Task 6	32	6	10	15	50%	R2	$3.00
7	Task 7	24	5	12	16		R3	$4.00
8	Task 8	40	7	4	10	100%	R4	$2.50
9	Task 9	48	8	4	11	100%	R5	$2.50
10	Task 10	64	12	4	15	50%	R6	$2.50

Task ID	DEP	Day 10 PV	Day 10 AC	Day 10 EV	Day 10 CV	Day 10 CV%	Day 10 CPI	Day 10 TCPI
1		$48.00	$60.00	$48.00	$(12.00)	−25%	0.80	1.01
2	1	$96.00	$96.00	$72.00	$(24.00)	−33%	0.75	1.03
3	1	$160.00	$110.00	$115.20	$5.20	5%	1.05	0.99
4		$80.00	$100.00	$128.00	$28.00	22%	1.08	0.97
5	4	$ −	$ −	$ −	$ −	0%	1.00	1.00
6	1	$24.00	$30.00	$48.00	$18.00	38%	1.60	0.98
7	1	$ −	$ −	$ −	$ −	0%	1.00	1.00
8	1	$100.00	$100.00	$100.00	$ −	0%	1.00	1.00
9	1	$100.00	$130.00	$120.00	$(10.00)	−8%	0.92	1.01
10	1	$100.00	$100.00	$80.00	$(20.00)	−25%	0.80	1.02
		$726.00	$711.20	$(14.80)	−2%	0.98	1.05	

Legend: **Red** **Yellow** **Green**

DEP: dependency.

tain point in a project. After a project has either gone beyond its total schedule or gone over the total budget allocated, the *point of no return* has been reached.

So when do we reach the point of no return? Let's continue with our example which has a total duration of 17 days (as shown in Table 3.1) and a total budget of $1036 (as shown in Table 3.2). Suppose at any point in the project that we exceed the total number of 17 days which has been allocated to the project. In this situation, we are already behind schedule. There is no way to bring the project back on schedule. Therefore, we have reached the point of no return. The to-complete schedule performance indicator (time) ($TSPI_t$) value will become negative and have no meaning.

Similarly, if at any point in time the project costs exceed the total budget of $1036, then this is a point of no return based on costs. Beyond this point, we must ensure that losses

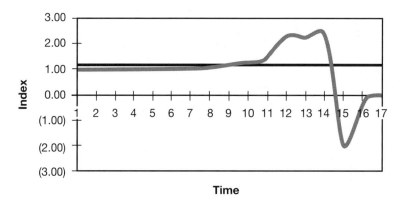

Figure 3.1. Effect of constant cost performance indicator on to-complete cost performance indicator.

are kept to a minimum because there is no way to get back funds already spent. After the point of no return, the to-complete cost performance indicator (TCPI) value will go negative and provide no meaningful value. At this point, it is better to not consider the TCPI value at all. (Note: To continue to use TSPI, $TSPI_t$, and TCPI beyond the point of no return, rebaseline the schedule with the revised total duration of the project and the revised total budget of the project.)

It is important to remember that with respect to the EVM forecasting performance measures they are indexes which if used (e.g., a 10% schedule variance) at the *beginning* of the project will yield a better TSPI value than if used during the middle or at the end of a project. If we plot a graph to show the effect of constant cost variance throughout a project on the TCPI (to-complete cost performance indicator), then we will see that the TCPI value increases with time and at the point of no return goes negative. It returns to zero at the end of a project (Table 3.18 and Figure 3.1).

In Table 3.18, the cost performance indicator (CPI) has been kept constant throughout the project. The to-complete cost performance indicator (TCPI) value increases as time progresses because as time progresses, bringing the project back on track with respect to schedule or cost becomes more and more difficult. The TCPI value goes negative on Day 15. Therefore, Day 15 becomes the point of no return because beyond this point the project cannot be brought back on track in terms of cost. Notice that the actual cost spent as of Day 15 is $1069, which is above the total project budget of $1036. Therefore, on Day 15, the project is already over budget by $63 which cannot be recovered.

Table 3.18. Effect on To-Complete Cost Performance Indicator with Constant Cost Performance Indicator

Task ID	Tasks	Effort Hours	Duration in Days	Start Day	End Day	% Complete	Resource	Resource Rate
1	Task 1	24	3	1	3	100%	R1	$2.00
2	Task 2	32	6	4	9	75%	R2	$3.00
3	Task 3	48	8	4	11	60%	R3	$4.00
4	Task 4	64	12	4	15	100%	R1	$2.00
5	Task 5	16	2	16	17		R1	$2.00
6	Task 6	32	6	10	15	50%	R2	$3.00
7	Task 7	24	5	12	16		R3	$4.00
8	Task 8	40	7	4	10	100%	R4	$2.50
9	Task 9	48	8	4	11	100%	R5	$2.50
10	Task 10	64	12	4	15	50%	R6	$2.50

Task ID	DEP	Day 1	Day 2	Day 3	Day 4	Day 5	Day 6	Day 7	Day 8	Day 9	Day 10	Day 11	Day 12	Day 13	Day 14	Day 15	Day 16	Day 17
1																		
2	1	$16	$16	$16	$24	$24			$24	$24								
3	1				$32	$32			$32	$32	$32							
4					$16	$16			$16	$16	$16	$16	$16			$16		
5	4																$16	$16
6	1										$24	$24	$24			$24		
7	1												$32			$32	$32	
8	1				$20	$20			$20	$20	$20							
9	1				$20	$20			$20	$20	$20	$20						
10	1				$20	$20			$20	$20	$20	$20	$20			$20		
	Total	$16	$16	$16	$132	$132	$ –	$ –	$132	$132	$132	$80	$92	$ –	$ –	$92	$48	$16
	PV	$16	$32	$48	$180	$312	$312	$312	$444	$576	$708	$788	$880	$880	$880	$972	$1,020	$1,036
	EV	$16	$32	$48	$180	$312	$312	$312	$444	$576	$708	$788	$880	$880	$880	$972	$1,020	$1,036
	AC	$18	$35	$53	$198	$312	$343	$343	$488	$634	$779	$867	$968	$968	$880	$1,069	$1,122	$1,140
	CPI	1.10	1.10	1.10	1.10	1.10	1.10	1.10	1.10	1.10	1.10	1.10	1.10	1.10	1.10	1.10	1.10	1.10
	TCPI	1.00	1.00	1.00	1.02	1.05	1.05	1.05	1.05	1.08	1.14	1.28	1.47	2.29	2.29	(1.93)	(0.19)	0.00

DEP: dependency

Notice in the graph in Figure 3.1 that the TCPI value keeps climbing until Day 14. On Day 14 the point of no return has not yet been reached, but on Day 15, we go past the point of no return, which is reflected by the dip in the graph. The TCPI value beyond this point is meaningless because now there is no way to bring the project back on track. When the point of no return is reached, look at the remaining work to be done and determine if the project can be rebaselined with a revised budget and schedule.

Table 3.19. Budget at Completion Calculation

Task ID	Tasks	Effort Hours	Duration in Days	Start Day	End Day	% Complete	Resource	Resource Rate	DEP	Total PV
1	Task 1	24	3	1	3	100%	R1	$2.00		$48.00
2	Task 2	32	6	4	9	75%	R2	$3.00	1	$96.00
3	Task 3	48	8	4	11	60%	R3	$4.00	1	$192.00
4	Task 4	64	12	4	15	100%	R1	$2.00		$128.00
5	Task 5	16	2	16	17		R1	$2.00	4	$32.00
6	Task 6	32	6	10	15	50%	R2	$3.00	1	$96.00
7	Task 7	24	5	12	16		R3	$4.00	1	$96.00
8	Task 8	40	7	4	10	100%	R4	$2.50	1	$100.00
9	Task 9	48	8	4	11	100%	R5	$2.50	1	$120.00
10	Task 10	64	12	4	15	50%	R6	$2.50	1	$160.00
									BAC =	$1,068.00

DEP: dependency.

Budget at Completion

Budget at completion (BAC) is the total budget allocated to a project. Budget at completion is generally plotted over time in reporting periods (weekly, monthly, etc). It is used to compute the estimate at completion (EAC). Budget at completion is also used to compute TCPI, $TSPI_t$, and TSPI. It can also be perceived as a total cumulative planned value (PV) for the project.

Using our example, let's see how budget at completion is computed (Table 3.19). BAC is the total of the planned value for each task at the end of a project. To calculate the total planned value for an individual task, multiply the effort hours by the resource rate for that task. Summing up the total planned value for all of the tasks gives the budget at completion for our project.

Budget at completion, when plotted over time and calculated as the cumulative planned value, yields the well-known S-curve. However, to get a strictly accurate S-curve, resources must be leveled optimally. (Note: Resource leveling is discussed in Chapter 5.)

Budget at Completion (Time)

Budget at completion (time) (BAC_t) is the total budgeted *duration* allocated to a project (as opposed to the total budgeted cost in budget at completion). BAC_t is generally plotted over time in reporting periods reporting (weekly, monthly, etc). It is used to compute the estimate at completion (time) (EAC_t). BAC_t is also used to compute the to-complete schedule performance (time) ($TSPI_t$).

Budget at completion (time) can also be looked at as the total elapsed time (ET) for a project. Using our example, let's see how budget at completion (time) is computed (Table

Table 3.20. Budget at Completion (Time) Calculation

Task ID	Tasks	Effort Hours	Duration in Days	Start Day	End Day	% Complete	Resource	Resource Rate	DEP	Total Project ET
1	Task 1	24	3	1	3	100%	R1	$2.00		3.00
2	Task 2	32	6	4	9	75%	R2	$3.00	1	9.00
3	Task 3	48	8	4	11	60%	R3	$4.00	1	11.00
4	Task 4	64	12	4	15	100%	R1	$2.00		15.00
5	Task 5	16	2	16	17		R1	$2.00	4	17.00
6	Task 6	32	6	10	15	50%	R2	$3.00	1	15.00
7	Task 7	24	5	12	16		R3	$4.00	1	16.00
8	Task 8	40	7	4	10	100%	R4	$2.50	1	10.00
9	Task 9	48	8	4	11	100%	R5	$2.50	1	11.00
10	Task 10	64	12	4	15	50%	R6	$2.50	1	15.00
									$BAC_t =$	17.00

DEP: dependency.

3.20). Remembering that BAC_t is the *total* amount of elapsed time (ET) at the end of a project, look at the task's **End Day** column for the total elapsed time for an individual task to see the total elapsed time for that task. The highest total elapsed time for any of the tasks (17.00 in the last column) is the budget at completion (time) or BAC_t for the project. Using the formula, the calculation would be (maximum task end day – minimum task start day + 1), which in our example is $17 – 1 + 1 = 17$.

Estimate to Complete

Estimate to complete (ETC) is the estimated cost required to complete the remainder of a project. Estimate to complete is calculated and applied when estimating assumptions made in the past become invalid and therefore new estimates are needed. It should be computed at the stage in a project when flaws are discovered in the assumptions used for the original estimates or when changes have occurred during the course of the project which cause the original estimates to no longer be valid. When this situation occurs, calculate the estimate to complete so that revised estimates can be applied to the project.

The calculation of an ETC can be needed for a positive or negative variance. Most often, however, an estimate to complete is calculated when a variance is negative because that is when a project is in trouble and additional funding approval might be needed from the project sponsor. If variances are large and positive, a new estimate might not be necessary. Sometimes a project with a large positive variance is completed "as is" because the course of the project is not affected and no additional approval is required from senior management. Even in the case of positive variances, a reestimate might be desirable so that some of the budget allocated to this project could be diverted to other projects in the organization that are in trouble.

Estimate to complete is sometimes used to show the value of the remaining budget in the project and is calculated by using the formula:

$$\textit{Estimate to complete (ETC)} = \textit{budget at completion (BAC)} - \textit{actual cost (AC)}$$
$$+ \textit{additional estimates for change requests}$$

Note: ETC is used to compute estimate at completion (EAC). ETC can be computed using the estimating techniques that have been discussed previously.

Estimate at Completion

Estimate at completion (EAC) is the estimated cost of a project at the end of the project based on the current performance of the project. Therefore, early in a project, the estimate at completion will be almost equal to the budget at completion. As the project progresses this value changes. Calculation of the estimate at completion involves three scenarios:

Scenario 1. Variances are typical. In this scenario, variances at the current stage of the project are considered to be typical and are not expected to occur in the future. That is, there are variances at this time, but these variances are not expected to continue; the remainder of the project is expected to be completed as planned. The estimate at completion for Scenario 1 is calculated using the formula:

$$\textit{EAC (1)} = \textit{AC} + (\textit{BAC} - \textit{EV})$$

In this formula, BAC is the total budget and EV is the earned value of the project as of a certain day/period. (BAC – EV) will give the remaining work on the project; when this is added to AC (actual cost), the estimate at completion (EAC) is obtained. So in this case, EAC is BAC plus the current variances. Current variances are used because we are assuming that current variances will not affect the remainder of the project.

Using our example, let's look at the estimate at completion for Scenario 1 (Table 3.21). The estimate at completion is calculated using the following values:

$$\textit{EAC (1)} = \$726 + (\$1068 - \$711.20) = \$1082.80$$

Scenario 2. Past estimating assumptions are not valid. In this scenario, past estimating assumptions are not valid and fresh estimates need to be applied to the project (see the discussion in the *Estimate to Complete* calculation section.) The estimate at completion for Scenario 2 is calculated using the formula:

$$\textit{EAC (2)} = \textit{AC} + \textit{ETC}$$

Table 3.21. Estimate at Completion Calculation using Scenario 1

Task ID	Tasks	Effort Hours	Duration in Days	Start Day	End Day	% Complete	Resource	Resource Rate	DEP	Total PV	Day 10 AC	Day 10 EV	Day 10 CV
1	Task 1	24	3	1	3	100%	R1	$2.00		$48.00	$60.00	$48.00	$(12.00)
2	Task 2	32	6	4	9	75%	R2	$3.00	1	$96.00	$96.00	$72.00	$(24.00)
3	Task 3	48	8	4	11	60%	R3	$4.00	1	$192.00	$110.00	$115.20	$5.20
4	Task 4	64	12	4	15	100%	R1	$2.00		$128.00	$100.00	$128.00	$28.00
5	Task 5	16	2	16	17		R1	$2.00	4	$32.00	$ —	$ —	$ —
6	Task 6	32	6	10	15	50%	R2	$3.00	1	$96.00	$30.00	$48.00	$18.00
7	Task 7	24	5	12	16		R3	$4.00	1	$96.00	$ —	$ —	$ —
8	Task 8	40	7	4	10	100%	R4	$2.50	1	$100.00	$100.00	$100.00	$ —
9	Task 9	48	8	4	11	100%	R5	$2.50	1	$120.00	$130.00	$120.00	$(10.00)
10	Task 10	64	12	4	15	50%	R6	$2.50	1	$160.00	$100.00	$80.00	$(20.00)
									BAC =	$1,068.00	$726.00	$711.20	$(14.80)
									EAC (1) =	$1,082.80			

DEP: dependency.

This formula is easy to decipher. In this situation we are saying that we will reestimate the remainder of the project and arrive at the estimate to complete (ETC) value and add this value to the actual costs (AC) incurred on the project to date.

Suppose this scenario is applied to our example and we arrive at an estimate to complete the remainder of the project of $550. The estimate at completion (EAC) is calculated as follows:

$$EAC\ (2) = \$726 + \$550 = \$1276$$

Scenario 3. Variances will be present in the future. In this scenario, the assumption is that current variances will continue to be present in the future and that the project will have these variances at the same level going forward. The estimate at completion for Scenario 3 is calculated using the formula:

$$EAC\ (3) = AC + (BAC - EV)/CPI$$

In deciphering this formula, notice that it is similar to the one used for Scenario 1 except that the cost performance indicator (CPI) is used in this formula. In this formula, (BAC − EV) will give the remaining work on the project. When remaining work on the project is divided by the current cost performance indicator, the current performance of the project is projected on the remainder of the project to arrive at the budget needed to complete the remainder of the project. If this amount is added to the actual costs (AC), the result is the estimate at completion.

Table 3.22. Estimate at Completion Calculation using Scenario 3

Task ID	Tasks	Effort Hours	Duration in Days	Start Day	End Day	% Complete	Resource	Resource Rate	DEP	Total PV	Day 10 AC	Day 10 EV	Day 10 CV	Day 10 CPI
1	Task 1	24	3	1	3	100%	R1	$2.00		$48.00	$60.00	$48.00	$(12.00)	0.80
2	Task 2	32	6	4	9	75%	R2	$3.00	1	$96.00	$96.00	$72.00	$(24.00)	0.75
3	Task 3	48	8	4	11	60%	R3	$4.00	1	$192.00	$110.00	$115.20	$5.20	1.05
4	Task 4	64	12	4	15	100%	R1	$2.00		$128.00	$100.00	$128.00	$28.00	1.25
5	Task 5	16	2	16	17		R1	$2.00	4	$32.00	$ —	$ —	$ —	0.00
6	Task 6	32	6	10	15	50%	R2	$3.00	1	$96.00	$30.00	$48.00	$18.00	1.60
7	Task 7	24	5	12	16		R3	$4.00	1	$96.00	$ —	$ —	$ —	0.00
8	Task 8	40	7	4	10	100%	R4	$2.50	1	$100.00	$100.00	$100.00	$ —	1.00
9	Task 9	48	8	4	11	100%	R5	$2.50	1	$120.00	$130.00	$120.00	$(10.00)	0.92
10	Task 10	64	12	4	15	50%	R6	$2.50	1	$160.00	$100.00	$80.00	$(20.00)	0.80
									BAC =	$1,068.00	$726.00	$711.20	$(14.80)	0.98
									EAC (3) =	$1,090.08				

DEP: dependency.

Using our example, let's apply Scenario 3 to see the effect on the estimate at completion (Table 3.22). Apply the formula for calculating the EAC to obtain the value of $1090.08:

$$EAC\ (3) = 726.00 + (1068.00 - 711.20)/0.98 = \$1090.08$$

Estimate at Completion (Time)

Estimate at completion (time) (EAC_t) is the time version of the estimate at completion in which the total time estimate to complete the project is calculated. Estimate at completion (time) is almost the same as budget at completion (time) (BAC_t) in the early part of a project. As the project progresses, the estimate at completion (time) value goes up depending on variances present in the project. Estimate at completion (time) is calculated using the formula:

$$EAC_t = \frac{BAC/SPI}{BAC/BAC_t}$$

Deciphering this formula is simple. The numerator part of the formula (BAC/SPI) gives the extrapolated (projected) value of the budget that is needed to complete the project according to the current schedule performance. The denominator gives the budget allocated for each reporting period. So the numerator (in another way) gives the estimate at completion in terms of cost/effort and the denominator gives the budget allocated per reporting period. When these two are divided, the result is the estimate at completion (in terms of reporting period) needed to complete the project.

Table 3.23. Variance at Completion Calculation

Task ID	Tasks	Effort Hours	Duration in Days	Start Day	End Day	% Complete
1	Task 1	24	3	1	3	100%
2	Task 2	32	6	4	9	75%
3	Task 3	48	8	4	11	60%
4	Task 4	64	12	4	15	100%
5	Task 5	16	2	16	17	
6	Task 6	32	6	10	15	50%
7	Task 7	24	5	12	16	
8	Task 8	40	7	4	10	100%
9	Task 9	48	8	4	11	100%
10	Task 10	64	12	4	15	50%

Task ID	Resource	Resource Rate	DEP	Total PV	Day 10 AC	Day 10 EV	Day 10 CV	Day 10 CPI
1	R1	$ 2.00		$48.00	$60.00	$48.00	$(12.00)	0.80
2	R2	$ 3.00	1	$96.00	$96.00	$72.00	$(24.00)	0.75
3	R3	$ 4.00	1	$192.00	$110.00	$115.20	$5.20	1.05
4	R1	$ 2.00		$128.00	$100.00	$128.00	$28.00	1.25
5	R1	$ 2.00	4	$32.00	$ —	$ —	$ —	0.00
6	R2	$ 3.00	1	$96.00	$30.00	$48.00	$18.00	1.60
7	R3	$ 4.00	1	$96.00	$ —	$ —	$ —	0.00
8	R4	$ 2.50	1	$100.00	$100.00	$100.00	$ —	1.00
9	R5	$ 2.50	1	$120.00	$130.00	$120.00	$(10.00)	0.92
10	R6	$ 2.50	1	$160.00	$100.00	$80.00	$(20.00)	0.80
			BAC =	$1,068.00	$726.00	$711.20	$(14.80)	0.98
			ETC =	$550.00				
			EAC (1) =	$1,082.80	VAC (1) =	$(14.80)		
			EAC (2) =	$1,276.00	VAC (2) =	$(208.00)		
			EAC (3) =	$1,090.22	VAC (3) =	$(22.00)		

DEP: dependency

Continuing with our example, let's apply this formula to see how the estimate at completion is reflected:

$$EAC_t = (1068/1)/(1068/17) = 17$$

With the current variances, the estimate at completion (time) is the same as the budget at completion (time), meaning the project is on track.

Variance at Completion

Variance at completion (VAC) is the variance in the total budget at the end of the project. Variance at completion is calculated using the formula:

$$VAC = BAC - EAC$$

Variation at completion can be negative or positive. When positive, based on current performance, a project will be under budget at the end of the project; a negative variance, based on current performance, indicates that a project will be over budget at the end of the project. In other words, variation at completion is the cost variance (CV) at the end of the project with the current status of the project.

Using our example, let's see how the variance at completion is reflected in the three scenarios used earlier (in the *Estimate at Completion* section). Table 3.23 shows the variance at completion calculations for the three scenarios. Notice in the VAC (1) calculation that the current cost variation (14.80) is assumed to be the final cost variation at the end of the project.

Variance at Completion (Time)

Variance at completion (time) (VAC_t) is the variance in total budgeted time at the end of a project. Variance at completion (time) is calculated using the formula:

$$VAC_t = BAC_t - EAC_t$$

Variance at completion (time) can be negative or positive. When VAC_t is positive, based on current performance, a project will be ahead of schedule at the end of the project; a negative VAC_t indicates that a project will be behind schedule at the end of the project. In other words, variance at completion (time) is the schedule variance (time) (SV_t) at the end of the project based on the current status of the project. In our example, we have variance at completion (time) as 0, meaning we are right on target.

4

WHY EVM?

Earned Value Management (EVM) has numerous benefits including continuous assessment of a project's performance, cost, and status. Using performance measurement techniques, the future performance of a project can be estimated, and corrective or preventive action taken, to help ensure that a project is completed on schedule and within its budget and scope. This chapter discusses several benefits of EVM.

BENEFITS OF EVM EXPLORED

Monitors a Project as It Progresses

Tasks can be monitored as they progress, allowing preventive/corrective action to be taken during the course of a project. In the sample project shown in Figure 4.1, some summary activities have negative schedule and cost variances; these tasks need special monitoring going forward. In Figure 4.1, the project manager has objective evidence that some tasks are delayed; he can also see the contribution of these tasks to the overall delay in the project. He also has objective evidence of cost variance at the task level as well as the contribution of these tasks to the overall cost overrun in the project. By having this objective view, the project manager can make calculated decisions to improve the status of the project.

ID	Task Name	BCWS	BCWP	ACWP	SV	CV	EAC	BAC	VAC
1	**XYZ Project**	**$4,005.50**	**$3,981.36**	**$3,794.12**	**($24.15)**	**$187.23**	**$5,942.86**	**$5,875.76**	**($67.10)**
2	Module Self Study	$360.00	$360.00	$360.00	$0.00	$0.00	$360.00	$360.00	$0.00
3	Module Training	$360.00	$360.00	$360.00	$0.00	$0.00	$360.00	$360.00	$0.00
4	ABC Project Hold	$0.00	$0.00	$0.00	$0.00	$0.00	$0.00	$0.00	$0.00
5	Reschedule	$8.00	$8.00	$8.00	$0.00	$0.00	$8.00	$8.00	$0.00
6	Reschedule	$24.00	$24.00	$24.00	$0.00	$0.00	$24.00	$24.00	$0.00
7	Reschedule	$0.00	$0.00	$0.00	$0.00	$0.00	$0.00	$0.00	$0.00
8	Hold for Regression Testing	$0.00	$0.00	$0.00	$0.00	$0.00	$0.00	$0.00	$0.00
9	Reschedule	$0.00	$0.00	$0.00	$0.00	$0.00	$8.00	$0.00	($8.00)
10	**Project Management**	**$0.00**	**$0.00**	**$0.00**	**$0.00**	**$0.00**	**$0.00**	**$0.00**	**$0.00**
62	**Screen Rework**	**$76.00**	**$75.00**	**$76.00**	**($1.00)**	**($1.00)**	**$76.00**	**$76.00**	**$0.00**
76	**Test Design Re-Validation**	**$416.00**	**$368.00**	**$416.00**	**($48.00)**	**($48.00)**	**$416.00**	**$416.00**	**$0.00**
108	**Report Design Rework**	**$216.90**	**$260.00**	**$222.70**	**$43.10**	**$37.30**	**$222.70**	**$216.90**	**($5.80)**
167	**Masters & Transactions**	**$1,953.42**	**$2,016.26**	**$1,679.44**	**$62.84**	**$336.82**	**$3,820.18**	**$3,786.48**	**($33.70)**
168	**Application -1**	**$46.74**	**$79.04**	**$38.04**	**$32.30**	**$41.00**	**$38.04**	**$46.74**	**$8.70**
188	**Application -2**	**$38.74**	**$79.04**	**$25.50**	**$40.30**	**$53.54**	**$25.50**	**$38.74**	**$13.24**
208	**Application -3**	**$33.24**	**$79.04**	**$20.00**	**$45.80**	**$59.04**	**$20.00**	**$33.24**	**$13.24**
228	**Application -4**	**$61.74**	**$79.04**	**$46.04**	**$17.30**	**$33.00**	**$46.04**	**$61.74**	**$15.70**
248	**Application -5**	**$72.04**	**$79.04**	**$47.04**	**$7.00**	**$32.00**	**$47.04**	**$72.04**	**$25.00**
268	**Application -6**	**$79.04**	**$79.00**	**$18.04**	**($0.04)**	**$60.96**	**$18.04**	**$79.04**	**$61.00**

Figure 4.1. Objective evidence of how a project is progressing.

In Figure 4.1, notice that overall variances of the tasks are at project level. A drill-down view of the tasks and their contribution to overall project-level variances is shown in the columns and rows in Figure 4.1. Also notice that some tasks are ahead of schedule. The drill-down view allows a project manager to move between macro-level (the project level) and micro-level (the task level) management easily and effectively.

In Figure 4.1, the circled tasks require the attention of the project manager. He needs to look into these tasks and take action. Knowing which tasks need attention allows a project manager to *manage by exception* rather than trying to focus his energy on the entire project. The key to obtaining this benefit is by periodically updating the schedule. The project manager must update the schedule periodically, depending on the size of the project, and then look into any variances so that he can take the necessary corrective/preventive action.

ID	Task Name	BCWS	BCWP	ACWP	SV	CV	EAC	BAC	VAC
1	**XYZ Project**	**$4,005.50**	**$3,981.36**	**$3,794.12**	**($24.15)**	**$187.23**	**$5,942.86**	**$5,875.76**	**($67.10)**
2	Module Self Study	$360.00	$360.00	$360.00	$0.00	$0.00	$360.00	$360.00	$0.00
3	Module Training	$360.00	$360.00	$360.00	$0.00	$0.00	$360.00	$360.00	$0.00
4	ABC Project Hold	$0.00	$0.00	$0.00	$0.00	$0.00	$0.00	$0.00	$0.00
5	Reschedule	$8.00	$8.00	$8.00	$0.00	$0.00	$8.00	$8.00	$0.00
6	Reschedule	$24.00	$24.00	$24.00	$0.00	$0.00	$24.00	$24.00	$0.00
7	Reschedule	$0.00	$0.00	$0.00	$0.00	$0.00	$0.00	$0.00	$0.00
8	Hold for Regression Testing	$0.00	$0.00	$0.00	$0.00	$0.00	$0.00	$0.00	$0.00
9	Reschedule	$0.00	$0.00	$0.00	$0.00	$0.00	$8.00	$0.00	($8.00)
10	**Project Management**	**$0.00**	**$0.00**	**$0.00**	**$0.00**	**$0.00**	**$0.00**	**$0.00**	**$0.00**
62	**Screen Rework**	**$76.00**	**$75.00**	**$76.00**	**($1.00)**	**($1.00)**	**$76.00**	**$76.00**	**$0.00**
76	**Test Design Re-Validation**	**$416.00**	**$368.00**	**$416.00**	**($48.00)**	**($48.00)**	**$416.00**	**$416.00**	**$0.00**
108	**Report Design Rework**	**$216.90**	**$260.00**	**$222.70**	**$43.10**	**$37.30**	**$222.70**	**$216.90**	**($5.80)**
167	**Masters & Transactions**	**$1,953.42**	**$2,016.26**	**$1,679.44**	**$62.84**	**$336.82**	**$3,820.18**	**$3,786.48**	**($33.70)**
168	**Application -1**	**$46.74**	**$79.04**	**$38.04**	**$32.30**	**$41.00**	**$38.04**	**$46.74**	**$8.70**
188	**Application -2**	**$38.74**	**$79.04**	**$25.50**	**$40.30**	**$53.54**	**$25.50**	**$38.74**	**$13.24**
208	**Application -3**	**$33.24**	**$79.04**	**$20.00**	**$45.80**	**$59.04**	**$20.00**	**$33.24**	**$13.24**
228	**Application -4**	**$61.74**	**$79.04**	**$46.04**	**$17.30**	**$33.00**	**$46.04**	**$61.74**	**$15.70**
248	**Application -5**	**$72.04**	**$79.04**	**$47.04**	**$7.00**	**$32.00**	**$47.04**	**$72.04**	**$25.00**
268	**Application -6**	**$79.04**	**$79.00**	**$18.04**	**($0.04)**	**$60.96**	**$18.04**	**$79.04**	**$61.00**

Figure 4.2. Variances at a glance—the earned value view.

Shows Schedule/Cost Performance at a Glance

Having overall project schedule and effort parameters available at any given point in time also allows a project manager to take immediate preventive or corrective action. Continuing with our sample project, notice in Figure 4.2 that there is a negative schedule variance (in circle) which means that the project is behind schedule; therefore, corrective action needs to be taken. Notice also that there is a positive cost variance, meaning the project is running under budget—a good situation, but one that needs monitoring.

Using MPP, schedule and effort overruns are calculated correctly, with costs rolled up to the summary tasks, and made available with the click of a button. In Figure 4.2, notice that schedule and cost variances are available at all levels, which helps monitoring the tasks independently. It is important to remember is that by using this technique after every reporting period, variance data are immediately available to indicate where/when action needs to be taken. Choosing to update a schedule on a daily basis, but to report it, say weekly, is best because real-time information about project variances is accurate day by day.

ID	ⓘ	Task Name	% Comp.	Actual Work	Work	Start	Finish	Predecessors
1		**XYZ Project**	**60%**	**4,214.38 hrs**	**9,531.17 hrs**	**Tue 3/15/05**	**Thu 3/2/06**	
2	✓	Module Self Study	100%	360 hrs	360 hrs	Tue 3/15/05	Mon 3/21/05	
3	✓	Module Training	100%	360 hrs	360 hrs	Tue 3/22/05	Mon 3/28/05	2
4	✓	ABC Project Hold	100%	0 hrs	0 hrs	Mon 3/28/05	Mon 3/28/05	3
5	✓	Reschedule	100%	8 hrs	8 hrs	Mon 6/20/05	Mon 6/20/05	
6	✓	Reschedule	100%	24 hrs	24 hrs	Tue 5/31/05	Tue 5/31/05	
7	✓	Reschedule	100%	0 hrs	0 hrs	Tue 3/15/05	Tue 3/15/05	
8	✓	Hold for Regression Testing	100%	0 hrs	0 hrs	Mon 6/27/05	Mon 6/27/05	
9		Reschedule	0%	0 hrs	8 hrs	Tue 3/29/05	Tue 3/29/05	
10		**Project Management**	**15%**	**18 hrs**	**90 hrs**	**Mon 4/4/05**	**Thu 3/2/06**	
62		**Screen Rework**	**56%**	**96.98 hrs**	**176.98 hrs**	**Mon 4/18/05**	**Fri 9/23/05**	4
76	✓	**Test Design Re-Validation**	**100%**	**416 hrs**	**416 hrs**	**Tue 3/15/05**	**Tue 8/30/05**	4FS-10 days
108		**Report Design Rework**	**100%**	**369.07 hrs**	**467.42 hrs**	**Mon 4/4/05**	**Wed 5/25/05**	
167		**Masters & Transactions**	**49%**	**1,864.55 hrs**	**4,288.17 hrs**	**Tue 3/15/05**	**Thu 2/16/06**	4
168	✓	**Application -1**	**100%**	**38.03 hrs**	**38.03 hrs**	**Tue 3/15/05**	**Fri 6/3/05**	
188	✓	**Application -2**	**100%**	**25.5 hrs**	**25.5 hrs**	**Tue 4/5/05**	**Fri 6/3/05**	
208	✓	**Application -3**	**100%**	**20 hrs**	**20 hrs**	**Tue 4/5/05**	**Fri 6/3/05**	
228	✓	**Application -4**	**100%**	**46.03 hrs**	**46.03 hrs**	**Thu 4/7/05**	**Fri 6/17/05**	
248	✓	**Application -5**	**100%**	**47.03 hrs**	**47.03 hrs**	**Thu 4/7/05**	**Fri 6/17/05**	
268	✓	**Application -6**	**100%**	**18.03 hrs**	**18.03 hrs**	**Wed 6/8/05**	**Fri 6/17/05**	6

Figure 4.3. Variances using dates—the traditional view; FS, finish to start.

Uses Numbers Rather than Dates

Dealing with numbers is easier and better than dealing with dates. Notice that Figure 4.2, the earned value view, uses numbers rather than dates. Figure 4.3 shows the traditional view and uses dates. Numbers provide quantitative information that is more specific and easier to use. *Important:* Dealing with dates is very difficult because dates must be remembered when checking a project to see if it is on or behind schedule. Additionally, dates do not give any indication of the effort/cost parameters and variances. Dates only show that tasks and the project are either behind or ahead of schedule. Using dates also makes estimating the effect of a delay in a particular task on the overall project very difficult—something that is easily done using the earned value view. Because quantitative values are not associated with dates, the use of dates is an ineffective method for tracking project progress.

Quantifies and Tracks Delays Caused by External Factors

By introducing **Holds** in MPP, a hold period (circled area in Figure 4.4) can be discarded from the calculation of schedule overruns. Using **Holds** is beneficial in two ways—to have a record of delays caused by factors beyond the control of the project team; and to have

ID	⚈	Task Name	% Comp.	Actual Work	Work	Start	Finish	Predecessors
1		**XYZ Project**	60%	**4,214.38 hrs**	**9,531.17 hrs**	**Tue 3/15/05**	**Thu 3/2/06**	
2	✓	Module Self Study	100%	360 hrs	360 hrs	Tue 3/15/05	Mon 3/21/05	
3	✓	Module Training	100%	360 hrs	360 hrs	Tue 3/22/05	Mon 3/28/05	2
4	✓	ABC Project Hold	100%	0 hrs	0 hrs	Mon 3/28/05	Mon 3/28/05	3
5	✓	Reschedule	100%	8 hrs	8 hrs	Mon 6/20/05	Mon 6/20/05	
6	✓	Reschedule	100%	24 hrs	24 hrs	Tue 5/31/05	Tue 5/31/05	
7	✓	Reschedule	100%	0 hrs	0 hrs	Tue 3/15/05	Tue 3/15/05	
8	✓	Hold for Regression Testing	100%	0 hrs	0 hrs	Mon 6/27/05	Mon 6/27/05	
9		Reschedule	0%	0 hrs	8 hrs	Tue 3/29/05	Tue 3/29/05	
10		**Project Management**	15%	**18 hrs**	**90 hrs**	**Mon 4/4/05**	**Thu 3/2/06**	
62		**Screen Rework**	56%	**96.98 hrs**	**176.98 hrs**	**Mon 4/18/05**	**Fri 9/23/05**	4
76	✓	**Test Design Re-Validation**	100%	**416 hrs**	**416 hrs**	**Tue 3/15/05**	**Tue 8/30/05**	4FS-10 days
108		**Report Design Rework**	100%	**369.07 hrs**	**467.42 hrs**	**Mon 4/4/05**	**Wed 5/25/05**	
167		**Masters & Transactions**	49%	**1,864.55 hrs**	**4,288.17 hrs**	**Tue 3/15/05**	**Thu 2/16/06**	4
168	✓	Application -1	100%	38.03 hrs	38.03 hrs	Tue 3/15/05	Fri 6/3/05	
188	✓	Application -2	100%	25.5 hrs	25.5 hrs	Tue 4/5/05	Fri 6/3/05	
208	✓	Application -3	100%	20 hrs	20 hrs	Tue 4/5/05	Fri 6/3/05	
228	✓	Application -4	100%	46.03 hrs	46.03 hrs	Thu 4/7/05	Fri 6/17/05	
248	✓	Application -5	100%	47.03 hrs	47.03 hrs	Thu 4/7/05	Fri 6/17/05	
268	✓	Application -6	100%	18.03 hrs	18.03 hrs	Wed 6/8/05	Fri 6/17/05	6

Figure 4.4. Quantifying and tracking delays; FS, finish to start.

correct reporting numbers for schedule and cost parameters. To adjust for a hold in a project, introduce a new task in MPP and rebaseline the new task with all its summary tasks and assign a higher priority (1000) to the task. This process ensures that the hold is scheduled ahead of other tasks.

MPP is a good way to keep track of delays caused by external factors or delays that are beyond the control of a project team. Keeping a record of delays in a project can facilitate negotiations with project sponsors for additional budget amounts and/or additional time, because evidence has been collected over the course of project execution. Delays caused by external factors can be excluded from the original project and actual variances caused by the project team are recorded and the reasons for them are reported. Keeping a record of delays in a project also allows tapping into contingency reserves which have been set aside for risks attributed to external factors.

Embraces Change in a Project

A familiar scenario in some projects is the frequent occurrence of changes in priority that result in significant schedule changes and/or the reordering of tasks. In particular, when a project's schedule undergoes frequent changes and tasks change priorities, preparing new schedules and updating them becomes a nightmare. Project managers often spend half of

ID	❶	Priority	Task Name	% Comp.	Actual Work	Work	Start	Finish	Predecessors
1		500	XYZ Project	60%	4,214.38 hrs	9,531.17 hrs	Tue 3/15/05	Thu 3/2/06	
2	✓	1000	Module Self Study	100%	360 hrs	360 hrs	Tue 3/15/05	Mon 3/21/05	
3	✓	1000	Module Training	100%	360 hrs	360 hrs	Tue 3/22/05	Mon 3/28/05	2
4	✓	1000	ABC Project Hold	100%	0 hrs	0 hrs	Mon 3/28/05	Mon 3/28/05	3
5	✓	1000	Reschedule	100%	8 hrs	8 hrs	Mon 6/20/05	Mon 6/20/05	
6	✓	1000	Reschedule	100%	24 hrs	24 hrs	Tue 5/31/05	Tue 5/31/05	
7	✓	1000	Reschedule	100%	0 hrs	0 hrs	Tue 3/15/05	Tue 3/15/05	
8	✓	1000	Hold for Regression Testing	100%	0 hrs	0 hrs	Mon 6/27/05	Mon 6/27/05	
9		500	Reschedule	0%	0 hrs	8 hrs	Tue 3/29/05	Tue 3/29/05	
10		500	**Project Management**	15%	18 hrs	90 hrs	Mon 4/4/05	Thu 3/2/06	
62		500	**Screen Rework**	56%	96.98 hrs	176.98 hrs	Mon 4/18/05	Fri 9/23/05	4
76	✓	500	**Test Design Re-Validation**	100%	416 hrs	416 hrs	Tue 3/15/05	Tue 8/30/05	4FS-10 days
108		500	**Report Design Rework**	100%	369.07 hrs	467.42 hrs	Mon 4/4/05	Wed 5/25/05	
167		500	**Masters & Transactions**	49%	1,864.55 hrs	4,288.17 hrs	Tue 3/15/05	Thu 2/16/06	4
168	✓	100	**Application -1**	100%	38.03 hrs	38.03 hrs	Tue 3/15/05	Fri 6/3/05	
188	✓	90	**Application -2**	100%	25.5 hrs	25.5 hrs	Tue 4/5/05	Fri 6/3/05	
208	✓	80	**Application -3**	100%	20 hrs	20 hrs	Tue 4/5/05	Fri 6/3/05	
228	✓	70	**Application -4**	100%	46.03 hrs	46.03 hrs	Thu 4/7/05	Fri 6/17/05	
248	✓	60	**Application -5**	100%	47.03 hrs	47.03 hrs	Thu 4/7/05	Fri 6/17/05	
268	✓	30	**Application -6**	100%	18.03 hrs	18.03 hrs	Wed 6/8/05	Fri 6/17/05	6

Figure 4.5. Changes caused by schedule and priority changes; FS, finish to start.

their time making project updates. When change is the "order of the day" for a project, project updating is particularly time consuming.

The traditional method of sequencing tasks uses the **Predecessor** field in MPP, which is very time consuming and cumbersome. However, problems associated with using the **Predecessor** field can be avoided by using the **Priority** field (Figure 4.5). The **Priority** field makes schedule changes and task sequencing for a particular resource quite simple, which can significantly reduce the amount of time spent on project plan updates. When schedule updates and resequencing of tasks is facilitated, change is more welcome because it can be more easily incorporated into a schedule.

Makes Project Monitoring Simple

Project plan monitoring at any level (summary/activity) of a project is simple using earned value analysis. Notice in Figure 4.6 that earned value analysis has been performed using MPP at a subtask level (circled area in Application 1). Having a consistent way to look at an entire project at different levels of the schedule is a strong point for MPP.

Remember also that keeping the WBS at a granular level will help resolve issues when they are quite small. When not managed, small issues have the potential to cause serious effects on variances at the project level. A WBS at a granular level also helps a project man-

ID	Task Name	BCWS	BCWP	ACWP	SV	CV	EAC	BAC	VAC
1	**XYZ Project**	**$4,005.50**	**$3,981.36**	**$3,794.12**	**($24.15)**	**$187.23**	**$5,942.86**	**$5,875.76**	**($67.10)**
2	Module Self Study	$360.00	$360.00	$360.00	$0.00	$0.00	$360.00	$360.00	$0.00
3	Module Training	$360.00	$360.00	$360.00	$0.00	$0.00	$360.00	$360.00	$0.00
4	ABC Project Hold	$0.00	$0.00	$0.00	$0.00	$0.00	$0.00	$0.00	$0.00
5	Reschedule	$8.00	$8.00	$8.00	$0.00	$0.00	$8.00	$8.00	$0.00
6	Reschedule	$24.00	$24.00	$24.00	$0.00	$0.00	$24.00	$24.00	$0.00
7	Reschedule	$0.00	$0.00	$0.00	$0.00	$0.00	$0.00	$0.00	$0.00
8	Hold for Regression Testing	$0.00	$0.00	$0.00	$0.00	$0.00	$0.00	$0.00	$0.00
9	Reschedule	$0.00	$0.00	$0.00	$0.00	$0.00	$8.00	$0.00	($8.00)
10	**Project Management**	**$0.00**	**$0.00**	**$0.00**	**$0.00**	**$0.00**	**$0.00**	**$0.00**	**$0.00**
62	**Screen Rework**	**$76.00**	**$75.00**	**$76.00**	**($1.00)**	**($1.00)**	**$76.00**	**$76.00**	**$0.00**
76	**Test Design Re-Validation**	**$416.00**	**$368.00**	**$416.00**	**($48.00)**	**($48.00)**	**$416.00**	**$416.00**	**$0.00**
108	**Report Design Rework**	**$216.90**	**$260.00**	**$222.70**	**$43.10**	**$37.30**	**$222.70**	**$216.90**	**($5.80)**
167	**Masters & Transactions**	**$1,953.42**	**$2,016.26**	**$1,679.44**	**$62.84**	**$336.82**	**$3,820.18**	**$3,786.48**	**($33.70)**
168	**Application -1**	**$46.74**	**$79.04**	**$38.04**	**$32.30**	**$41.00**	**$38.04**	**$46.74**	**$8.70**
169	Analysis and Bridge Doc Preparation	$9.60	$9.60	$4.00	$0.00	$5.60	$4.00	$9.60	$5.60
170	Bridge Doc Review	$3.20	$3.20	$1.00	$0.00	$2.20	$1.00	$3.20	$2.20
171	Bridge Doc Review Feedback Implementation	$3.20	$3.20	$0.00	$0.00	$3.20	$0.00	$3.20	$3.20
172	Coding/Rework	$14.40	$14.40	$12.00	$0.00	$2.40	$12.00	$14.40	$2.40
173	Unit Testing	$9.60	$9.60	$6.00	$0.00	$3.60	$6.00	$9.60	$3.60
174	Release to Code review R1	$0.00	$0.00	$0.00	$0.00	$0.00	$0.00	$0.00	$0.00
175	Code Review Round1	$3.20	$3.20	$3.00	$0.00	$0.20	$3.00	$3.20	$0.20
176	Code Review Feedback Implementation Round1	$4.80	$4.80	$1.50	$0.00	$3.30	$1.50	$4.80	$3.30

Figure 4.6. Monitoring at subtask level.

ager to focus on a *particular* resource assigned to a task so that the necessary corrective or preventive action for this resource may be taken.

Another view of earned value analysis through MPP is at the resource level. Earned value analysis can be performed at the resource level to see which resources are contributing positively and which ones are contributing negatively to variances at the project level (Figure 4.7). When indicated, using earned value analysis in this way helps a project manager to improve the efficiency of certain resources by encouraging these resources to perform at higher efficiency levels.

Notice in Figure 4.7 that all of the basic elements of earned value and the variances at each resource level are spread across time. The view in Figure 4.7 helps a project manager to reallocate critical work to resources that are performing at higher efficiency levels (as shown by earned value analysis) and to move less critical work to resources who are performing at lower efficiency levels. Remember: In every project, resources perform at different levels. No two resources will have the same efficiency levels throughout a project. However, there might be a specific reason for variance which is due to the work done by a particular resource. If this is the case, a project manager can quickly assess the situation so that future variances may be corrected or prevented.

	Resource Name ▾	Work ▾	Details	Qtr 2, 2005				Qtr 3, 2005
				Mar	Apr	May	Jun	Jul
1	⊞ Rajeev	323.58 hrs	BCWS	$86.00	$143.60	$225.20	$329.52	$415.44
			BCWP	$83.20	$138.60	$159.20	$211.92	$277.80
			ACWP	$81.00	$110.00	$128.50	$181.50	$273.98
			CV	$2.20	$28.60	$30.70	$30.42	$3.82
			SV	($2.80)	($5.00)	($66.00)	($117.60)	($137.64)
2	⊞ Krishna	220.5 hrs	BCWS	$80.00	$88.00	$243.20	$296.00	$414.60
			BCWP	$80.00	$89.60	$172.10	$236.80	$236.80
			ACWP	$80.00	$89.00	$167.30	$220.50	$220.50
			CV	$0.00	$0.60	$4.80	$16.30	$16.30
			SV	$0.00	$1.60	($71.10)	($59.20)	($177.80)
3	⊞ Joby	589.8 hrs	BCWS	$80.00	$88.00	$262.40	$417.60	$545.20
			BCWP	$80.00	$80.00	$88.00	$88.00	$158.40
			ACWP	$80.00	$80.00	$88.00	$88.00	$149.00
			CV	$0.00	$0.00	$0.00	$0.00	$9.40
			SV	$0.00	($8.00)	($174.40)	($329.60)	($386.80)
4	⊞ Tilak	284 hrs	BCWS	$80.00	$88.00	$219.20	$343.60	$483.92
			BCWP	$80.00	$80.00	$88.00	$200.45	$204.80
			ACWP	$80.00	$80.00	$88.00	$240.50	$251.00
			CV	$0.00	$0.00	$0.00	($40.05)	($46.20)
			SV	$0.00	($8.00)	($131.20)	($143.15)	($279.12)
5	⊞ Rajkishore	648.5 hrs	BCWS	$80.00	$88.00	$136.00	$263.20	$389.60
			BCWP	$89.60	$215.20	$262.63	$389.91	$445.42
			ACWP	$84.00	$143.50	$181.50	$280.56	$408.50
			CV	$5.60	$71.70	$81.13	$109.35	$36.92
			SV	$9.60	$127.20	$126.63	$126.71	$55.82
6	⊞ Vamsikrishna	1,200.33 hrs	BCWS	$80.00	$88.00	$218.00	$350.40	$491.04
			BCWP	$80.00	$137.00	$235.67	$318.38	$418.96
			ACWP	$80.00	$140.00	$257.00	$399.50	$508.82
			CV	$0.00	($3.00)	($21.33)	($81.12)	($89.86)
			SV	$0.00	$49.00	$17.67	($32.02)	($72.08)
7	⊞ Chika	969 hrs						

Figure 4.7. Earned value analysis—resources.

Facilitates Having Projects On Time and Under Budget

Using EVM and MPP effectively, monitoring the schedule periodically, and taking the necessary steps to keep variances under control ensure delivery of projects that are on time and under budget (Figure 4.8). The chance of failure due to schedule and cost overruns is drastically minimized. This degree of control and the intensity with which projects are monitored using EVM and MPP are not possible using conventional methods of tracking dates and budgets separately. Although EVM and MPP involve significant intensity in the monitoring process, the amount of time actually spent by a project manager using these techniques is quite small—the reason why EVM and MPP will become the most preferred monitoring technique for all types of projects, small, medium, or large, going forward.

Important: Early indications of problems in a project revealed by EVM and MPP allow early corrective and/or preventive measures to be taken or approvals for an increase in the budget or time to be obtained (for external factors in the project for which the project team has no control). Remember: Costs of corrections at an early stage in a project are low compared to corrections taken during the late stages.

ID	Task Name	BCWS	BCWP	ACWP	SV	CV	EAC	BAC	VAC
1	**XYZ Project**	$4,005.50	$3,981.36	$3,794.12	($24.15)	$187.23	$5,942.86	$5,875.76	($67.10)
2	Module Self Study	$360.00	$360.00	$360.00	$0.00	$0.00	$360.00	$360.00	$0.00
3	Module Training	$360.00	$360.00	$360.00	$0.00	$0.00	$360.00	$360.00	$0.00
4	ABC Project Hold	$0.00	$0.00	$0.00	$0.00	$0.00	$0.00	$0.00	$0.00
5	Reschedule	$8.00	$8.00	$8.00	$0.00	$0.00	$8.00	$8.00	$0.00
6	Reschedule	$24.00	$24.00	$24.00	$0.00	$0.00	$24.00	$24.00	$0.00
7	Reschedule	$0.00	$0.00	$0.00	$0.00	$0.00	$0.00	$0.00	$0.00
8	Hold for Regression Testing	$0.00	$0.00	$0.00	$0.00	$0.00	$0.00	$0.00	$0.00
9	Reschedule	$0.00	$0.00	$0.00	$0.00	$0.00	$8.00	$0.00	($8.00)
10	**Project Management**	$0.00	$0.00	$0.00	$0.00	$0.00	$0.00	$0.00	$0.00
62	**Screen Rework**	$76.00	$75.00	$76.00	($1.00)	($1.00)	$76.00	$76.00	$0.00
76	**Test Design Re-Validation**	$416.00	$368.00	$416.00	($48.00)	($48.00)	$416.00	$416.00	$0.00
108	**Report Design Rework**	$216.90	$260.00	$222.70	$43.10	$37.30	$222.70	$216.90	($5.80)
167	**Masters & Transactions**	$1,953.42	$2,016.26	$1,679.44	$62.84	$336.82	$3,820.18	$3,786.48	($33.70)
627	**Process/Report**	$585.38	$510.09	$647.98	($75.29)	($137.89)	$647.98	$622.58	($25.40)

Figure 4.8. Project which is on time and under budget.

Improves Customer Satisfaction

Customer satisfaction is improved because progress is provided to a customer and/or sponsor on a periodic basis in a status report (weekly in the case of Figure 4.9). Throughout a project, periodic presentation of earned value analysis as part of status reporting ensures that there is transparency in reporting and also ensures that the customer is aware of problems and the corrective or preventive actions that have been taken.

XYZ Project Weekly Status Report

		Project	XYZ			
		Status Date	22-Aug			
		Legend		Performance measure is out of control. Needs attention.		
				Performance measure is out of control. Controllable.		
				Performance measure is in control.		
				Help on Abbreviations		
Week	Performance Parameter	Performance Measure	Value	Performance Measure Outcome	Reasons	Corrective Action
22-Aug	Schedule/Time	BAC(t-wks)	52.50	Total of 52.5 weeks budgeted for the project		
22-Aug	Schedule/Time	SV(t-wks)	9.70	We are ahead of schedule by 9.7 weeks.	Huge schedule underruns are due to introduction of Links to Enhancements. Underruns will come down going forward	None
22-Aug	Schedule/Time	SPI(t-wks)	1.43	We are at 143% efficiency in use of time.		
22-Aug	Schedule/Time	EAC(t-wks)	37.03	If we continue to work at past performance levels, 37 weeks will be needed to complete the project compared to the 52.5 weeks budgeted.		
22-Aug	Cost/Effort	CV	40.64	We have spent 40 hours less than hours actually budgeted.		None.
22-Aug	Cost/Effort	CPI	1.01	We are at 101% efficiency in use of budgeted effort.		
22-Aug	Cost/Effort	TCPI	0.97	We need to work at 97% efficiency on effort going forward.		
22-Aug	Cost/Effort	TSPI	0.68	We need to work at 68% efficiency on the schedule going forward.		
22-Aug	Effort	BAC	5,995.52	Total of 5995.52 hours budgeted for the project		
22-Aug	Cost/Effort	EAC(effort)	5,954.88	Assuming that variances will not exist in the project going forward, we will need 5925 hours to complete the project.		
22-Aug	Cost/Effort	VAC	40.64	We will spend 40 hours less than hours budgeted at the end of the project.		
22-Aug	Schedule/Time	ETC	2,238.26	We will need 2238 hours to complete remaining project work.		

Figure 4.9. Sample weekly project status report; wks, weeks.

For the project team, the end result is that the customer develops a higher comfort level and hence customer satisfaction increases.

Less time-consuming negotiations are another benefit of periodic, transparent reporting. If a customer is aware of or involved in the decision-making process for project issues, and the need arises, less effort is required in negotiations between the project manager and the customer. Negotiating with a poorly informed customer is much more difficult and will likely require lengthy explanations.

A high level of customer satisfaction almost always translates into new revenue for service-oriented companies, which emphasizes the importance of service-oriented companies keeping their customers satisfied. Suggestion: Conduct a customer satisfaction survey periodically to keep track of the customer satisfaction index (CSI).

Forecasts Cost/Effort and Time Required

Forecasting the effort and time required to complete the remainder of a project gives a clear picture of how a project is likely to end (e.g., with/without schedule/effort overruns). As you can see from Figure 4.10, the project is estimated to be completed earlier than the budgeted time, BAC (t-wks). Forecasting the future performance of a project using earned value analysis (as done in Chapter 3 using various estimate at completion scenarios) provides an understanding of the impact of current variances on the end result, which enables a project manager and project stakeholders to interject an appropriate amount of urgency into project monitoring to bring the project back on track.

For example, utilizing EVM, a project manager can use several scenarios to present views of the future performance of a project to stakeholders:

- Assuming that current variances *will exist* in the future, how much longer will the project continue?
- Assuming that current variances *will exist* in the future, how much more will the project cost?
- Assuming that current variances *will not exist* in the future, how much longer will the project continue?
- Assuming current variances *will not exist* in the future, how much more will the project cost?
- Assuming that original estimates *are no longer valid,* and using a new set of estimates, how long will the project continue?
- Assuming that original estimates *are no longer valid*, and using a new set of estimates for the remaining work to be done, how much will the project cost?

XYZ Project Weekly Status Report

		Project	XYZ		
		Status Date	22-Aug		
		Legend		Performance measure is out of control. Needs attention.	
				Performance measure is out of control. Controllable.	
				Performance measure is in control.	
				Help on Abbreviations	

Week	Performance Parameter	Performance Measure	Value	Performance Measure Outcome	Reasons	Corrective Action
22-Aug	Schedule/Time	BAC(t-wks)	52.50	Total of 52.5 weeks budgeted for the project		
22-Aug	Schedule/Time	SV(t-wks)	9.70	We are ahead of schedule by 9.7 weeks.	Huge schedule underruns are due to introduction of Links to Enhancements. Underruns will come down going forward.	None
22-Aug	Schedule/Time	SPI(t-wks)	1.43	We are at 143% efficiency in use of time.		
22-Aug	Schedule/Time	EAC(t-wks)	37.03	If we continue to work at past performance levels, 37 weeks will be needed to complete the project compared to the 52.5 weeks budgeted.		
22-Aug	Cost/Effort	CV	40.64	We have spent 40 hours less than hours actually budgeted.		None.
22-Aug	Cost/Effort	CPI	1.01	We are at 101% efficiency in use of budgeted effort.		
22-Aug	Cost/Effort	TCPI	0.97	We need to work at 97% efficiency on effort going forward.		
22-Aug	Cost/Effort	TSPI	0.68	We need to work at 68% efficiency on the schedule going forward.		
22-Aug	Effort	BAC	5,995.52	Total of 5995.52 hours budgeted for the project		
22-Aug	Cost/Effort	EAC(effort)	5,954.88	Assuming that variances will not exist in the project going forward, we will need 5925 hours to complete the project.		
22-Aug	Cost/Effort	VAC	40.64	We will spend 40 hours less than hours budgeted at the end of the project.		
22-Aug	Schedule/Time	ETC	2,238.26	We will need 2238 hours to complete remaining project work.		

Figure 4.10. Weekly status report showing forecast of current schedule underruns; wks, weeks.

Imagine the value obtained from having this information. It is available at a project manager's fingertips using the EVM technique.

Forecasts Future Efficiency Needed

Forecasting the efficiency parameters required to complete a project on time and under budget gives a project manager a heads-up about conducting team meetings. For example, notice the circled values in Figure 4.11. Based on these values, at the next meeting, the project manager should charge-up the team or perhaps just make a subtle comment about the level of team performance (efficiency) needed going forward (Figure 4.11)

Forecasting the future efficiency needed to bring a project back on track can be done using earned value analysis. Future efficiency needed provides another forecast view. Future efficiency needed uses the efficiency performance measures of TCPI (to-complete cost performance indicator) and TSPI (to-complete schedule performance indicator) and allows a project manager to assess *quantitatively* the amount of extra work needed to be done within the same time frame. For example, if we have a TCPI of 1.25, the project team needs to work 25% more efficiently. In a situation in which a team must work 25% more efficiently, suppose a task needs $100 to be completed. With a current TCPI of 1.25, a proj-

XYZ Project Weekly Status Report

		Project		XYZ		
		Status Date		22-Aug		
		Legend		Performance measure is out of control. Needs attention.		
				Performance measure is out of control. Controllable.		
				Performance measure is in control.		
				Help on Abbrevations		
Week	**Performance Parameter**	**Performance Measure**	**Value**	**Performance Measure Outcome**	**Reasons**	**Corrective Action**
22-Aug	Schedule/Time	BAC(t-wks)	52.50	Total of 52.5 weeks budgeted for the project		
22-Aug	Schedule/Time	SV(t-wks)	9.70	We are ahead of schedule by 9.7 weeks.	Huge schedule underruns are due to introduction of Links to Enhancements. Underruns will come down going forward.	None
22-Aug	Schedule/Time	SPI(t-wks)	1.43	We are at 143% efficiency in use of time.		
22-Aug	Schedule/Time	EAC(t-wks)	37.03	If we continue to work at past performance levels, 37 weeks will be needed to complete the project compared to the 52.5 weeks budgeted.		
22-Aug	Cost/Effort	CV	40.64	We have spent 40 hours less than hours actually budgeted.		None.
22-Aug	Cost/Effort	CPI	1.01	We are at 101% efficiency in use of budgeted effort.		
22-Aug	Cost/Effort	TCPI	0.97	We need to work at 97% efficiency on effort going forward.		
22-Aug	Cost/Effort	TSPI	0.68	We need to work at 68% efficiency on the schedule going forward.		
22-Aug	Effort	BAC	5,995.52	Total of 5995.52 hours budgeted for the project		
22-Aug	Cost/Effort	EAC(effort)	5,954.88	Assuming that variances will not exist in the project going forward, we will need 5925 hours to complete the project.		
22-Aug	Cost/Effort	VAC	40.64	We will spend 40 hours less than hours budgeted at the end of the project.		
22-Aug	Schedule/Time	ETC	2,238.26	We will need 2238 hours to complete remaining project work.		

Figure 4.11. Weekly status report showing summary of forecast of needed performance efficiency; wks, weeks.

ect team must complete this task with $75. This efficiency rate applies to all remaining tasks in the project.

However, if some tasks are completed with higher efficiency, depending on their weight (weighted average), TCPI will change. Therefore, computation of TCPI and TSPI is required for every reporting period, with adjustments made accordingly. Periodic tracking allows a project team to shift between working at higher efficiency levels in some periods to working at a more relaxed pace in other periods, which boosts team motivation. The team soon becomes aware that if extra effort is given in one reporting period, they might be able to ease off a bit during the periods that follow. However, this give-and-take mentality does not mean that a project manager can allow momentum to drop as soon as TCPI and TSPI reach 1 or below 1. Momentum must be maintained so that positive variances are maximized to the benefit of the end customer.

Figure 4.12 shows another view of forecast values. This time BAC (budget at completion) and EAC (estimate at completion) are used. In Figure 4.12, plotting BAC and EAC values has produced an S-curve or another way to view forecasts. At all points ensure that the EAC curve is always below the BAC curve, which results in a successful project.

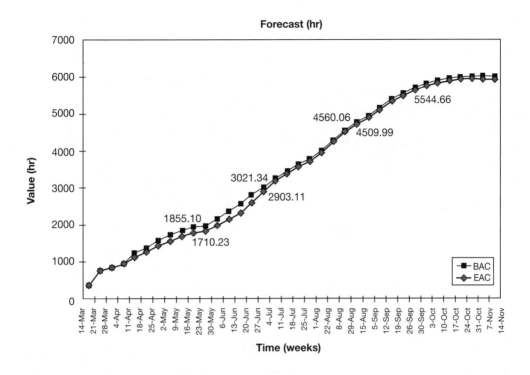

Figure 4.12. S-curve showing forecast of needed future performance efficiency.

Manages Trends

Trends in effort/schedule parameters indicate to a project manager if serious action needs to be taken or if a subtle discussion of the situation in a team meeting will suffice. Managing trends in variances is another way to monitor a project and keep it on track or bring it back on track. If trends in a project are obtained period by period, a project manager can assess the situation and take steps as necessary to reverse a negative trend or try to maximize positive trends to benefit the project and the end customer.

Notice in Figure 4.13 that two areas have been circled. In the left circle, this part of the trend has variances that are moving in an upward, positive direction. The circle on the right has a downward trend. Clearly the trend moves upward during the initial stages, but reverses in the weeks that follow. Looking at this trend over several days will allow a project manager to assess this situation and maximize the positive trend.

Also notice schedule variance in Figure 4.13. Clearly schedule variance moves downward toward a negative trend, but then comes back on track. Notice the spikes on the neg-

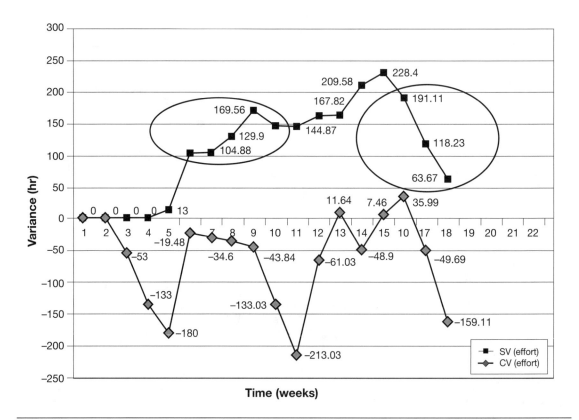

Figure 4.13. Managing trends—effort variance.

ative side in downward trends. During downward trends, a project manager needs to take corrective and/or preventive actions to reverse the trend in the weeks that follow.

Trend analysis provides "triggers" that indicate potential risks in a project and allow a project manager to proactively assess a situation and take corrective and/or preventive action as required. Trend analysis also allows the addition of a trend line (linear, polynomial, logarithmic, etc.) which will indicate where variances are headed based on past performance data. Linear, polynomial, and logarithmic methods predict (forecast) the future with available past data. For example, a linear trend line indicates the linear path that will be taken by variances in the future based on past data. A moving average trend line, which smoothes out a trend to show an even better picture of the trend of past data, may also be used to predict the future performance of a project.

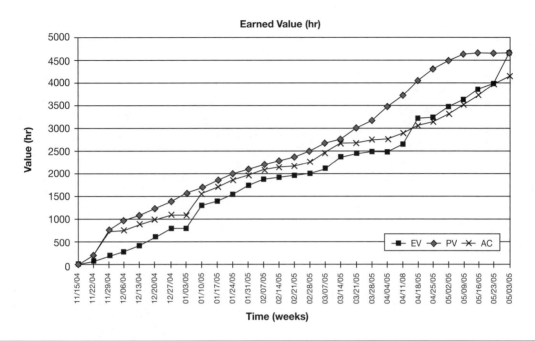

Figure 4.14. Curves illustrating total control of a project.

Allows Total Control of a Project

Figure 4.14 shows the curves produced by plotting three performance measures (earned value, planned value, and actual cost) for a project. In Figure 4.14, earned value is lower than actual cost throughout most of the project. With continuous improvement efforts by the project manager and his team, the project is back under control near the end of the project. The curves in Figure 4.14 are classic examples of project monitoring to perfection. The project is delivered on time and under budget.

The curves in Figure 4.14 are the result of periodic targeted management by the project manager which allowed him to have total control of the project. Total control not only enables the project manager and his project team to deliver the project on time and under budget, but it also helps reduce management time for the project manager—which is not possible without the use of EVM techniques and tools.

Needless to say, having total control of a project translates into increased customer satisfaction, increased team productivity, and as a result, better performance appraisals for the project manager—all with reduced management effort by the project manager.

5

CREATING A SCHEDULE

SCHEDULE PREPARATION

Preparing a schedule properly is crucial. Proper preparation ensures that you will be able to use the EVM report template effectively and save significant time when maintaining a schedule. Follow the setup steps described in the sections that follow to create a schedule. This directive does not mean that the EVM report template cannot be used without following these steps. The template can be used with conventional schedule creation and tracking methods. However, using the techniques discussed in this chapter saves significant time in tracking progress and when adjusting the schedule as a project progresses.

As discussed in Chapter 2 (*Schedule Management*), five basic elements are required to prepare a schedule and to apply the rules of schedule preparation. Having a good work breakdown structure at the beginning is also very important. The work breakdown structure (WBS) needs to be structured hierarchically (see Chapter 2). This WBS structure must be reflected in MPP when you create a schedule. For example, the project must be the top-level task to obtain earned value numbers from MPP easily (without having to perform manual calculations). Let's recap the basic elements of a schedule:

- Work breakdown structure
- Estimates
- Resources
- Resource costs
- Task dependencies

These elements are necessary to complete a schedule.

SETTING UP MICROSOFT® OFFICE PROJECT—MPP OPTIONS

Before you start to create a project schedule, several things need to be set up in MPP as *first-time* settings (see also Chapter 1). The MPP setup also depends on project requirements. Understanding a few of the available options will facilitate better use of the tool.

The Schedule Screen

First, go into the **Tools > Options** menu item to open up a dialog box (shown in Figure 5.1). This dialog box provides various setup options which should be chosen before creating a schedule. Although most of the options can be left as the default values provided, some still need to be adjusted according to your project's requirements.

The most commonly changed options are in the **Schedule** tab of the **Options** dialog box. In this box, options can be specified about how MPP is to track **Duration**, **Work**, and **Default task type**.

Before we begin, remember the definition of the terms duration and work. Duration is typically the time in *calendar* days required to complete the work. Work is the *effort required* to complete the work. For example, for a task that is performed by two people for 5 days, the duration of the task is 5 days and the effort for the task is 5 days multiplied by 8 hours per day multiplied by the number of resources (two), i.e., 80 hours or 10 workdays. With an understanding of the difference between work and duration, we are ready to create a schedule.

The unit to be used for calculation of **Duration** and **Work** may also be chosen, e.g., minutes, hours, days, weeks, or months. Technically, a choice may be made to have MPP calculate duration and work in days, but for the purpose of distinguishing between the two parameters easily, using days for **Duration** and hours for **Work** is advisable. (Note: Depending on the size of a project, the choice could be to have duration calculated in weeks or months. The advantage of choosing the unit used is basically to ensure that numbers are manageably small.)

Another parameter to set up is the **Default task type**. **Default task type** can be fixed; **Fixed Units**, **Fixed Duration**, and **Fixed Work**. These options basically indicate which parameter is fixed and which others are variable. This choice instructs MPP about the parameters that will need to be calculated and the parameters that will be entered by the user.

Suppose you specify the **Default task type** as **Fixed Units**. This choice specifies that the amount of resource units assigned to a particular task is fixed and the other two parameters of duration and work are variable. So in this case you specify the resource units and

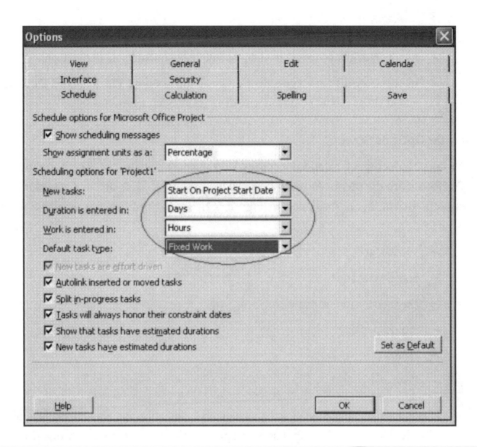

Figure 5.1. MPP **Options** dialog box.

their duration and work will be calculated. Similarly, for the **Fixed Duration** option, duration is fixed and the work and resource units are variable.

Setting this parameter depends on the type of task and project. For most projects, the **Fixed Work** option is typically used, with duration and resource units remaining as variables, because you will have an effort estimate for the project. For some projects, duration is available; therefore you vary the effort and resource units to achieve duration. For these projects, the **Fixed Duration** option is used.

Steps:

> In the menu, go to the **Tools** menu and choose the **Options** menu item.

> Navigate to **Schedule** by clicking on the **Schedule** tab.

> In the **New tasks** dropdown, choose **Start On Project Start Date** as the option.

> ➤ In the **Duration is entered in** dropdown, choose **Days** as the option.

> ➤ In the **Work is entered in** dropdown, choose **Hours** as the option.

> ➤ In the **Default task type** dropdown, choose **Fixed Work**, **Fixed Duration**, or **Fixed Units** as the option depending on the requirement.

The Calendar Options Screen

Next is the setup of calendar options (Figure 5.2). Go to the **Tools** menu and select **Options** from the menu. A dialog box will be displayed. Click on the **Calendar** tab to enter choices for the items displayed in Figure 5.2. Several options are available for calendar setup:

> ➤ Week start

> ➤ Fiscal year start

> ➤ Day start and end time

> ➤ Hours per day

> ➤ Hours per week

> ➤ Days per month

These settings allow MPP to calculate the duration of the schedule and adjust it accordingly. For example, suppose you specify that your team will work 6 days a week instead of the regular 5 days a week. The end date to complete the project will be earlier because the available time has been increased by 1 day per week. Therefore, correctly setting this option is important when creating a schedule.

Steps:

> ➤ In the menu, go to the **Tools** menu and choose the **Options** menu item.

> ➤ Navigate to **Calendar** by clicking on the **Calendar** tab.

> ➤ In the **Week starts on** dropdown, choose **Sunday** as the option (or as required by the project).

> ➤ In the **Fiscal year starts in** dropdown, choose **January** as the option (or as required by the project).

> ➤ In the **Default start time** dropdown, choose **9:00 AM** as the option (or as required by the project).

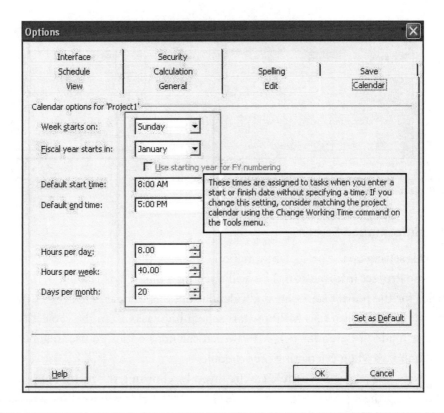

Figure 5.2. Calendar **Options** dialog box.

> In the **Default end time** dropdown, choose **6:00 PM** as the option (or as required by the project).

> In the **Hours per day** spinner, update to **8** as the number of hours per workday (or as required by the project).

> In the **Hours per week** spinner, update to **40** as the number of hours per week (or as required by the project).

> In the **Days per month** spinner, update to **20** as the number of workdays in the month (or as required by the project).

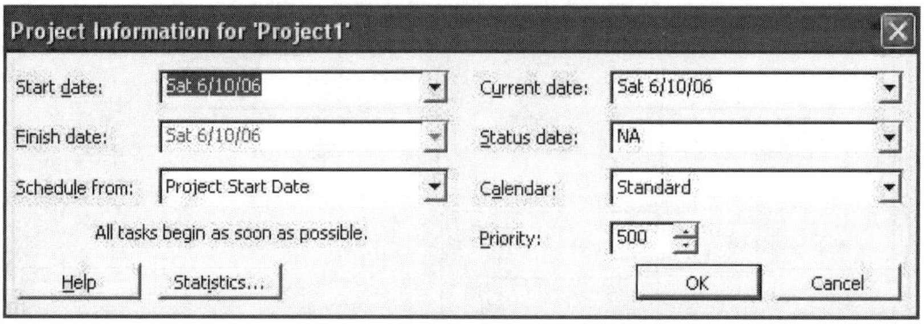

Figure 5.3. Project Information dialog box.

The Project Information Screen

Next is setting up the project information screen. In the menu, go to the **Project** menu and choose **Project Information**. This will open up a dialog box (Figure 5.3). This screen has fields for the project start date and calendar options to be entered. The **Start date** choice made on this screen tells MPP to start scheduling tasks from the project's start date. The choice made in **Calendar** tells MPP which calendar option to use to apply working days and holidays when calculating the schedule.

Now, the project's schedule can be saved by choosing the menu option of **File > Save** and giving the schedule a name. (Note: The other fields will be discussed later. For now, leave the default values in these fields.)

Steps:

➤ In the menu, go to the **Project** menu and choose the **Project Information** menu item.

➤ In the **Start date** dropdown, choose the date on which the project is expected to start. (Note: This date can always be changed before baselining a schedule.)

➤ In the **Schedule from** dropdown, choose **Project Start Date** as the option.

➤ In the **Calendar** dropdown, choose **Standard** as the option. (If you have created a new project calendar, other than the default calendar, choose the **New Project** calendar as the option.)

➤ Leave the **Current date** dropdown as it is. This field reflects the current date and depends on the date in your system.

➤ Leave the **Status date** dropdown as it is. By default this field has a value of NA.

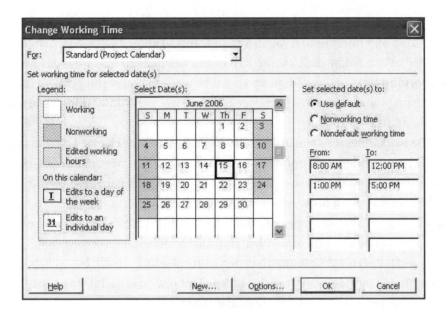

Figure 5.4. Change Working Time dialog box.

The Project Calendar

One more step is needed to complete MPP setup—the project calendar. Setting up a project calendar before creating a schedule is important because the schedule will be calculated based on the settings made in **Project Calendar**. Settings in **Project Calendar** include workdays, weekends, company holidays, work times, etc. If this screen is not set up with the proper/correct information, the schedule will be calculated without taking holidays, etc. into consideration, which will almost certainly result in an earlier project end date that definitely causes a schedule overrun.

Go to the **Tools > Change Working Time** menu item to set up the project calendar (Figure 5.4). Enter details such as workdays, weekends, company holidays, work times, etc. Mark company holidays on the project calendar for each month included in the project. The accuracy of schedule calculations depends on inclusion of holidays. Unless holidays are specified, calculations will be incorrect.

To set (or change) the work times for a particular day, select the day (note bolded date on calendar) and then select the **Nondefault working time** option on the right-hand side of the screen. Enter the work time (or changed work time) under the **From** and **To** columns.

By default MPP has a 5-day work week with Saturday and Sunday as nonworking days. Depending on project needs, you can change this to allow a 6- or 7-day work week. To set up a day as a holiday, click on the day in the calendar that is a holiday and choose the **Nonworking time** option. To set up an entire week as nonworking, select the entire week by dragging the mouse across that week; then select the **Nonworking time** option on the right-hand side.

The work times for a single day or multiple days may be changed by selecting the day(s) and the **Nonworking time** option and then changing the times on the right-hand side. This option allows you to increase/decrease the work time for a particular period or day.

The **Nonworking time** option is very useful during a project when you need to bring a schedule back on track, especially if it is lagging behind by a few days. The work time for a few days can be changed or another shift can be added.

By default, **Project Calendar** has two shifts of 4 hours each, but as many as five shifts for a period or particular day may be added. This option is useful if a project has shifts and work on the project goes on for nearly the entire day.

Now you can appreciate how important the project calendar is in preparing and changing your schedule. With these options selected, you are finished with the setup of your project schedule in MPP.

Steps:

➤ In the menu, go to the **Tools** menu and choose the **Change Working Time** menu item.

➤ To mark a particular day as a holiday, select the day on the calendar in the middle of the screen. On the right-hand side of the screen, select the **Nonworking time** button.

➤ To change the work time for a particular day, select that day on the calendar. On the right-hand side, select the **Nondefault working time** button and enter the changed work times for that particular day.

➤ To mark a group of consecutive days as holidays, select the first day and drag the mouse over the remaining days on the calendar. On the right-hand side, select the **Nonworking time** button.

➤ To change the work time for a group of consecutive days, select the first day and drag the mouse over the remaining days on the calendar. On the right-hand side, select the **Nondefault working time** button and enter the changed work times for those particular days.

➤ To mark a group of nonconsecutive days as holidays, select the first day and keep the **Ctrl** key pressed on the keyboard. Select the other days on the calendar. On the right-hand side, select the **Nonworking time** button.

➤ To change the working time of a group of nonconsecutive days, select the first day and keep the **Ctrl** key pressed on the keyboard. Select the other days on the calendar. On the right-hand side, select the **Nondefault working time** button and enter the changed work times.

➤ To mark an entire week as a holiday, select the week column heading on the calendar. On the right-hand side, select the **Nonworking time** button.

➤ To change the work time for a day of the week, select the week column heading on the calendar. On the right-hand side, select the **Nondefault working time** button and enter the changed work times for that weekday.

CREATING A WBS

The WBS is another important aspect of project planning. Ensure that you create a deliverables-oriented WBS so that tracking is easy and issues may be resolved quickly and attributed to a phase or deliverable.

Typically a deliverables-oriented WBS has the project at the top-most level followed by phases in the next level, deliverables in the third level, and activities required to finish the deliverables in the fourth level. (Note: This setup is for a software project. A similar pattern could be followed for other projects.)

A sample software project will be used to demonstrate the various aspects discussed in this book (Figure 5.5). This sample project does not represent any actual project. It is also not exhaustive enough to cover all aspects of all types of projects. Notice that the project is at level 1 in Figure 5.5. Lowest-level tasks are identified by regular face type and summary level tasks are identified by boldface type.

Steps:

➤ In the menu, go to the **View** menu and choose the **Gantt Chart** menu item.

➤ In this menu, go to the **View** menu and choose the **Table** menu item. Under the **Table** menu, choose the **Entry** submenu item.

➤ To insert a row, click the **Insert** button and add a **Task Name**.

➤ To indent a row, on the formatting toolbar, choose the ➔ icon on the menu.

ID		Task Name	Duration	Start	Finish	Predecessors	Resource Names
	ⓘ						
1		**Sample Software Project**	**1 day?**	**Mon 6/12/06**	**Mon 6/12/06**		
2		**Initiation**	**1 day?**	**Mon 6/12/06**	**Mon 6/12/06**		
3		Project Kick Off Meeting	1 day?	Mon 6/12/06	Mon 6/12/06		
4		**Project Charter**	**1 day?**	**Mon 6/12/06**	**Mon 6/12/06**		
5		Prepare Project Charter	1 day?	Mon 6/12/06	Mon 6/12/06		
6		Review Project Charter	1 day?	Mon 6/12/06	Mon 6/12/06		
7		Sign Off Project Charter	1 day?	Mon 6/12/06	Mon 6/12/06		
8		**Planning**	**1 day?**	**Mon 6/12/06**	**Mon 6/12/06**		
9		**Estimation**	**1 day?**	**Mon 6/12/06**	**Mon 6/12/06**		
13		**Project Plan**	**1 day?**	**Mon 6/12/06**	**Mon 6/12/06**		
17		**Requirements**	**1 day?**	**Mon 6/12/06**	**Mon 6/12/06**		
18		**SRS Module 1**	**1 day?**	**Mon 6/12/06**	**Mon 6/12/06**		
22		**SRS Module 2**	**1 day?**	**Mon 6/12/06**	**Mon 6/12/06**		
26		**SRS Final**	**1 day?**	**Mon 6/12/06**	**Mon 6/12/06**		
30		**Design**	**1 day?**	**Mon 6/12/06**	**Mon 6/12/06**		
31		**Design Module 1**	**1 day?**	**Mon 6/12/06**	**Mon 6/12/06**		
35		**Design Module 2**	**1 day?**	**Mon 6/12/06**	**Mon 6/12/06**		
39		**Design Final**	**1 day?**	**Mon 6/12/06**	**Mon 6/12/06**		
43		**Development**	**1 day?**	**Mon 6/12/06**	**Mon 6/12/06**		
44		**Develop Module 1**	**1 day?**	**Mon 6/12/06**	**Mon 6/12/06**		
48		**Develop Module 2**	**1 day?**	**Mon 6/12/06**	**Mon 6/12/06**		
52		**Develop Final**	**1 day?**	**Mon 6/12/06**	**Mon 6/12/06**		
56		**Testing**	**1 day?**	**Mon 6/12/06**	**Mon 6/12/06**		
57		**Develop Module 1**	**1 day?**	**Mon 6/12/06**	**Mon 6/12/06**		
61		**Develop Module 2**	**1 day?**	**Mon 6/12/06**	**Mon 6/12/06**		
65		**Develop Final**	**1 day?**	**Mon 6/12/06**	**Mon 6/12/06**		

Figure 5.5. WBS for a sample software project.

> ➤ To remove an indent from a row, on the formatting toolbar, choose the ← icon on the menu.

> ➤ Enter an entire WBS by inserting new rows and indenting (and changing indents) to arrive at the final form of the WBS. Ensure that the project is at the top-most level of the WBS.

ASSIGNING ESTIMATES

The next step is to assign estimates to the lowest-level tasks. When assigning estimates, be sure to enter effort in the **Work** column (see Figure 5.8) not in the **Duration** column as is traditionally done. **Duration** is calculated automatically once resources are assigned to a task.

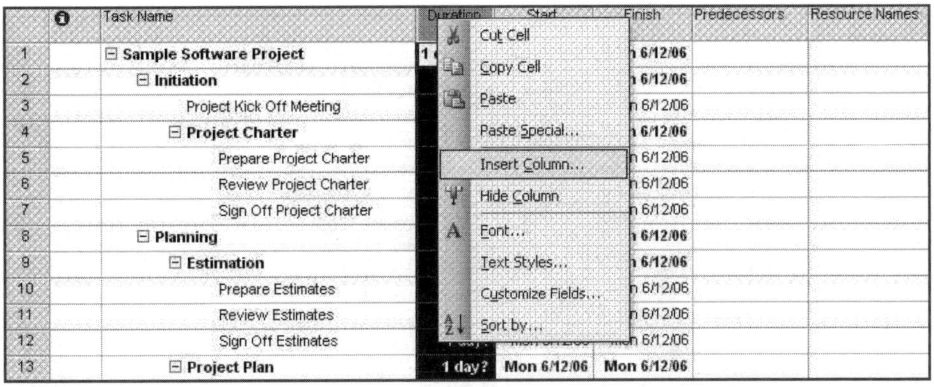

Figure 5.6. Duration column dropdown showing **Insert Column** option.

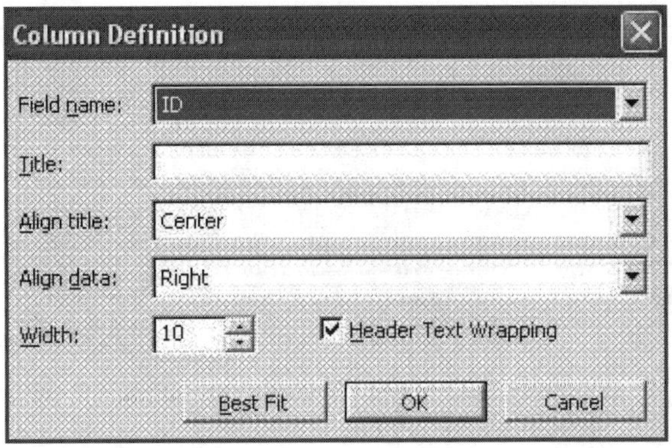

Figure 5.7. Column Definition dialog box.

First, right click on the **Duration** column and choose the menu item **Insert Column** (Figure 5.6). Next, in the **Column Definition** dialog box (Figure 5.7), click on the **Field name** dropdown and choose the **Work** field and click **OK** to insert the **Work** column before the **Duration** column. Now that the **Work** column has been inserted, the next screen will contain a **Work** column (Figure 5.8). To adjust the **Duration** column to remove the "?" symbols, enter 1 in the **Duration** column (Figure 5.9).

Tip: You can enter 1 in the first editable task (Task 3, Project Kick-Off Meeting, in our example) and select all of the rows in the **Duration** column and press **Ctrl+D** to populate all of the **Duration** rows to a 1-day default.

ID	ⓘ	Task Name	Work	Duration	Start	Finish	Predecessors	Resource Names
1		**Sample Software Project**	**0 hrs**	**1 day?**	**Mon 6/12/06**	**Mon 6/12/06**		
2		**Initiation**	**0 hrs**	**1 day?**	**Mon 6/12/06**	**Mon 6/12/06**		
3		Project Kick Off Meeting	0 hrs	1 day?	Mon 6/12/06	Mon 6/12/06		
4		**Project Charter**	**0 hrs**	**1 day?**	**Mon 6/12/06**	**Mon 6/12/06**		
5		Prepare Project Charter	0 hrs	1 day?	Mon 6/12/06	Mon 6/12/06		
6		Review Project Charter	0 hrs	1 day?	Mon 6/12/06	Mon 6/12/06		
7		Sign Off Project Charter	0 hrs	1 day?	Mon 6/12/06	Mon 6/12/06		
8		**Planning**	**0 hrs**	**1 day?**	**Mon 6/12/06**	**Mon 6/12/06**		
9		**Estimation**	**0 hrs**	**1 day?**	**Mon 6/12/06**	**Mon 6/12/06**		
10		Prepare Estimates	0 hrs	1 day?	Mon 6/12/06	Mon 6/12/06		
11		Review Estimates	0 hrs	1 day?	Mon 6/12/06	Mon 6/12/06		
12		Sign Off Estimates	0 hrs	1 day?	Mon 6/12/06	Mon 6/12/06		
13		**Project Plan**	**0 hrs**	**1 day?**	**Mon 6/12/06**	**Mon 6/12/06**		

Figure 5.8. Project with addition of **Work** column.

ID	ⓘ	Task Name	Work	Duration	Start	Finish	Predecessors	Resource Names
1		**Sample Software Project**	**0 hrs**	**1 day**	**Mon 6/12/06**	**Mon 6/12/06**		
2		**Initiation**	**0 hrs**	**1 day**	**Mon 6/12/06**	**Mon 6/12/06**		
3		Project Kick Off Meeting	0 hrs	1 day	Mon 6/12/06	Mon 6/12/06		
4		**Project Charter**	**0 hrs**	**1 day**	**Mon 6/12/06**	**Mon 6/12/06**		
5		Prepare Project Charter	0 hrs	1 day	Mon 6/12/06	Mon 6/12/06		
6		Review Project Charter	0 hrs	1 day	Mon 6/12/06	Mon 6/12/06		
7		Sign Off Project Charter	0 hrs	1 day	Mon 6/12/06	Mon 6/12/06		
8		**Planning**	**0 hrs**	**1 day**	**Mon 6/12/06**	**Mon 6/12/06**		
9		**Estimation**	**0 hrs**	**1 day**	**Mon 6/12/06**	**Mon 6/12/06**		

Figure 5.9. Project with **1** entered in **Duration** column to remove "?."

Now assign estimates to all the lowest-level tasks in hours. Note: Effort in hours must be entered for each task. In this context, let's review effort and duration in MPP. From earlier reminders, we know that effort is different from duration. Effort is the amount in hours that one person would need to work on a task to finish it; duration is the calendar time needed to finish the work. Therefore, for a task that needs 8 hours of effort to complete, and if one resource is assigned to this task for 50% of his time, the **Work** column would show 8 hours and the duration column would show 2 days.

One more thing needs attention. When entering hours in the **Work** column, hours must be multiplied by the number of resources being used for a task. For example, Task 3, the Kick-Off Meeting, is done by four people for 1 hour each; therefore, the **Work** column for Task 3 is updated with 4 hours. Note: Effort estimates need to only be assigned to the

ID		Task Name	Work	Duration	Start	Finish	Predecessors	Resource Names
	❶							
1		**Sample Software Project**	**693 hrs**	**1 day**	**Mon 6/12/06**	**Mon 6/12/06**		
2		**Initiation**	**27 hrs**	**1 day**	**Mon 6/12/06**	**Mon 6/12/06**		
3		Project Kick Off Meeting	4 hrs	1 day	Mon 6/12/06	Mon 6/12/06		
4		**Project Charter**	**23 hrs**	**1 day**	**Mon 6/12/06**	**Mon 6/12/06**		
5		Prepare Project Charter	20 hrs	1 day	Mon 6/12/06	Mon 6/12/06		
6		Review Project Charter	2 hrs	1 day	Mon 6/12/06	Mon 6/12/06		
7		Sign Off Project Charter	1 hr	1 day	Mon 6/12/06	Mon 6/12/06		
8		**Planning**	**66 hrs**	**1 day**	**Mon 6/12/06**	**Mon 6/12/06**		
9		**Estimation**	**21 hrs**	**1 day**	**Mon 6/12/06**	**Mon 6/12/06**		
10		Prepare Estimates	18 hrs	1 day	Mon 6/12/06	Mon 6/12/06		
11		Review Estimates	2 hrs	1 day	Mon 6/12/06	Mon 6/12/06		
12		Sign Off Estimates	1 hr	1 day	Mon 6/12/06	Mon 6/12/06		
13		**Project Plan**	**45 hrs**	**1 day**	**Mon 6/12/06**	**Mon 6/12/06**		
14		Prepare Project Plan	40 hrs	1 day	Mon 6/12/06	Mon 6/12/06		
15		Review Project Plan	4 hrs	1 day	Mon 6/12/06	Mon 6/12/06		
16		Sign Off Project Plan	1 hr	1 day	Mon 6/12/06	Mon 6/12/06		

Figure 5.10. Estimates assigned to lowest-level tasks in **Work** column and rolled up to summary level.

lowest-level tasks, not the summary tasks; the estimates will roll up to the summary tasks. Summary tasks are in boldface in MPP (Figure 5.10).

Steps:

➤ In the **Gantt Chart** view, right click on the **Duration** column and select the **Insert Column** option.

➤ In the **Insert Column** dialog box, select the **Work** field and click **OK**.

➤ In **Duration** enter 1 day in the first lowest-level task and select the **Duration** column for the entire WBS; press **Ctrl+D** to copy the value 1 to the entire WBS (to remove "?" from the **Duration** column).

➤ Now enter the estimates in hours in the **Work** column for all of the lowest-level tasks. Lowest-level tasks are identified by regular-face type; summary-level tasks are identified by boldface type. Estimates when entered in the lowest-level tasks will roll up to the summary tasks.

➤ If the project is the top-level task, then the **Work** column for this task displays the total effort in hours for the project. (Note: This number can be cross-checked/verified with your estimates.)

ID	❶	Resource Name	Type	Material Label	Initials	Group	Max. Units	Std. Rate	Ovt. Rate	Cost/Use	Accrue At	Base Calendar	Code
1		Sham	Work		S		100%	$1.00/hr	$0.00/hr	$0.00	Prorated	Standard	
2		Shailaja	Work		S		100%	$1.00/hr	$0.00/hr	$0.00	Prorated	Standard	
3		Jim	Work		J		100%	$1.00/hr	$0.00/hr	$0.00	Prorated	Standard	
4		Kerry	Work		K		100%	$1.00/hr	$0.00/hr	$0.00	Prorated	Standard	
5		Claudia	Work		C		100%	$1.00/hr	$0.00/hr	$0.00	Prorated	Standard	

Figure 5.11. Resource Sheet screen.

CREATING RESOURCES

The next step in creating a schedule creation process is setting up the resources to be used in MPP. Human, machinery, and material resources for the project are created in the **Resources** tab of MPP. In the **View** menu, click on the **Resource Sheet** menu item to go to the **Resource Sheet** (Figure 5.11).

Cost calculations and earned value measurements require that rates be assigned to the resources. Actual costs or efforts may be used to calculate earned value measurements. If actual cost is chosen, a per-hour rate must be entered in the **Std. Rate** column for each resource. If effort is chosen, enter $1.00/hr in the **Std. Rate** column. Note: Using the actual cost will give more accurate results than using effort. However, if actual costs are not available efforts may be used. The cost per use rate is beneficial for machinery utilized in the project.

Steps:

➤ In the menu, go to the **View** menu and choose the **Resource Sheet** menu item. (If you have the view bar on the right-hand side of MPP, choose the **Resource Sheet** icon.)

➤ Press the **Insert** button to insert new rows.

➤ Enter the resource names in the **Resource Name** column.

➤ In the **Type** column, enter the type of resource (e.g., **Work** or **Material**).

➤ In the **Max. Units** column, enter the allocation percent for each project resource.

➤ In the **Std. Rate** column, enter the rate/hr for each resource.

➤ In the **Ovt. Rate** column, enter the rate/hr for overtime work by each resource.

➤ In the **Cost/Use** column, enter the cost per use of each resource if the resource is a machine.

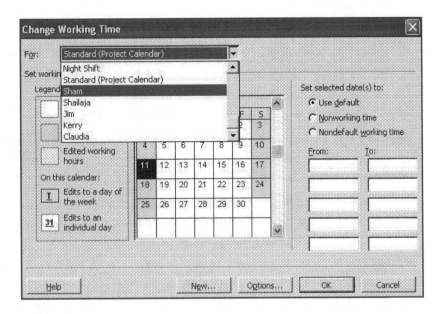

Figure 5.12. Change Working Time screen.

> In the **Accrue At** column, enter **Prorated** as the option.

> In the **Base Calendar** column, choose the base calendar for each resource.

SETTING UP THE RESOURCE CALENDAR

Now that resources have been set up, the calendars for the resources need to be set up. Specify their work times if they are different from the standard calendar. Specify their vacation plans.

To set up the resource calendar, go to the **Tools > Change Working Time** menu item (Figure 5.12). Perform the same operations as described earlier for changing work times or setting vacation times for the standard calendar. Another important element in calculations is including vacation time at the resource level. Vacation time drives the end date of a project. If the vacation time of resources is not input into a schedule, the end date for a project will be earlier than the date that can actually be achieved. By the end of the project, it will definitely be behind schedule. A good practice is to compile the vacation schedules of resources at this stage and set them up in the project schedule to ensure that there are minimal schedule problems.

Steps:

➤ In the menu, go to the **Tools** menu and choose the **Change Working Time** menu item.

➤ In the **For** dropdown, select the resource for whom you want to set up a calendar by specifying his vacation time, weekends, work time, etc.

➤ To mark a particular day, such as a holiday, select the day on the calendar in the center of the screen. On the right-hand side of the screen, select the **Nonworking time** button.

➤ To change the work times of a particular day, select the day on the calendar. On the right-hand side, select the **Nondefault working time** button and enter the changed working times for that particular day.

➤ To mark a group of consecutive days as holidays, select the first day and drag the mouse over the remaining days on the calendar. On the right-hand side, select the **Nonworking time** button.

➤ To change the work time for a group of consecutive days, select the first day and drag the mouse over the remaining days on the calendar. On the right-hand side, select the **Nondefault working time** button and enter the changed work times for that particular day.

➤ To mark a group of nonconsecutive days as holidays, select the first day and keep the **Ctrl** key pressed on the keyboard and select the other days on the calendar. On the right-hand side, select the **Nonworking time** button.

➤ To change the working time of a group of nonconsecutive days, select the first day and keep the **Ctrl** key pressed on the keyboard and select the other days on the calendar. On the right-hand side, select the **Nondefault working time** and enter the changed work times.

➤ To mark an entire week as a holiday, select the week column heading on the calendar. On the right-hand side, select the **Nonworking time** button.

➤ To change the work time of a day of the week, select the week column heading on the calendar. On the right-hand side, select the **Nondefault working time** and enter the changed working times for that weekday.

⬤	Task Name	Work	Duration	Start	Finish	Predecessors	Resource Names
1	⊟ **Sample Software Project**	**693 hrs**	**1 day**	**Mon 6/12/06**	**Mon 6/12/06**		
2	⊟ **Initiation**	**27 hrs**	**1 day**	**Mon 6/12/06**	**Mon 6/12/06**		
3	Project Kick Off Meeting	4 hrs	1 day	Mon 6/12/06	Mon 6/12/06		
4	⊟ **Project Charter**	**23 hrs**	**1 day**	**Mon 6/12/06**	**Mon 6/12/06**		Sham
5	Prepare Project Charter	20 hrs	1 day	Mon 6/12/06	Mon 6/12/06		Shailaja
6	Review Project Charter	2 hrs	1 day	Mon 6/12/06	Mon 6/12/06		Jim
7	Sign Off Project Charter	1 hr	1 day	Mon 6/12/06	Mon 6/12/06		Kerry
8	⊟ **Planning**	**66 hrs**	**1 day**	**Mon 6/12/06**	**Mon 6/12/06**		Claudia

Figure 5.13. Dropdown menu for **Resource Names** column.

ASSIGNING RESOURCES

Resources can be assigned to tasks by clicking on the dropdown menu in the **Resource Names** column and selecting the resource you want to assign to a particular task (see the lower right-hand side of Figure 5.13). When a resource is assigned using this technique, MPP assumes that you intend to assign the resource to the task at 100% and adjusts the **Duration** column accordingly, depending on the estimates entered in the **Work** column. (Note: Remember from Figure 5.1 that the **Fixed Work** option was chosen when we set up MPP. If we had chosen **Fixed Duration**, the **Work** column would be adjusted accordingly.)

Look at the Project Kick-Off Meeting task. The estimate given is 4 hours. If Jim is chosen as the resource, 50% will appear for Jim. This means that Jim can finish the task using 50% of his time on this task. However, if you reassign Jim to the task by choosing Jim from the dropdown, Jim is now assigned at 100%. You will not see 50% beside Jim's name. Instead, the **Duration** column will be adjusted to 0.5 days. Therefore, if Jim is assigned full time for this task, and we have an 8-hour workday, then Jim requires a half day or 4 hours of work. Alternatively, multiple resources can be assigned by going into the **Task Information** dialog box (Figure 5.14), which comes up by double clicking on the task.

The percentage of time allocated to a task for a resource can be adjusted by entering a percentage value in the percent column. *Important:* If a resource is assigned to a particular task at a percentage lower than the maximum available units for that resource as defined in the **Resource Sheet**, MPP will assign the remaining time of the resource to other tasks to which the resource has been assigned.

Let's look at a simple example. If a resource has maximum units of 100% as defined in the **Resource Sheet** and the resource workday is 8 hours, and if the resource is assigned to a particular task at 50% and the task requires 8 hours of work, then this resource should need to work 2 calendar days to finish the task.

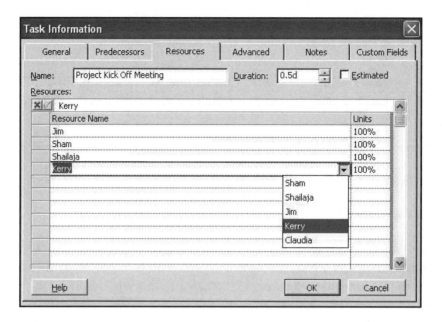

Figure 5.14. Task Information dialog box.

Tip: Assigning the same resources to multiple tasks can be easily accomplished by assigning the resources to the first task and then selecting the remaining tasks by pressing the **Ctrl** key. Select the tasks and press **Ctrl+D**. Sometimes doing this assigns the resources with different units and therefore a percentage different from the original task will appear on remaining tasks. If this happens, keep the selection and press **Ctrl+D** once again and the assignment will be done correctly. This situation occurs because MPP keeps **Duration** and **Work** intact and tries to make fixes in the resource units. The next time you copy the resource details, **Duration** is adjusted, keeping resource units the same.

This procedure will copy the resources to all of the selected tasks. In this case, the resource units (in percentage of time the resources are allocated to the task) vary depending on the **Work** and **Duration** columns. For the same allocation, keep the selection as is and press **Ctrl+D** on the keyboard once again. This time MPP knows that you want to retain the resource units as done in the first task and adjusts the duration accordingly.

Steps:

> In the **Gantt Chart** view, go to the **Resource Names** column. Select the resource from the dropdown to assign a single resource to the task at a 100% utilization level.

➢ To assign multiple resources at different utilization levels, right click on the task row. Select the **Task Information** menu item (or simply double click on the task row to which you want to assign a resource).

➢ Navigate to the **Resources** by clicking on the **Resources** tab.

➢ Click on **Table Resources**.

➢ Press **Insert** to insert a row for a resource.

➢ Choose the resource's name from the dropdown.

➢ In the **Units** column, specify the percentage allocation of this resource to the particular task.

➢ After finishing entries for all resources, click **OK** to apply the changes.

Tip: To copy the same set of resources at the same levels of utilization to other tasks, simply select the tasks by dragging the mouse over the resource column for consecutive tasks or by pressing the **Ctrl** key and selecting nonconsecutive tasks and press **Ctrl+D**. This may have to be done twice on each set to ensure that the same levels of utilization are applied.

SEQUENCING LOWEST-LEVEL TASKS

If lowest-level tasks need to be sequenced, select all of the tasks that need to be sequenced and click on the **Link tasks** button on the menu. This will assign predecessors to all of the tasks except the first task (Figure 5.15).

Alternatively, the predecessor of each task can be set manually to sequence the tasks, i.e., the tasks are sequenced by assigning predecessors to each one. This method means that

	❶	Task Name	Work	Duration	Start	Finish	Predecessors	Resource Names
1		⊟ **Sample Software Project**	**693 hrs**	**10 days**	**Mon 6/12/06**	**Fri 6/23/06**		
2		⊟ **Initiation**	**27 hrs**	**2.5 days**	**Mon 6/12/06**	**Wed 6/14/06**		
3		Project Kick Off Meeting	4 hrs	0.13 days	Mon 6/12/06	Mon 6/12/06		Jim, Sham
4		⊟ **Project Charter**	**23 hrs**	**2.5 days**	**Mon 6/12/06**	**Wed 6/14/06**		
5		Prepare Project Charter	20 hrs	2.5 days	Mon 6/12/06	Wed 6/14/06		Shailaja
6		Review Project Charter	2 hrs	0.25 days	Mon 6/12/06	Mon 6/12/06		Jim
7		Sign Off Project Charter	1 hr	0.13 days	Mon 6/12/06	Mon 6/12/06		Jim
8		⊟ **Planning**	**66 hrs**	**5 days**	**Mon 6/12/06**	**Fri 6/16/06**		

Figure 5.15. Lowest-level tasks to be sequenced.

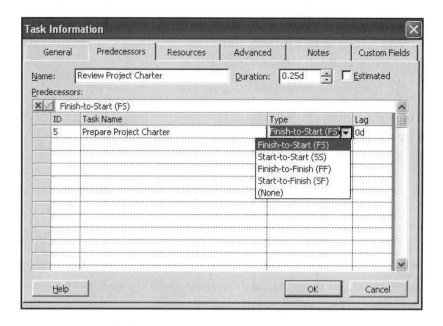

Figure 5.16. Relationships for sequencing tasks.

only after the first task is completed can the second task start—the finish-to-start relationship. In MPP, four relationships can be used to sequence tasks (Figure 5.16).

- Finish-to-Start (FS)
- Start-to-Start (SS)
- Finish-to-Finish (FF)
- Start-to-Finish (SF)

Finish-to-Start. Finish-to-start is the default relationship. Finish-to-start means that the task which is assigned as the predecessor to the current task must be completed before this task can start.

Start-to-Start. In a start-to-start relationship, the task which is assigned as the predecessor to the current task and the current task must start at the same time. A start-to-start relationship is seldom used.

Finish-to-Finish. In a finish-to-finish relationship, the task which is assigned as the predecessor to the current task and the current task must finish at the same time. The finish-to-finish relationship is seldom used.

Start-to-Finish. In a start-to-finish relationship, the current task should finish by the start date of the task assigned as the predecessor. The start-to-finish relationship is seldom used.

Although the last three of these relationships are seldom used, any of them may be used to sequence the tasks. Lag time for any of these relationships can also be specified. Lag time must be specified in days.

For example, suppose you specify a lag time of 10 days for a finish-to-start relationship. This specification means that a current task will start 10 days after a task assigned as the predecessor finishes. Therefore, if you want to start a current task 10 days before its predecessor is completed, specify the lag time as –10 days. The negative assignment is also called lead time.

Tip: You can specify the relationships directly in the **Predecessors** column instead of opening the task information dialog box. Suppose you wish to specify a **Lag** time of 10 days and the predecessor as Task 5. If so, put **5FS+10** in the **Predecessors** column. Similarly, start to start, finish to finish, and start to finish may be used for other relationships.

Steps:

- ➢ In the **Gantt Chart** view, go to the **Predecessors** column. Enter the task number of the task which precedes this task. This procedure creates a finish-to-start relationship between these two tasks.

- ➢ To set the predecessor for a group of tasks with finish-to-start relationships, select the tasks on the **Gantt Chart** view and click on the **Link tasks** icon. This procedure will link tasks with the finish-to-start relationship starting from the first task down to the last task selected.

- ➢ To create more complex relationships between tasks, right click on the task row. Select the **Task Information** menu item (or simply double click on the task row to which you would like to assign a resource).

- ➢ Navigate to the **Predecessors** by clicking on the **Predecessors** tab.

- ➢ Click on **Table Predecessors**.

- ➢ Press **Insert** to insert a row for a resource.

- ➢ Choose the **Task Name** from the dropdown.

- ➢ In the **Type** column specify the relationship.

0	Priority	Task Name	Work	Duration	Start	Finish	Predecessors	Resource Names
1	800	⊟ Sample Software Project	693 hrs	14 days	Mon 6/12/06	Thu 6/29/06		
2	800	⊞ Initiation	27 hrs	2.88 days	Mon 6/12/06	Wed 6/14/06		
8	700	⊞ Planning	66 hrs	5.63 days	Mon 6/12/06	Mon 6/19/06		
17	600	⊞ Requirements	69 hrs	3.38 days	Mon 6/12/06	Thu 6/15/06		
30	500	⊞ Design	119 hrs	5.88 days	Mon 6/12/06	Mon 6/19/06		
43	400	⊞ Development	256 hrs	14 days	Mon 6/12/06	Thu 6/29/06		
56	300	⊞ Testing	156 hrs	6.5 days	Mon 6/12/06	Tue 6/20/06		

Figure 5.17. Project with a gap of 100 between each summary task.

> In the **Lag** column, specify the lead or lag time by specifying a negative value for **Lead** and a positive value for **Lag** time.

> After finishing the entry of all relationships, click **OK** to apply the changes.

ASSIGNING PRIORITIES TO SUMMARY TASKS

The **Priority** field can be used to sequence tasks. (Note: The author advises use of the **Priority** field to sequence summary tasks and use of standard relationships to sequence lowest-level tasks.) Insert the column **Priority** in MPP (see the *Assigning Estimates* section about how to insert a column).

Using the **Priority** field, a priority can be assigned to tasks that will define the sequence of the tasks. The **Priority** field accepts values from 0 to 1000. Priority must be assigned in reverse order, meaning a task with 1000 priority is the first task and a task with 0 priority is the last task. By default, priority is set at 500 for all tasks. This number can be changed by entering the appropriate number in the **Priority** field.

First, assign priorities to second-level tasks. Choose the **Show > Outline Level 2** menu option to collapse the schedule to the second level. Assign priorities in descending order. Suggestion: As appropriate for your project, leave a gap between each summary task. Notice in Figure 5.17 that a gap of 100 has been left between each summary task. Having a gap of 100 will help you when assigning priorities for tasks below this level.

Expand to one level further to assign priorities to the next level (Figure 5.18). As can be seen, priority needs to be assigned to third-level summary tasks and third-level tasks using the numbers between second-level summary tasks. For example, notice that the **Initiation** task has a priority of 800 and the **Planning** task has a priority of 700; therefore the Project Kick Off Meeting and **Project Charter** tasks must have priorities between 800 and 700. Suggestion: Leave a gap between the numbers assigned to level 2 summary tasks

❶	Priority	Task Name	Work	Duration	Start	Finish	Predecessors	Resource Names
1	800	⊟ Sample Software Project	693 hrs	14 days	Mon 6/12/06	Thu 6/29/06		
2	800	⊟ Initiation	27 hrs	2.88 days	Mon 6/12/06	Wed 6/14/06		
3	790	Project Kick Off Meeting	4 hrs	0.13 days	Mon 6/12/06	Mon 6/12/06		Jim, Sham
4	780	⊞ Project Charter	23 hrs	2.88 days	Mon 6/12/06	Wed 6/14/06		
8	700	⊟ Planning	66 hrs	5.63 days	Mon 6/12/06	Mon 6/19/06		
9	690	⊞ Estimation	21 hrs	2.63 days	Mon 6/12/06	Wed 6/14/06		
13	680	⊞ Project Plan	45 hrs	5.63 days	Mon 6/12/06	Mon 6/19/06		
17	600	⊟ Requirements	69 hrs	3.38 days	Mon 6/12/06	Thu 6/15/06		
18	590	⊞ SRS Module 1	27 hrs	3.38 days	Mon 6/12/06	Thu 6/15/06		
22	580	⊞ SRS Module 2	27 hrs	3.38 days	Mon 6/12/06	Thu 6/15/06		
26	570	⊞ SRS Final	15 hrs	1.88 days	Mon 6/12/06	Tue 6/13/06		
30	500	⊟ Design	119 hrs	5.88 days	Mon 6/12/06	Mon 6/19/06		
31	490	⊞ Design Module 1	47 hrs	5.88 days	Mon 6/12/06	Mon 6/19/06		
35	480	⊞ Design Module 2	47 hrs	5.88 days	Mon 6/12/06	Mon 6/19/06		
39	470	⊞ Design Final	25 hrs	3.13 days	Mon 6/12/06	Thu 6/15/06		
43	400	⊟ Development	256 hrs	14 days	Mon 6/12/06	Thu 6/29/06		
44	390	⊞ Develop Module 1	112 hrs	14 days	Mon 6/12/06	Thu 6/29/06		
48	380	⊞ Develop Module 2	112 hrs	14 days	Mon 6/12/06	Thu 6/29/06		
52	370	⊞ Develop Final	32 hrs	4 days	Mon 6/12/06	Thu 6/15/06		
56	300	⊟ Testing	156 hrs	6.5 days	Mon 6/12/06	Tue 6/20/06		
57	290	⊞ Develop Module 1	52 hrs	6.5 days	Mon 6/12/06	Tue 6/20/06		
61	280	⊞ Develop Module 2	52 hrs	6.5 days	Mon 6/12/06	Tue 6/20/06		
65	270	⊞ Develop Final	52 hrs	6.5 days	Mon 6/12/06	Tue 6/20/06		

Figure 5.18. Project with levels expanded to assign priorities to next level.

as required by your project. The gap should be sufficient to allow prioritizing of the lower-level tasks.

Continue this process for the remaining levels and for the lowest-level tasks that use the standard relationships (finish-to-start, start-to-start, etc.). Repeat the priority of summary-level tasks (Figure 5.19).

The **Priority** field works like a finish-to-start relationship if two tasks with different priorities have the same resource assigned to them. The **Priority** field goes one level down in bringing the resource into consideration for sequencing the tasks.

In most projects, the **Priority** field can be used to sequence the summary tasks, thereby avoiding the process of assigning relationships through the use of predecessors. However, in some complex projects, using relationships by assigning predecessors will still be needed. You will need to make this decision, depending on the project and relationships of tasks.

	❶	Priority	Task Name	Work	Duration	Start	Finish	Predecessors	Resource Names
1		800	⊟ Sample Software Project	693 hrs	14 days	Mon 6/12/06	Thu 6/29/06		
2		800	⊟ Initiation	27 hrs	2.88 days	Mon 6/12/06	Wed 6/14/06		
3		790	Project Kick Off Meeting	4 hrs	0.13 days	Mon 6/12/06	Mon 6/12/06		Jim, Sham
4		780	⊞ Project Charter	23 hrs	2.88 days	Mon 6/12/06	Wed 6/14/06		
8		700	⊟ Planning	66 hrs	5.63 days	Mon 6/12/06	Mon 6/19/06		
9		690	⊟ Estimation	21 hrs	2.63 days	Mon 6/12/06	Wed 6/14/06		
10		690	Prepare Estimates	18 hrs	2.25 days	Mon 6/12/06	Wed 6/14/06		Shailaja
11		690	Review Estimates	2 hrs	0.25 days	Wed 6/14/06	Wed 6/14/06	10	Jim
12		690	Sign Off Estimates	1 hr	0.13 days	Wed 6/14/06	Wed 6/14/06	11	Jim

Figure 5.19. Project with further expansion to assign priorities to lowest-level tasks.

Steps:

➢ In the **Gantt Chart** view, right click on the **Task Name** column and select the **Insert Column** option.

➢ In the **Insert Column** dialog box, select **Priority** field and click **OK**.

➢ In the formatting **Tool** bar, select the **Show > Outline Level 2** menu option.

➢ In the **Priority** field, enter the priorities of level 2 summary tasks in descending order, leaving a gap of 100 or so numbers between the summary tasks. (Note: This gap is determined by the project and the WBS. Leaving a gap allows priorities to be assigned to tasks at a lower level than level 2.)

➢ Repeat the process in the above step until all summary tasks are finished.

➢ For lowest-level tasks, assign the same priority to all the tasks because these tasks will be linked through the **Predecessors** field.

CREATING RECURRING TASKS

Depending on the project, most projects generally have recurring tasks such as team meetings, brainstorming sessions, team outings, etc. Because these tasks are recurring in nature, they often occur at a predefined frequency throughout the duration of a project. Often these tasks are not included in a schedule which ultimately results in the cost of these tasks and the time associated with them to not be accounted for in the schedule. If many of these tasks occur in a project, they can lead to a significant budget or schedule overrun. Including all recurring tasks in a schedule is always a good practice.

Recurring tasks can be created in MPP. From the menu, choose the option **Insert > Recurring Task** (Figure 5.20). Then recurring tasks can be created using the **Recurring**

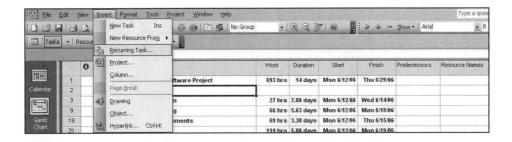

Figure 5.20. Dropdown menu for inserting a recurring task.

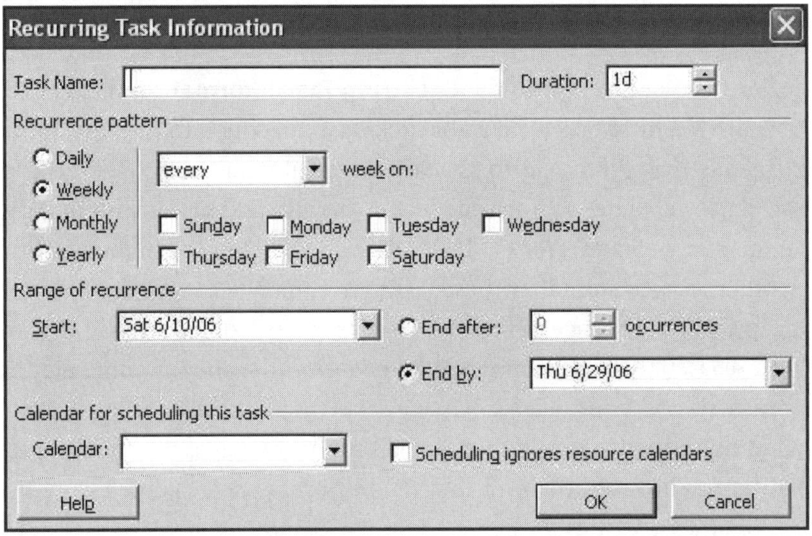

Figure 5.21. Recurring Task Information dialog box.

Task Information dialog box (Figure 5.21). **Task Name** can be entered; **Duration**, the **Recurrence pattern** or frequency, a date range of recurrence, and a calendar to be used for scheduling the task can be specified. Additionally, you can specify if MPP is to ignore the resource calendars. This option is particularly useful for team meetings. Even though some resources are taking vacation time, team meetings will continue.

Notice in Figure 5.22 that team meetings have been given the highest priority (1000) because team meetings are held at a specified time and day of the week/month regardless of other activities in the project. Specifying a 1000 priority for team meeting tasks will ensure that they are scheduled on the appropriate day and other activities are shifted in the

	❶	Priority	Task Name	Work	Duration	Start	Finish	Predecessors	Resource Names
1		800	⊟ Sample Software Project	693 hrs	14 days	Mon 6/12/06	Thu 6/29/06		
2	⟳🗍	1000	⊟ Team Meetings	0 hrs	########	Mon 6/12/06	Mon 6/26/06		
3	▦🗍	1000	Team Meetings 1	0 hrs	0.13 days	Mon 6/12/06	Mon 6/12/06		
4	▦🗍	1000	Team Meetings 2	0 hrs	0.13 days	Mon 6/19/06	Mon 6/19/06		
5	▦🗍	1000	Team Meetings 3	0 hrs	0.13 days	Mon 6/26/06	Mon 6/26/06		
6		800	⊞ Initiation	27 hrs	2.88 days	Mon 6/12/06	Wed 6/14/06		
12		700	⊞ Planning	66 hrs	5.63 days	Mon 6/12/06	Mon 6/19/06		
21		600	⊞ Requirements	69 hrs	3.38 days	Mon 6/12/06	Thu 6/15/06		
34		500	⊞ Design	119 hrs	5.88 days	Mon 6/12/06	Mon 6/19/06		
47		400	⊞ Development	256 hrs	14 days	Mon 6/12/06	Thu 6/29/06		
60		300	⊞ Testing	156 hrs	6.5 days	Mon 6/12/06	Tue 6/20/06		

Figure 5.22. Team Meetings showing a priority of 1000.

schedule. You also need to get to the **Recurring Task Information** dialog box by selecting all of the **Team Meeting** tasks and right clicking and going into the **Task Information** dialog box. In this dialog box, go to the **Advanced** tab and select the task type as **Fixed Duration**. This will allow MPP to schedule recurring tasks along with other work. If these tasks are marked as **Fixed Work**, MPP will schedule them as highest priority tasks and move all other tasks to start after these tasks are completed.

You can change the range of recurrence or frequency of recurrence anytime during the project and rebaseline the schedule. It does not affect the already completed tasks and creates new recurring tasks or deletes existing recurring tasks depending on the change.

Keep in mind that you need to assign all of the resources who participate in this task at a 100% level. This would ensure that the resources are scheduled to perform this task regardless of other activities in the schedule.

Steps:

➢ In the **Insert** menu, choose the **Recurring Task** option to view the **Recurring Task Information** dialog box.

➢ In the **Recurring Tasks Information** dialog box, enter data for the following fields:

- Enter the task name in the **Task Name** field.
- Enter the duration of each recurring task in the **Duration** field.
- Select the **Recurrence pattern**: **Daily**, **Weekly**, **Monthly**, or **Yearly**.
- For the recurrence pattern **Daily**, enter the recurrence pattern: every day of the week or every workday of the week.

- For the recurrence pattern **We<u>e</u>kly**, enter the recurrence pattern: every day, every other day, etc. and select the day of the week that the task needs to recur.
- For the recurrence pattern **Mont<u>h</u>ly**, enter the recurrence pattern: the first, second, third, etc. day of every, every other, etc. month. (The recurrence pattern can also be chosen to be every first, second, etc. day of the week or Monday, Tuesday, etc. of every, every other, etc. month.)
- **Range of recurrence**: enter a **<u>S</u>tart** date for recurrence.
- Enter the number of **o<u>c</u>currences** of the recurring task (**End after**) or an end date for the recurrence (**End <u>b</u>y**).
- Calendar for scheduling this task: choose the **Cale<u>n</u>dar** to be considered for generating the recurring tasks.
- Click **OK** to apply the changes.

RESOURCE LEVELING

So far we have discussed creating a WBS, assigning estimates, assigning resources, and sequencing tasks. Yet to use our schedule, these activities are not enough. At this point, we have not resolved overallocation of resources.

When we assign resources, MPP takes the sequencing of tasks which we have specified and allocates resources to the tasks, but this process does not ensure allocation of resources at the optimum level. Optimum level means that the resources have an 8-hour workday and that they can work only for 8 hours per day; any work over 8 hours should move to the next day.

Allocating resources at the optimum level is achieved by the resource leveling feature of MPP. Resource leveling is an *automated feature* in MPP which levels resources at their maximum level, depending on hours per workday, vacation plans of the resources, holiday plans for the project, the maximum number of units of the resource (see Figures 5.11 and 5.14), and the percentage of the units allocated to the task. Few practitioners, however, use the resource leveling feature of MPP. Instead they choose to level the resources manually by inputting complex relationships between tasks and manually adjusting the work for each of the resources.

Also, a popular myth exists among project managers—"the resource leveling feature in MPP always moves the end date of a project to unusual levels and therefore it is better to not use the feature." However, as said, this statement is only a myth and not fact. If the resource leveling feature is well understood and leveling is performed correctly, having a

❶	Resource Name	Work	Details	5						Jun 18, '06					
				M	T	W	T	F	S	S	M	T	W	T	F
1 ◇	⊞ Sham	4 hrs	Work	2h							1h				
2 ◇	⊞ Shailaja	242 hrs	Work	74h	68h	46h	24h	24h			9h				
3 ◇	⊞ Jim	43 hrs	Work	2h	3h	14h	7h				16h				
4 ◇	⊞ Kerry	84 hrs	Work	2h		4h	6h				25h	6h			
5 ◇	⊞ Claudia	335 hrs	Work	49h	48h	44h	42h	40h			17h	22h	16h	16h	16h
			Work												

Figure 5.23. Resource Sheet screen indicating overallocated resources.

well-scheduled project with a realistic date is ensured. An important added benefit is that significant time will be saved for the project manager while tracking progress of the project.

In the **Resource Sheet** in Figure 5.23, some/all of the resources in the **Resource Name** column would appear in red in MPP, which indicates that some or all of these resources have been overallocated on one or more days. (Note: On an actual MPP screen, the resources *and* their overallocated hours and days of work will be in red.)

On the right-hand side of Figure 5.23, notice the hours allocated to each resource day by day. Clearly the hours allocated on some days are more than each resource could work in a single day. (Note: In Figure 5.23, only the hours for Sham [M, 1h], Jim [T, 3h], and Kerry [W, 4h, and T, 6h] will appear in black in MPP; these hours are in boldface type.)

Let's now look at how resource leveling is done. From the menu, choose the option **Tools > Level Resources**. The **Resource Leveling** dialog box is displayed (Figure 5.24). The leveling calculation has two options: **Automatic** and **Manual**. When chosen, the **Automatic** calculation option will be in force while the schedule is being edited. As soon as a task is changed or new tasks are added or any information is changed that would lead to a change in the schedule, the resource leveling feature is triggered and resources are leveled "on the fly." When the **Manual** calculation option is chosen, the user is expected to go to the dialog box, change the options, and click on the **Level Now** button to trigger resource leveling.

The next choice is to select the basis for overallocations. The options are **Minute by Minute**, **Hour by Hour**, **Day by Day**, **Week by Week**, and **Month by Month**. When the week-by-week option is chosen to perform resource leveling, MPP will ensure that each resource has a total of 40 hours of work in a week, assuming an 8-hour workday and a 5-day week. MPP ignores daily overallocations. When the week-by-week option is chosen, it is possible that some resources might have more than 8 hours of work assigned in a day and more than 60 minutes of work assigned in an hour, but they will definitely not have more than 40 hours of work allocated in a week.

The best option for most projects is the hour-by-hour option, which will resolve all of the overallocations. The minute-by-minute option is not needed for most projects.

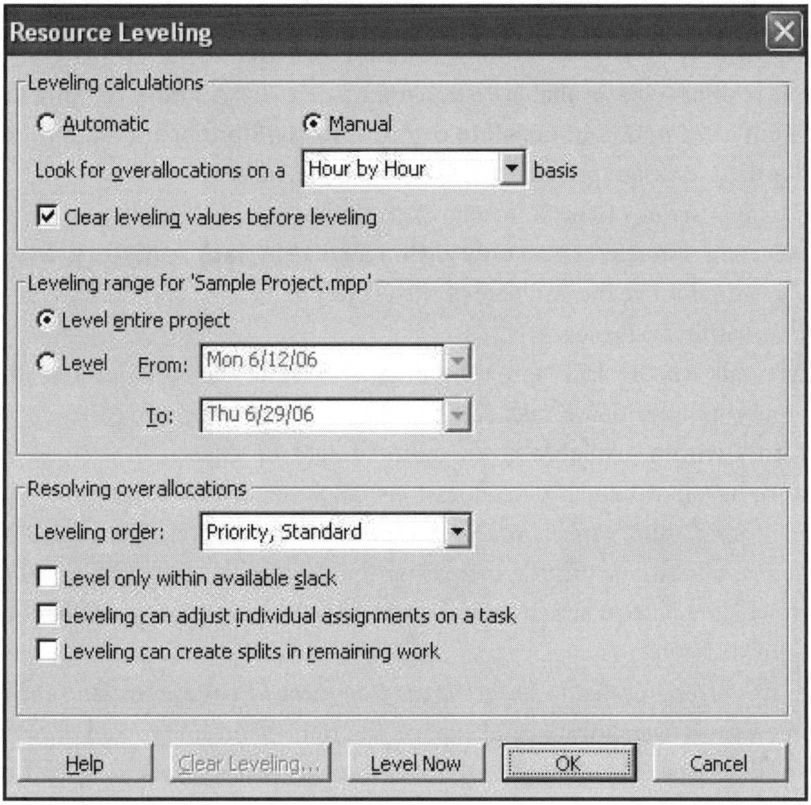

Figure 5.24. Resource Leveling dialog box.

The next option is a check box: **Clear leveling values before leveling**. By checking this box, whenever resource leveling is done, all leveling values are cleared before MPP performs resource leveling once again for all of the tasks. Otherwise, resource leveling is performed with the existing values and only for the overallocated resources.

The next option is the **Leveling range**. A choice can be made to **Level entire project** or to **Level** between **From** and **To** date ranges. Generally, a choice is made to **Level entire project** when schedule leveling is done for the first time. Yet the **Level entire project** choice is helpful—either when leveling an entire project for the first time or later when tracking the project.

The next option on the **Resource Leveling** sheet is **Resolving overallocations/ Leveling order**. The options in **Leveling order** are **ID Only**, **Standard**, and **Priority/ Standard**. The order chosen in **Leveling order** will dictate the way MPP performs resource leveling. The **ID Only** option ensures that MPP considers task ID first before other aspects such as relationships, available resource units, etc. The **Standard** option looks at relationships, available resource units, etc. for resource leveling and is the most commonly used option in **Leveling order**. **Priority/Standard** is an option used with the **Priority** field to assign priority to tasks (discussed earlier).

Next is a series of check boxes which defines to MPP what needs to be considered when leveling resources. **Level only within available slack** indicates to MPP that resource leveling cannot move the end date of the project and that it should try and resolve overallocations within available slack.

Let's talk about slack for a moment. Slack at the task level is the number of days/hours/minutes that a task can be delayed without delaying the entire project. The **Level only within available slack** option might be chosen in a situation when some resources have not had all overallocations resolved. In this situation, should overallocations be found, other aspects of the task need to be adjusted. Things that can be done to resolve overallocations include increasing the duration of the workday for the particular day on which a particular resource is overallocated or assigning a different resource who has more slack, etc.

To find overallocated tasks, go to the **Resource Sheet** and expand the task list of any resource who is overallocated and expand the right-hand side spread of hours to daily and look for days when the resource is allocated more than 8 hours a day and take the necessary steps:

Level only within available slack. Unchecking this option indicates to MPP to delay the end date of the project if necessary while resolving overallocations.

Leveling can adjust individual assignments on a task. This option indicates to MPP that to resolve overallocations, resource leveling can adjust the percent of allocation of the resources on a task. For example, when resource leveling cannot resolve an overallocation, MPP will increase the percent of allocation of the resource on the task to resolve the overallocation. The resource, therefore, must put in extra effort on that particular task to finish it.

Leveling can create splits in the remaining work. This option indicates to MPP that resource leveling can split a task while performing resource leveling. Use of this option generally comes into effect only after tracking the project has started and some tasks are partially complete. When performing resource leveling, if needed, MPP will split a task. Splitting is actually starting a task and finishing perhaps 40% of the task and then going to

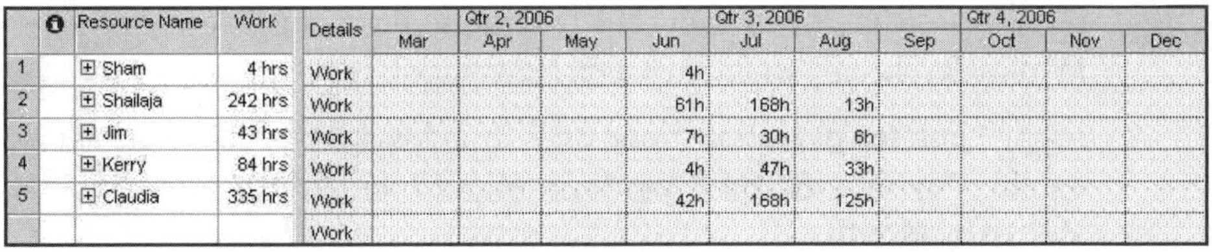

		Resource Name	Work	Details	Qtr 2, 2006			Qtr 3, 2006				Qtr 4, 2006		
	❶				Mar	Apr	May	Jun	Jul	Aug	Sep	Oct	Nov	Dec
1		⊞ Sham	4 hrs	Work				4h						
2		⊞ Shailaja	242 hrs	Work				61h	168h	13h				
3		⊞ Jim	43 hrs	Work				7h	30h	6h				
4		⊞ Kerry	84 hrs	Work				4h	47h	33h				
5		⊞ Claudia	335 hrs	Work				42h	168h	125h				
				Work										

Figure 5.25. Resource Utilization screen.

another task to finish that task before returning to the original task. Splitting can be useful if it is done *purposely*, but splitting creates a mess when resource leveling does it automatically. Keep this option **unchecked** unless using it is an absolute necessity and only if overallocations are being resolved by this option.

All of the options have been explained in the **Resource Leveling** dialog box. Depending on your project, you can now choose the options as needed. For most projects, the settings shown in Figure 5.24 will work perfectly well.

Apart from automatic resource leveling, check the **Resource Usage** tab to see if all resources are utilized fully on the project and if tasks can be reassigned to resources who are relatively free compared to others. This is a manual exercise that must be done a few times to get things right. Notice in Figure 5.25 that the resources Sham, Jim, and Kerry are not utilized at their optimum available time. You might want to consider assigning some tasks to these resources to reduce overall duration of the schedule. Checking that all resources are fully utilized greatly helps to reduce the duration of the project and to ensure that all resources are fully occupied.

Steps:

> In the menu, go to the **View** menu and choose the **Resource Usage** menu item (or choose the **Resource Usage** icon if you have the view bar on the right-hand side of MPP).

> In this view, some resources might have been overallocated. (Note: In MPP, overallocated resources will appear in red.)

> In the menu, go to the **Tools** menu and choose the **Level Resources** menu screen to view the **Resource Leveling** dialog box.

> In **Leveling calculations**, choose the **Automatic** or the **Manual** button. (Note: The difference between these two options is that **Automatic** levels the

resources on the fly as soon as there are some changes to the schedule and **Manual** levels only when the **Level Now** button is clicked.)

➤ In the **Look for overallocations on a** dropdown box, choose the appropriate option: **Day by Day**, **Hour by Hour**, **Minute by Minute**, **Week by Week**, or **Month by Month**.

➤ Check the **Clear leveling values before leveling** box.

➤ In the **Leveling Range for 'Sample project. mpp'**, select the **Level entire project** button.

➤ In the **Resolving overallocations/Leveling order** box, choose the **Priority/Standard** option for the leveling order.

➤ Uncheck the **Level only within available slack** box.

➤ Uncheck the **Leveling can adjust individual assignments on a task** box.

➤ Uncheck the **Leveling can create splits in remaining work** box.

➤ Click on the **Level Now** button to level resources. (Note: You will have an option to choose between **All Resources** and **Individual Resources**. Choose the **All Resources** option.)

➤ Resource leveling is complete and resources are leveled and allocated at the correct percentages. Now check the individual assignments of each resource and the overall schedule for end date of the project.

BASELINING THE SCHEDULE

The final step before starting a project is to baseline the schedule. A schedule is baselined *after* approval has been received from project stakeholders. Baselining is done to ensure that the original data used to set up the schedule are in place for future calculations and reference. A schedule baseline "freezes" all of the important data for every task, e.g., duration, work, start date, finish date, etc.

To baseline a schedule, from the **Tools** menu, choose the **Tracking > Save Baseline** option (Figure 5.26) to open the **Save Baseline** dialog box (Figure 5.27). (Note: As many as ten baselines can be saved using MPP, and a choice can be made about the baseline to be saved, e.g., the baseline for an entire project or for selected tasks. Saving multiple baselines is usually done in projects in which the project's schedule changes and the original baseline information will be needed for future reference and comparison.) Although the

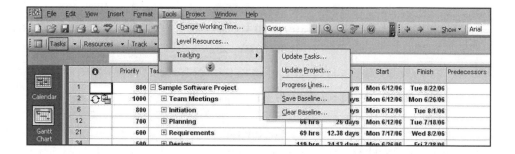

Figure 5.26. Save Baseline option.

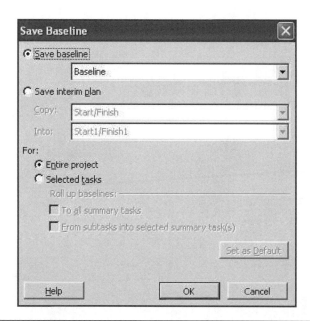

Figure 5.27. Save Baseline dialog box.

baseline for an entire project or for selected tasks can be saved, for now, because our schedule is a new schedule, we will save the baseline for the entire project. (Note: Saving interim plans and selected tasks will be discussed in Chapter 9.)

Steps:

> In the menu, go to the **Tools** menu and choose the **Tracking** menu item and then choose the **Save Baseline** submenu item to view the **Save Baseline** dialog box.

➢ Choose the **Save Baseline** button. (Note: From the dropdown, you can also choose the **Baseline Number to be saved as**. At this point, just choose the **Save baseline** button without changing this drop down.)

➢ Choose the **Entire Project** option in the **For** box.

➢ Click **OK** to save a baseline of the project.

You have now saved the baseline of the project. Any tracking done going forward will be against this saved baseline. (Note: A schedule can be rebaselined. This topic will be discussed in Chapter 9.)

6

SETTING UP THE EVM REPORT TEMPLATE

PREPARING THE TEMPLATE FOR A NEW PROJECT

Project Options

First, open the EVM template. (Note: Microsoft® Office Excel 2003 must be installed on your computer to open the tool; see also Chapter 1.) The template has the company name, project name, project manager's name, project start date, and project end date embedded in it. Enter the company address, company contact person's name, and budgeted cost of the project (Figure 6.1).

Note: The project manager field cannot be edited because the tool is licensed on a *named user basis.* When you request a fully licensed version of this tool, a license will be generated in your name and then sent to you. Also note that the tool that comes with this book is a full version which allows tracking of projects for a limited time of 6 months. A fully licensed version may be purchased from www.connoizor.com with discounts available for purchasers of this book.

Steps:

➢ Open the EVM report template.

➢ Navigate to the main menu tab as shown at the bottom of the screen (see Figure 6.1).

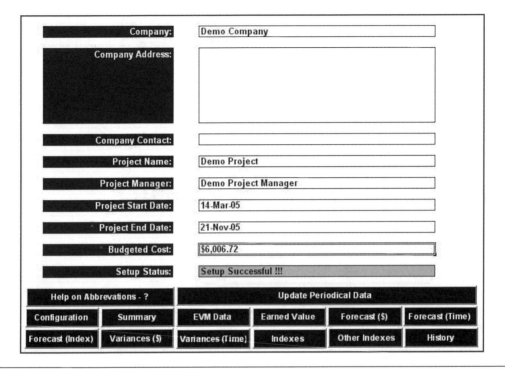

Figure 6.1. EVM report template—initial screen.

> ➤ Enter the **Company** name.

> ➤ Enter the **Company Address**.

> ➤ Enter the **Company Contact** person's name.

> ➤ Enter the **Project Name**.

> ➤ The **Project Manager** field cannot be edited.

> ➤ Enter the **Project Start Date**.

> ➤ Enter the **Project End Date**.

> ➤ Enter the **Budgeted Cost** of the project.

> ➤ Save the template to apply the changes made which completes the setup of the project options in the EVM report template.

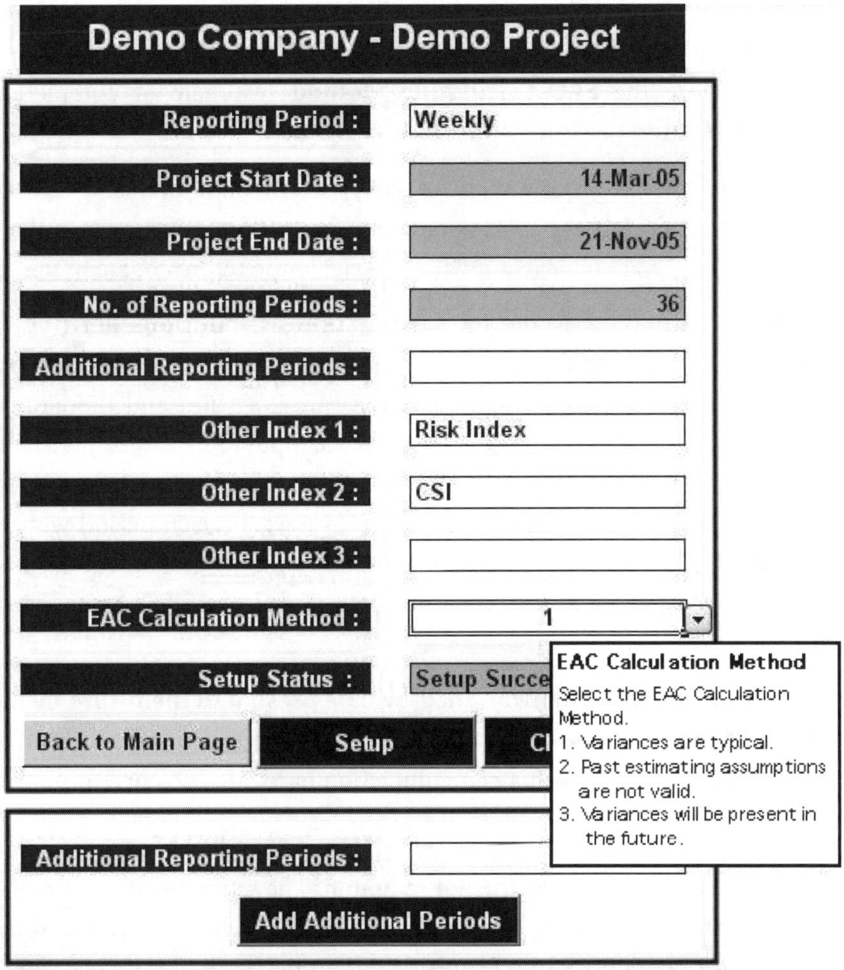

Demo Company - Demo Project

Reporting Period :	Weekly
Project Start Date :	14-Mar-05
Project End Date :	21-Nov-05
No. of Reporting Periods :	36
Additional Reporting Periods :	
Other Index 1 :	Risk Index
Other Index 2 :	CSI
Other Index 3 :	
EAC Calculation Method :	1
Setup Status :	Setup Succe

Back to Main Page   **Setup**   Cl

EAC Calculation Method

Select the EAC Calculation Method.
1. Variances are typical.
2. Past estimating assumptions are not valid.
3. Variances will be present in the future.

Additional Reporting Periods :	

Add Additional Periods

Figure 6.2. Configuration screen.

Configuration Options

Next is to configure the EVM template so it will accept data. Click on the **Configuration** button on the initial setup screen and go into the **Configuration** screen (Figure 6.2). Select a **Reporting Period** (options are **Weekly**, **Fortnightly**, **Monthly**, and **Bi-Monthly**). Once an option is selected, the reporting periods are calculated and displayed in the **No. of Reporting Periods** field. Additional reporting periods can be added by entering a number in the **Additional Reporting Periods** field. Three other tracking indexes that are not part of EVM can also be chosen and trend analysis can be performed on these indexes as well, e.g., the risk index, customer satisfaction index (CSI), etc.

Next, choose the **EAC Calculation Method** (estimate at completion). The **EAC Calculation Method** has three options: **1**, **2**, and **3**:

Option 1. Option 1 is the **Variances are typical** method. Choosing this method enables the template to calculate the EAC component based on the assumption that current variances in the project are typical and will not exist in the future course of the project.

Option 2. Option 2 is the **Past estimating assumptions are not valid** method. Choosing this method enables the template to calculate the EAC component based on the assumption that past estimating assumptions are not valid and therefore the estimates must be revised. Because this option requires the input of ETC (estimate to complete) values, enter the revised estimates in the **ETC** column. The revised estimates will then be used in the calculation of EAC. Also enter the ETC values for each period when you enter the periodic data. (Note: We will discuss how to enter the ETC value for each of the remaining periods in Chapter 7, *Tracking Schedule Progress*, and Chapter 8, *Monitoring the Schedule*.)

Option 3. Option 3 is the **Variances will be present in the future** method. Choosing this method enables the template to extrapolate current variances to future performance variances and shows the estimate at completion based on the current performance of the project.

The next step is to click on the **Setup** button. The setup process is usually done quickly on a fast machine, but may be slower using an older machine. To ensure that the setup has been successful, check the **Setup Status** field. This field indicates if the setup was successful.

Important: A setup can be cleared by using the **Clear Setup** button which allows the process to be redone if a mistake has been made. When you click the **Clear Setup** button, the template will prompt you to select an option of **Delete/Cancel**. Choose **Delete** for all charts. If **Delete** is not chosen, the template will stop working.

Steps:

➢ Navigate to the **Configuration** tab by clicking on this tab on the main menu screen.

➢ Select the **Reporting Period** that has been chosen for the project. Available options are **Weekly**, **Fortnightly**, **Monthly**, and **Bi-Monthly**. Base the period chosen on the size of the project, e.g., for a 6-month project, weekly is a good option (see Figure 6.2).

➤ The **Project Start Date**, **Project End Date**, and **No. of Reporting Periods** fields cannot be edited. The number of reporting periods is automatically calculated as soon as the reporting period is chosen.

➤ In **Additional Reporting periods**, enter additional reporting periods as needed. (Note: In some cases, adding a few additional reporting periods is beneficial because the project's status might need to be reported for an additional period or two after the planned reporting periods.)

➤ Enter other indexes in **Other Index 1**, **2** or **3** to track additional indexes which are not tracked as part of the template.

➤ Choose the **EAC Calculation Method** based on the needs of the project. At the beginning of the project, you might choose **1** and later change to another method as the need arises.

➤ Click on **Setup** to set up the template with the reporting periods and other indexes.

➤ Once the setup is completed, **Setup Status** shows a success message. The template cannot be used until it is set up correctly.

Now, configuring the template is finished. You can start populating the data.

Populating Reporting Periods

Now that the reporting periods have been created in the EVM template, the next step is to populate the reporting periods with data. The only data needed for the template at the setup stage is the baseline cost for the reporting periods.

Go into the **Task Usage** view of MPP by choosing the option **View > Task Usage** to see the screen illustrated in Figure 6.3. On the right-hand side of the screen, expand/collapse the details by using the + and – buttons shown in Figure 6.4. These buttons are on the MPP menu.

As you can see in Figure 6.3, the details have been expanded to show data by the week. Expand/collapse to display the data according to the reporting periods specified earlier in the template (weeks/fortnights/months). For the bi-monthly option, take the monthly data and sum up the data of 2 months to obtain bi-monthly data.

Notice in the **Details** column of Figure 6.3 that the data shown is **Work**, but you need to get the baseline cost values. To do this, right click on the **Details** column and choose the

	❶	Task Name	Work		Details	'06				Jul '06				Aug '06		
						4	11	18	25	2	9	16	23	30	6	
1		⊟ Sample Software Proje	708 hrs	5	Work		30h	5h	83h	85h	105h	90h	110h	77h	50h	
2	↻🗐	⊞ Team Meetings	15 hrs	1	Work		5h	5h	5h							
6		⊞ Initiation	27 hrs	3	Work	Detail Styles...							11h	12h		
12		⊞ Planning	66 hrs		Work ✓	Work				35h	10h					
21		⊞ Requirements	69 hrs	1	Work	Actual Work					40h	14h	15h			
34		⊞ Design	119 hrs	2	Work	Cumulative Work		39h	45h	10h		25h				
47		⊞ Development	256 hrs		Work	Baseline Work		39h	40h	60h	40h	21h				
60		⊞ Testing	156 hrs	2	Work	Cost						39h	50h	50h		
					Work	Actual Cost										
					Work											
					Work											

Figure 6.3. Task Usage screen.

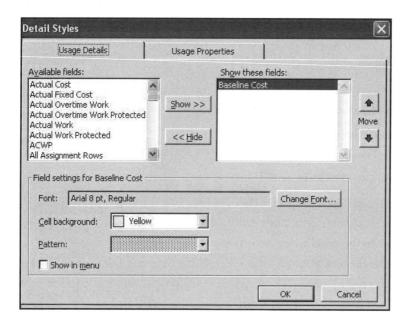

Figure 6.4. Expand (+) and collapse (–) buttons.

Figure 6.5. Dialog box to select **Baseline Cost** field.

Detail Styles option. This will open up a dialog box (shown in Figure 6.5). Use this dialog box to select the **Baseline Cost** field by using the **Show/Hide** buttons. This dialog will enable display of the baseline cost values which will appear on the right side of the screen shown in Figure 6.3. Next copy these cost values into the baseline cost field of the EVM

Demo Company - Demo Project - Periodical Data

Parameter	21-Mar-05	28-Mar-05	4-Apr-05	11-Apr-05	18-Apr-05	25-Apr-05	2-May-05
% Complete	5.00%	11.00%	11.00%	13.00%	19.00%	21.00%	24.00%
Baseline Cost	$357.00	$416.00	$80.00	$95.00	$286.20	$148.27	$184.73
EV	$360.00	$720.00	$720.00	$768.00	$1,214.72	$1,354.58	$1,532.60
PV	$357.00	$773.00	$853.00	$948.00	$1,234.20	$1,382.47	$1,567.20
AC	$360.00	$720.00	$720.00	$755.00	$1,113.20	$1,249.70	$1,402.70
BAC	$357.00	$773.00	$853.00	$948.00	$1,234.20	$1,382.47	$1,567.20
ETC	$0.00	$0.00	$0.00	$0.00	$0.00	$0.00	$0.00
EAC	$357.00	$773.00	$853.00	$935.00	$1,132.68	$1,277.59	$1,437.30
VAC	$0.00	$0.00	$0.00	$13.00	$101.52	$104.88	$129.90
ET (Periods)	1	2	3	4	5	6	7
PT (Periods)	1.80	3.96	3.96	4.68	6.84	7.56	8.64
SPI ($)	$1.01	$0.93	$0.84	$0.81	$0.98	$0.98	$0.98
CPI	1.00	1.00	1.00	1.02	1.09	1.08	1.09
TCPI	1.00	1.00	1.00	1.00	0.98	0.98	0.97
SV ($)	$3.00	-$53.00	-$133.00	-$180.00	-$19.48	-$27.89	-$34.60
CV ($)	$0.00	$0.00	$0.00	$13.00	$101.52	$104.88	$129.90
SV ($) %	1%	-7%	-16%	-19%	-2%	-2%	-2%
CV ($) %	0%	0%	0%	2%	8%	8%	8%
SV (Time)	0.80	1.96	0.96	0.68	1.84	1.56	1.64
SV (Time)%	80%	98%	32%	17%	37%	26%	23%
SPI (Time)	1.80	1.98	1.32	1.17	1.37	1.26	1.23
Tot Weeks	36	36	36	36	36	36	36
EAC (Time)	20.00	18.18	27.27	30.77	26.32	28.57	29.17
TSPI (Time)	0.98	0.94	0.97	0.98	0.94	0.95	0.94
Risk Index	0.00	0.00	0.00	0.00	0.00	0.00	0.00
CSI	0.00	0.00	0.00	0.00	0.00	0.00	0.00
Not Defined	0.00	0.00	0.00	0.00	0.00	0.00	0.00

Back to Main Page

Figure 6.6. EVM report template—periodic data screen.

template data screen as shown in Figure 6.6. Figure 6.7 displays the BAC (budget at completion) and EAC (estimate at completion) graphs that have been populated.

Now you are ready to start using the template for tracking and reporting project progress and status and to forecast the future performance of the project.

Steps:

➤ In the menu, go to the **View** menu and choose the **Task Usage** menu item to view **Task Usage**.

➤ On the left-hand side is the WBS; on the right is the **Work** for each task spread over time (see Figure 6.3).

➤ Right click on the **Details** column and uncheck **Work**.

➤ Right click and select **Detail Styles**.

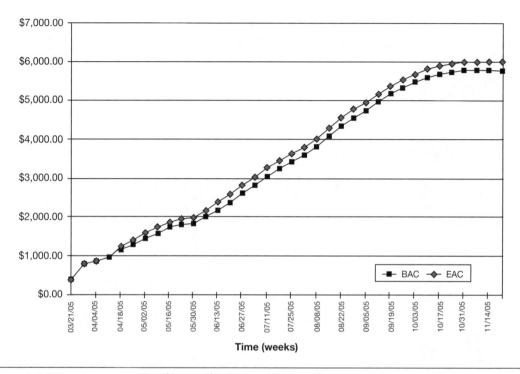

Figure 6.7. Demo Company project forecast ($)—BAC and EAC graphs.

➢ In the **Usage Details** tab, select the **Baseline Cost** field and click on **Show** (see Figure 6.5).

➢ Click **OK** to see the baseline costs on the right-hand side of the screen.

➢ Expand/collapse the **Time Period** to match the reporting periods (weeks, months, etc.) chosen in your template (by using the buttons shown in Figure 6.4).

➢ Copy the data from the top-level task (the project level).

➢ Starting with the first column in the row for **Baseline Cost**, paste the data into the data sheet of the template. (Note: The fields in white are the only fields in the EVM template data sheet that can be edited.)

➢ See that the data fit exactly into all of the reporting periods in the data sheet of the EVM template. If data do not match, remove the data by undoing the paste operation with **Ctrl+Z** and add additional periods from the **Configuration** sheet.

7

TRACKING PROGRESS IN THE SCHEDULE

TRACKING PROGRESS IN MPP

Now that you have set up the project and the EVM template, you are ready to start tracking progress in MPP and the EVM template on a periodic basis. Remember that the period tracked depends on the option that you selected when configuring the EVM template (weekly, fortnightly, monthly, etc.).

In our example of a simple software project, we have chosen the weekly reporting period option. So, your first reporting will start with the first week, which is 7 days from the project start date, and continue in this manner until the end of the project. Therefore, 7 days will be in every reporting period. In our example, the project start date is March 14, 2005; therefore, the first reporting period will be March 21, 2005 (see Figure 6.6).

Tracking progress in MPP can be accomplished in different ways and with differing rigor levels. The method and the rigor level depend on the project. In the sections that follow, three ways of tracking progress in MPP are discussed:

➢ Summary level tracking—a less rigorous method of tracking progress

➢ Task level day-wise (or period) tracking—tracking progress by tasks and days/periods

➢ Resource level day-wise tracking—tracking progress by resources and days/periods

	Task Name	Act. Star	Act. Finis	% Com	Phys Comp	Act. Dι	Rem. Dι	Act. Cos	Work	Act. Wc
1	☐ **Sample Software Project**	**Mon 10/2/06**	**NA**	**16%**	**0%**	**7.45 days**	**40.42 days**	**$114.00**	**700 hrs**	**114 hrs**
2	☐ **Team Meeting**	**Mon 10/2/06**	**NA**	**11%**	**0%**	**4.46 days**	**35.67 days**	**$1.00**	**9 hrs**	**1 hr**
3	Team Meeting 1	Mon 10/2/06	Mon 10/2/06	100%	0%	0.13 days	0 days	$1.00	1 hr	1 hr
4	Team Meeting 2	NA	NA	0%	0%	0 days	0.13 days	$0.00	1 hr	0 hrs
5	Team Meeting 3	NA	NA	0%	0%	0 days	0.13 days	$0.00	1 hr	0 hrs
6	Team Meeting 4	NA	NA	0%	0%	0 days	0.13 days	$0.00	1 hr	0 hrs
7	Team Meeting 5	NA	NA	0%	0%	0 days	0.13 days	$0.00	1 hr	0 hrs
8	Team Meeting 6	NA	NA	0%	0%	0 days	0.13 days	$0.00	1 hr	0 hrs
9	Team Meeting 7	NA	NA	0%	0%	0 days	0.13 days	$0.00	1 hr	0 hrs
10	Team Meeting 8	NA	NA	0%	0%	0 days	0.13 days	$0.00	1 hr	0 hrs
11	Team Meeting 9	NA	NA	0%	0%	0 days	0.13 days	$0.00	1 hr	0 hrs
12	☐ **Initiation**	**Mon 10/2/06**	**Wed 10/4/06**	**100%**	**0%**	**2.88 days**	**0 days**	**$29.00**	**29 hrs**	**29 hrs**
13	Project Kick Off Meeting	Mon 10/2/06	Mon 10/2/06	100%	0%	0.25 days	0 days	$8.00	8 hrs	8 hrs
14	☐ **Project Charter**	**Mon 10/2/06**	**Wed 10/4/06**	**100%**	**0%**	**2.63 days**	**0 days**	**$21.00**	**21 hrs**	**21 hrs**
15	Prepare Project Charter	Mon 10/2/06	Wed 10/4/06	100%	0%	2.25 days	0 days	$18.00	18 hrs	18 hrs
16	Review Project Charter	Wed 10/4/06	Wed 10/4/06	100%	0%	0.25 days	0 days	$2.00	2 hrs	2 hrs
17	Sign Off Project Charter	Wed 10/4/06	Wed 10/4/06	100%	0%	0.13 days	0 days	$1.00	1 hr	1 hr

Figure 7.1. Tracking Table in the **Tracking Gantt** option.

Summary Level Tracking

Summary level tracking is a method that tracks progress by tasks and at the summary level. In this method, actual values are continually updated in the **Tracking Gantt** option until a task is completed.

To update with actual values, go to the **View > Tracking Gantt** option to enter the actual values for tasks. In the **Tracking Gantt** option, choose the **Tracking Table**. You will see the screen shown in Figure 7.1. In this screen, enter the % complete (**% Comp.**), actual duration (**Act. Dur.**), actual cost (**Act. Cost**), and actual work (**Act. Work**) for each of the tasks.

For every period, you will need to continue updating the values for each task. If some tasks are not completed in a period, and they are carried forward to the next period, you will need to update these tasks in the next period, but you will update with a *cumulative* value for the actual value. For example, suppose that Task 2 in Figure 7.1 is only 75% complete in this period and that it has **Act. Work** of 24 hours. In the next period, suppose additional work of 24 hours has been completed on this task. When you update the schedule for the next period, you would update with 24 + 24 = 48 as the **Act. Work**.

Steps:

➢ In the menu, go to the **View** menu and choose the **Tracking Gantt** menu item to view the **Tracking Gantt**.

> In this menu, go to the **View** menu and from the **Tables** submenu choose the **Tracking Table**.

> Update the **Actual Start Date** of the tasks.

> Update the **Actual End Date** of tasks that have been completed in the reporting period for which the schedule is being updated.

> Update the % complete (**% Comp.**) for any task not yet completed.

> Update actual duration (**Act. Dur.**) for any task not yet completed.

> Update actual work (**Act. Work**) with the actual effort taken so far for the task.

Task Level Day-Wise Tracking

Task level day-wise tracking is a method that tracks the progress of a schedule at the task level. Actual values are entered in the schedule by the day or by some other specified time period. Compared to summary level tracking, this method allows tracking the progress at the day level for each individual lowest-level task. Schedule progress can be tracked using this method by going into the **View > Task Usage** screen and choosing the **Act. Work/Act. Cost** column on the right-hand side of the screen (shown in Figure 7.2).

In the view shown in Figure 7.2, enter the actual hours by day (or any period that has been chosen, depending on project requirements). Enter the amount of work done by each resource assigned to the task on any particular day (or any period chosen).

The task level day-wise tracking method is time consuming, but it is a more accurate tracking method than using the summary level method—the amount of actual work that

	❶	Task Name	Work	Details	6						Jan 7, '07		
					M	T	W	T	F	S	S	M	T
1		⊟ Project	392 hrs	Act. Work	8h	8h	8h	56h	56h			48h	36.8h
2	✓	⊟ Task 1	24 hrs	Act. Work	8h	8h	8h						
		R1	24 hrs	Act. Work	8h	8h	8h						
3		⊟ Task 2	32 hrs	Act. Work				8h	8h			8h	
		R2	32 hrs	Act. Work				8h	8h			8h	
4		⊞ Task 3	48 hrs	Act. Work				8h	8h			8h	4.8h
5	✓	⊞ Task 4	64 hrs	Act. Work				8h	8h			8h	8h
6		⊞ Task 5	16 hrs	Act. Work									
7		⊞ Task 6	32 hrs	Act. Work				8h	8h				
8		⊞ Task 7	24 hrs	Act. Work									
9	✓	⊞ Task 8	40 hrs	Act. Work				8h	8h			8h	8h
10	✓	⊞ Task 9	48 hrs	Act. Work				8h	8h			8h	8h
11		⊞ Task 10	64 hrs	Act. Work				8h	8h			8h	8h

Figure 7.2. Task Usage screen showing actual work/cost column at day level and task level.

you enter is spread equally, meaning that if you have entered 40 hours as the actual work for a week, it is spread across the entire week at 8 hours per day. The amount of work is spread evenly, even if a resource worked 10 hours on a particular day and then worked 6 hours on another day. The task level day-wise tracking method allows you to enter the actual hours spent day-wise by the resource on the task.

To use the task level day-wise tracking method, you will need to get input from your team by task. If you have modules which are handled by smaller teams, get input from the module leader for all of his team members to ensure that this is a good method to track schedule progress.

Steps:

> In the menu, go to the **View** menu and choose the **Task Usage** menu item to view **Task Usage**.

> On the left-hand side is the WBS and on the right is the **Work** for each task spread over time (see Figure 7.2).

> Right click on the **Details** column and uncheck **Work**.

> Right click and select **Detail Styles**.

> In the **Usage Details** tab, select the **Actual Work** field and click on **Show**.

> Click **OK** to see the **Actual Work** in the right-hand side of the screen.

> Expand/collapse the **Time Period** by using the +/– buttons (see Figure 6.4) to match the reporting period (days, weeks, months, etc.) that has been chosen to track progress of the schedule.

> Expand the left-hand side WBS to show the lowest-level tasks.

> On the right-hand side, enter the actual hours spent on a particular lowest-level task for each day/period.

Resource Level Day-Wise Tracking

Resource level day-wise tracking is a method that tracks the progress of a schedule by resource and by the tasks performed by each resource during the reporting period. Actual values by resource and task are entered in MPP by the day/period chosen to track the progress of the schedule. This method is similar to task level day-wise tracking, but in resource level day-wise tracking the *resource* is the primary group for tracking schedule progress on the schedule, whereas in task level day-wise tracking, tasks are the primary group.

ⓘ	Resource Name	Work	Details	6							Jan 7, '07			
				M	T	W	T	F	S	S	M	T	W
1	⊟ R1	104 hrs	Act. Work	8h	8h	8h	8h	8h			8h	8h	8h
	Task 1	24 hrs	Act. Work	8h	8h	8h							
	Task 4	64 hrs	Act. Work				8h	8h			8h	8h	8h
	Task 5	16 hrs	Act. Work										
2 ◈	⊟ R2	64 hrs	Act. Work				16h	16h			8h		
	Task 2	32 hrs	Act. Work				8h	8h			8h		
	Task 6	32 hrs	Act. Work				8h	8h					
3	⊟ R3	72 hrs	Act. Work				8h	8h			8h	4.8h	
	Task 3	48 hrs	Act. Work				8h	8h			8h	4.8h	
	Task 7	24 hrs	Act. Work										
4	⊟ R4	40 hrs	Act. Work				8h	8h			8h	8h	8h
	Task 8	40 hrs	Act. Work				8h	8h			8h	8h	8h
5	⊟ R5	48 hrs	Act. Work				8h	8h			8h	8h	8h
	Task 9	48 hrs	Act. Work				8h	8h			8h	8h	8h
6	⊟ R6	64 hrs	Act. Work				8h	8h			8h	8h	
	Task 10	64 hrs	Act. Work				8h	8h			8h	8h	

Figure 7.3. Resource Usage screen showing resources, tasks they are working on, and their times worked.

You can track progress of the schedule using this method by going into **View > Resource Usage** screen shown in Figure 7.3. In Figure 7.3, the resources and the tasks they are working on are on the left-hand side. On the right is the time-phased **Act. Work** column where the actual work done by each resource on each task by day (or period chosen to track the progress of the schedule) is entered. When actual work is updated, MPP automatically adjusts the **Actual Start Date**, **Actual Finish Date**, **% Comp.**, **Remaining Work**, and **Remaining Duration** of the task. Apply the same technique used in the task level day-wise tracking method to get the actual work data on the right-hand side of the screen.

To use the resource level day-wise tracking method you need to get the data for the actual values by resource so that these figures can be input into the schedule. The resource level day-wise tracking method is generally suitable when all resources send out a status report at the end of each day or each reporting period.

Steps:

➢ In the menu, go to the **View** menu and choose the **Resource Usage** menu item to view **Resource Usage**.

➢ On the left-hand side are the resources and their tasks. On the right is the **Work** for each task spread over time (see Figure 7.3).

➢ Right click on the **Details** column and uncheck **Work**.

➢ Right click and select **Detail Styles**.

➢ In the **Usage Details** tab, select the **Actual Work** field and click on **Show**.

➤ Click **OK** to see **Actual Work** on the right-hand side of the screen.

➤ Expand/collapse the **Time Period** by using the +/− buttons (see Figure 6.4) to match the reporting period (days, weeks, months, etc) that has been chosen to track schedule progress.

➤ Expand the left-hand side resources to the task level.

➤ On the right hand side, by resource, enter the actual hours spent on each task for each day/period.

Adjusting the Schedule While Tracking

Most tasks in a schedule just will not be completed as originally planned. There are bound to be differences in the actual work and actual duration spent on tasks by different resources. Therefore, you need to track the progress, but also keep adjusting the schedule to some extent so that MPP can give an accurate picture of the current status of the project.

More time than planned. In most projects, some tasks will take more time than planned. For example, suppose a task which is originally planned to be done in 40 hours will instead require 56 hours. In this situation, you will adjust the **Work** column in the schedule to 56 hours instead of the 40 hours that is in the schedule right now. This update will tell MPP that the task will take longer than planned and the % complete will be adjusted accordingly as you track progress of the schedule each day. However, if the **Work** column is not updated, after 40 hours of effort, MPP will automatically mark the task as 100% complete which is incorrect.

Keeping a schedule current and updating small variations are important. If the variations are small, you might not need approval from the stakeholders because at the overall level, the project could still be doing well (e.g., as we learned when we were calculating the EVM performance measures).

Less time than planned. Similarly, some tasks will be completed with less effort. For example, suppose a task which was originally planned for 40 hours of effort has instead taken only 20 hours to complete. In this situation you will also adjust the **Work** column, but this time to 20 hours so that MPP can mark the task as 100% complete.

More effort than planned. Another scenario is that you are midway through a task and you know that more effort will be required than planned. You therefore need to estimate the extra effort needed for this task and update the **Work** column accordingly.

Change in utilization level. Some tasks that were planned to be completed at a 100% utilization level of a resource might have a change in utilization level. For example, due to changes in other tasks, a resource is now no longer able to spend 100% of his time on the task; instead he is able to spend only 50%. In this situation, the effort in the **Work** column will remain the same, but the duration, start date, and end date of the task will change. Tracking changes in utilization levels is also important so MPP can project the end date based on current tracking.

In all of the tracking methods that we have discussed, additional columns will need to be added to the screen for **Work** and **Duration**. These columns will need to be adjusted as you track the progress of the schedule. (Note: See Chapter 5, the *Assigning Estimates* section, for a discussion of adding columns to a screen). Although small differences that occur when executing a project do not necessarily need to be brought to the attention of the stakeholders, you still need to keep a schedule current and adjust the **Work** column accordingly.

The work columns. Let's briefly review the three different types of columns in MPP that contain similar data—**Work, Baseline Work,** and **Actual Work**. The **Work** column stores the *current work* planned for the task. Current work *continually changes* as a project progresses. **Baseline Work** is the work *planned and agreed upon* with stakeholders of the project. Baseline work *does not change* without specific approval. Baseline work is the value against which performance is measured. **Actual Work** is the column in which the *actual values of the effort used so far* to execute the task are stored (which applies to **Cost** and **Duration** as well).

Having an accurate % complete at every task level is important to enable you to correctly report the status and the progress of a project. Having an accurate schedule is also important when the schedule is distributed to the stakeholders—an accurate schedule enables them to have an accurate picture at every task level. Additionally, they can also see the extra effort/time that will be needed to complete a task. By following the steps we have discussed, accurate reporting of project status can be achieved.

TRACKING PROGRESS WITH THE EVM TOOL

Once you have updated the project schedule for the period, go to the EVM template to update data so that the template can calculate the EVM performance measures for that particular reporting period. You do not have to perform any of the calculations that have been described earlier for earned value analysis—the template takes care of all calculations.

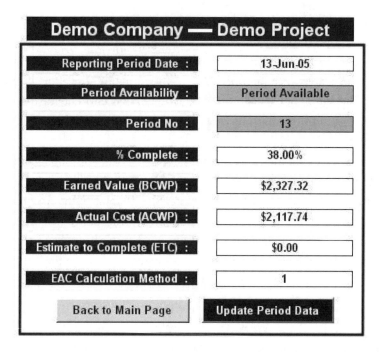

Figure 7.4. Periodic data update screen.

To finish the template, only the periodic data needs to be entered. Then you can concentrate on the analysis part of project management (see Chapter 8).

Click on the **Update Periodical Data** button on the main menu to update periodic data. Clicking on the button opens up the screen shown in Figure 7.4. Enter the **Reporting Period Date**. The **Period Availability** field will show if the date you have entered exists as a reporting period. If the reporting period is not available, key in the correct date. Go into the EVM **Data Sheet** from the main menu to find the correct date. The **Period No** field will then display the number of the reporting period.

Next, enter data in the **% Complete, Earned Value (BCWP)**, and **Actual Cost (ACWP)** fields. These data are available from MPP after you have updated the periodic data. Choose the option **View > Table > More Tables** screen (Figure 7.5), which will open up a new dialog box (Figure 7.6). In this dialog box, scroll to select **Earned Value** and then click on **Apply**. Now you will have the MPP screen shown in Figure 7.7.

This screen has values for BCWP (earned value) and ACWP (actual cost). The % complete can be obtained from the original screen (see Figure 7.1). Enter all three values—%

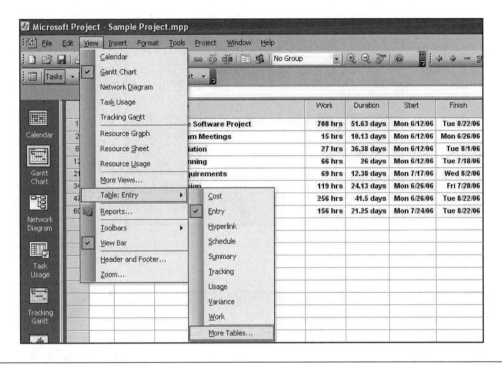

Figure 7.5. More Tables submenu.

complete, BCWP, and ACWP—in the EVM template (see Figure 7.4). Note: BCWP and ACWP should be taken from the project level which is always Task 1 or the first line.

Additionally, you can choose to enter the ETC (estimate to complete) and EAC calculation method. Remember: The default for ETC is always **0**; the default for the EAC calculation method is **1**. The **ETC** column is used *only* when the EAC calculation method is **2**.

Now data entry is complete. You are ready to update these details in the template. Click on the **Update Period Data** button. Updating the period data is now finished. The next step is to check the variances and trend charts.

Steps:

➢ Open the EVM report template.

➢ Navigate to the main menu tab as shown at the bottom of the screen (see Figure 6.1).

➢ Click on the **Update Periodical Data** button to go to the **Update Periodical Data** screen (see Figure 7.4).

➢ Go to MPP.

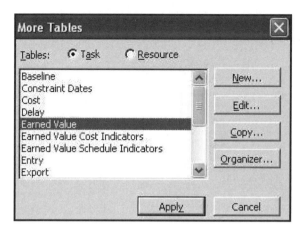

Figure 7.6. Dialog box in **More Tables** option.

	Task Name	BCWS	BCWP	ACWP	SV	CV	EAC	BAC	VAC
1	⊟ Sample Software Proje	$708.00	$0.00	$0.00	($708.00)	$0.00	$708.00	$708.00	$0.00
2	⊞ Team Meetings	$15.00	$0.00	$0.00	($15.00)	$0.00	$15.00	$15.00	$0.00
6	⊞ Initiation	$27.00	$0.00	$0.00	($27.00)	$0.00	$27.00	$27.00	$0.00
12	⊞ Planning	$66.00	$0.00	$0.00	($66.00)	$0.00	$66.00	$66.00	$0.00
21	⊞ Requirements	$69.00	$0.00	$0.00	($69.00)	$0.00	$69.00	$69.00	$0.00
34	⊞ Design	$119.00	$0.00	$0.00	($119.00)	$0.00	$119.00	$119.00	$0.00
47	⊞ Development	$256.00	$0.00	$0.00	($256.00)	$0.00	$256.00	$256.00	$0.00
60	⊞ Testing	$156.00	$0.00	$0.00	($156.00)	$0.00	$156.00	$156.00	$0.00

Figure 7.7. MPP screen showing value for BCWP (earned value) and ACWP (actual cost).

➤ Take the **% Comp.** from the top level task and update **% Complete** in the EVM template.

➤ In the menu, go to the **View** menu and from the **Table** submenu choose the **More Tables** submenu shown in Figure 7.5 to view the dialog box.

➤ In the **Tables** dialog, navigate to and select **Earned Value** and click **Apply** (see Figure 7.6).

➤ Click **OK** to see the earned value table (see Figure 7.7).

➤ Take the BCWP and ACWP values from Task 1 (the **Sample Software Project** task).

➤ Enter these values in the EVM template (see Figure 7.4).

➢ Click the **Update Period Data** button to update the period data.

➢ Now you have completed updating the periodic data in the EVM template and are ready to perform analysis of that data.

8

MONITORING THE SCHEDULE

We have discussed setting up MPP and the EVM template and also updating details in the EVM template. Now let's see how the EVM template can be used for monitoring a project and taking corrective/preventive actions.

THE SUMMARY SHEET—CHECKING AND UPDATING

For a summary of the status/progress of a project as of a specific reporting period, from the main page go to the **Summary Sheet** by clicking on the **Summary** button to see the screen in Figure 8.1. In the **Summary Sheet**, enter the date desired in the **Status Date** field. The status date must be the starting date in the specified reporting period. Then click on the **Update Status Date** button to get the status for the current reporting period. A value for each attribute will appear in the **Value** column. For each attribute, the data value is color coded (red, yellow, or green) based on performance. (Note: In Figure 8.1, red is indicated by dark gray; yellow is indicated by light gray; and green is indicated by medium gray.) If the project is ahead of schedule, the color is green (0% or above); for a schedule variance of 0 to –10%, the color is yellow; otherwise, the color is red (below –10%). Although color coding gives a concise visual picture of the status of the project, we can clearly see from the **Value** column that the project is ahead of schedule and slightly over budget.

Next, in the **Performance Measure Outcome** field, record the outcome of each performance measure, the reasons for the outcome, and the corrective action planned (if needed). The information in this screen gives a snapshot view of the project's performance.

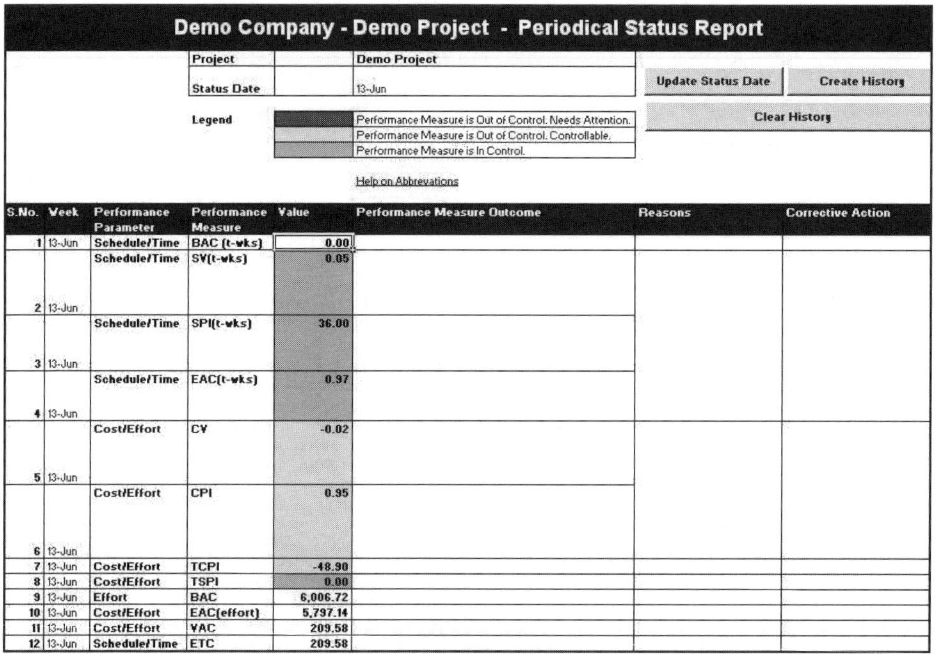

S.No.	Week	Performance Parameter	Performance Measure	Value	Performance Measure Outcome	Reasons	Corrective Action
1	13-Jun	Schedule/Time	BAC (t-wks)	0.00			
2	13-Jun	Schedule/Time	SV(t-wks)	0.05			
3	13-Jun	Schedule/Time	SPI(t-wks)	36.00			
4	13-Jun	Schedule/Time	EAC(t-wks)	0.97			
5	13-Jun	Cost/Effort	CV	-0.02			
6	13-Jun	Cost/Effort	CPI	0.95			
7	13-Jun	Cost/Effort	TCPI	-48.90			
8	13-Jun	Cost/Effort	TSPI	0.00			
9	13-Jun	Effort	BAC	6,006.72			
10	13-Jun	Cost/Effort	EAC(effort)	5,797.14			
11	13-Jun	Cost/Effort	VAC	209.58			
12	13-Jun	Schedule/Time	ETC	209.58			

Figure 8.1. Periodical Status Report screen.

The data in this sheet can be stored in the **History Sheet** by clicking on the **Create History** button. By creating a history of performance over the reporting periods, you will be able to identify the lessons learned at the end of the project. Throughout the project you can look back at some of the causes of trends.

Steps:

- ➢ Open the EVM report template.
- ➢ Navigate to the main menu tab as shown at the bottom left corner of the screen (see Figure 6.1).
- ➢ Click on the **Summary** button to go to the summary screen.
- ➢ Enter the desired status date in the **Status Date** field.
- ➢ Click on **Update Status Date** to view the performance measures for that period. The performance measures are automatically color coded (red, yellow, or green) based on the value returned for the period.
- ➢ In the **Performance Measure Outcome** field, record the outcome of each performance measure and the reasons for this outcome.

➤ Click on the **Create History** button to store the **Performance Measure Outcome** information for the period in the **History Sheet** for future reference and to create a report of lessons learned from the project.

THE EARNED VALUE GRAPH

The graph in Figure 8.2 is useful in the sense that it gives a high-level understanding of how the project is progressing with respect to the schedule and cost. If the earned value (EV) line in the graph is above the planned value (PV) and actual cost (AC) lines, the project is under budget and ahead of schedule. Figure 8.2 also shows this data over all of the project periods, which can indicate a trend and allow for corrective or preventive action to be taken.

In Figure 8.2, the three lines represent the cumulative data of earned value, planned value, and actual cost plotted over time. Notice the progression of earned value over time in comparison to planned value and actual cost. Also notice that planned value follows an S-curve which is typical for any project. Additionally, after a certain point in the project, notice that the lines for earned value and actual cost become flat—this situation occurs because the project has progressed to the point at which the earned value and actual cost measures become the same for the remaining periods.

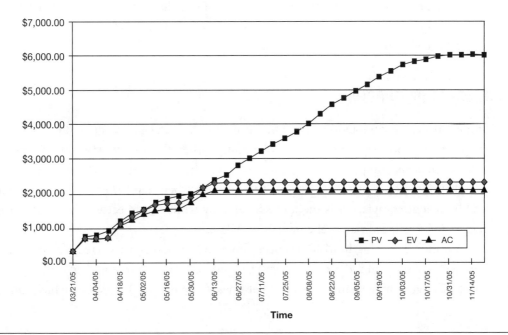

Figure 8.2. Earned value graph.

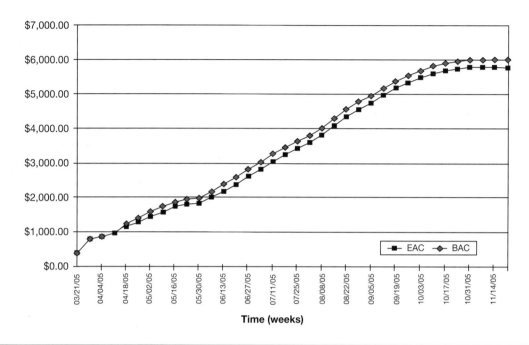

Figure 8.3. Forecast ($) graph.

For a project to be under budget and ahead of schedule, period by period, ensure that the earned value line is above or close to the planned value and actual cost lines. Figure 8.2 is the basic view of earned value analysis.

THE FORECAST ($) GRAPH

If the estimate at completion (EAC) line is below the budget at completion (BAC) line, a project is in good shape and will be under budget when the project is finished. Conversely, if the estimate at completion is over the BAC line, the project is forecast to be over budget and therefore needs corrective action. The difference between the estimate at completion and budget at completion is the *forecast* value by which a project will be under or over budget (also called variance at completion, VAC).

If resource leveling in MPP has been done and resources are correctly being utilized, a project will have an S-curve as shown in Figure 8.3. The S-curve indicates that effort on the project goes up and then becomes flat toward the end of the project, which indicates

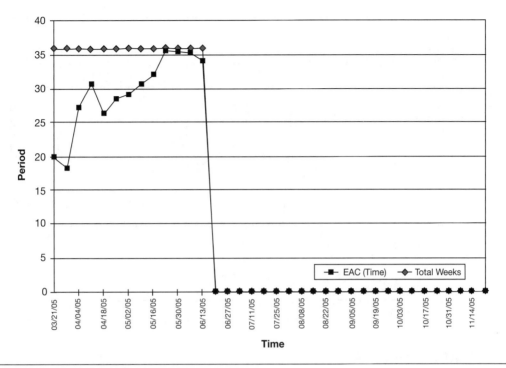

Figure 8.4. Forecast (time) graph.

the project is coming to a close. The S-curve in Figure 8.3 also shows how resources are ramped up and down in a project.

THE FORECAST (TIME) GRAPH

A forecast (time) graph plots the total budgeted reporting periods of a project against the estimate at completion (time), or EAC (time), which is the time aspect of estimate at completion. EAC (time) actually provides the estimated number of reporting periods that the project is expected to continue based on the current performance of the project.

Again, as shown in Figure 8.4, keeping the estimate at completion line below the total periods line is important. This indicates that the project is ahead of schedule. The graph in Figure 8.4 also shows the estimated completion time, in number of reporting periods, for the project on any given reporting period date (in this case, total budgeted periods are 36 weeks). In the graph, the estimate at completion line has always been below the total budgeted periods line, which is indicative that the project has stayed ahead of schedule to date.

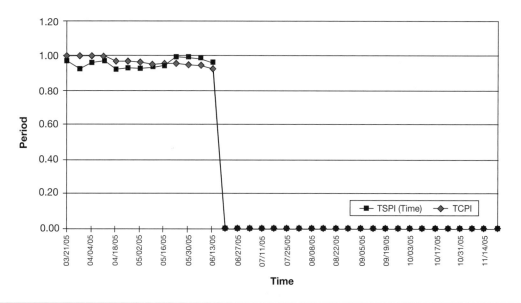

Figure 8.5. Forecast (index) graph.

THE FORECAST (INDEX) GRAPH

The graph in Figure 8.5 plots the to-complete cost performance index (TCPI) against the to-complete schedule performance index (TSPI). TCPI and TSPI are forecasting measures that are indexes which indicate what the original cost performance index (CPI) and schedule performance index (SPI) need to be going forward in order for the project to be on schedule and on budget. Keeping the TCPI and TSPI indexes at 1 is also important.

TCPI. A TCPI *at* 1 indicates that to complete the project on budget, project resources need to maintain effort at the level estimated in the budget. A TCPI *less than* 1 indicates that to keep the project on budget, resources can be lenient in using the budget; they can relax *a bit.* A TCPI *above* 1 is cause for concern because to keep the project on budget, resources must put in extra effort. For example, if TCPI is 1.05, the project team needs to be 105% efficient in using resources and effort. The team must finish the remaining work using 5% less effort than the amount of effort budgeted.

TSPI. A TSPI *at* 1 indicates that to complete the project on schedule, project resources need to use time as budgeted; there is no cause for concern about the use of time. A TSPI *less than* 1 indicates that to keep the project on schedule, resources can relax their efficiency. A TSPI *above* 1 is cause for concern because to keep the project on schedule, resources must use their time more efficiently. *More efficiently* means that from now until the end of the proj-

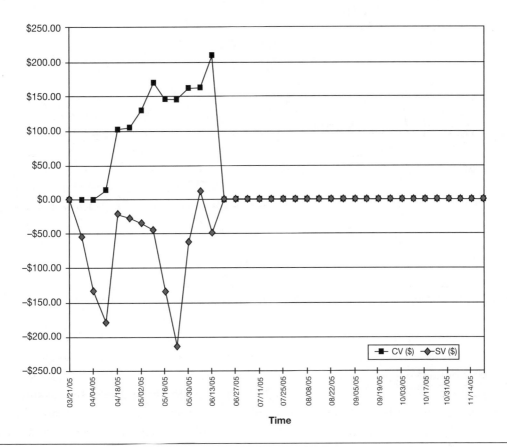

Figure 8.6. Variances ($) graph.

ect, resources must complete tasks ahead of time, either by putting in extra effort or by working more efficiently (e.g., using tools and techniques). For example, if TSPI is 1.05, the project team needs to be 105% efficient in using time; the team must finish the remaining work using 5% less time than was originally budgeted.

THE VARIANCES ($) GRAPH

A variances graph plots schedule variance and cost variance against time. In Figure 8.6, schedule variance and cost variance are shown over reporting periods and indicate trends in these two measures. Ideally a project should maintain cost variance and schedule variance at a level of zero, i.e., both measures are zero at each reporting period. However, projects are bound to have schedule and cost variances; nevertheless project managers must manage these variances and keep them under control.

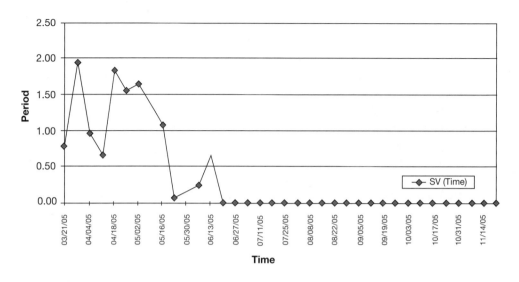

Figure 8.7. Variances (time) graph.

Both schedule and cost variance measures are indicated as a dollar ($) value in the standard EVM technique. Therefore, a positive $100 cost variance indicates that the project is under budget by $100; a negative cost variance indicates that the project is over budget by $100. Similarly, a positive $100 schedule variance indicates that planned work costing $100 has been completed ahead of schedule; therefore, the project is ahead of budgeted time. Again, a negative schedule variance indicates that the project is behind schedule. Although schedule variance can be measured in terms of cost ($), doing so is problematic—at the end of the project, even if the project has been delayed by a couple of weeks, schedule variance ($) will reflect a 0 because schedule variance is always compared to planned work and the actual work done (earned value). Therefore, using schedule variance (time), or SV (weeks), is best.

THE VARIANCES (TIME) GRAPH

A variances (time) graph plots the schedule variance (time) factor by reporting period, which shows schedule variance in terms of reporting period (e.g., weeks) and also shows the trend of schedule variance (time) over the reporting periods (Figure 8.7).

Note in Figure 8.7 that we have a schedule variance of almost 2 early in the project. This schedule variance indicates that the project was ahead of schedule by two reporting periods (in this case, weeks). The graph in Figure 8.7 gives a clear picture of schedule variance in terms of duration instead of cost.

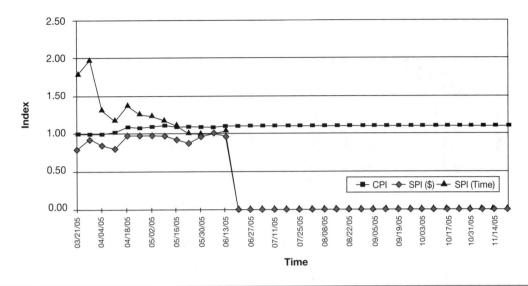

Figure 8.8. Indexes graph.

THE INDEXES GRAPH

An indexes graph plots various indexes by reporting period. In Figure 8.8, the schedule performance indicator (SPI), cost performance indicator (CPI), and schedule performance indicator (time), or SPI (time), indexes are plotted by reporting period.

The SPI index indicates the performance of the project with respect to schedule. Keeping SPI *at* 1 or *above* should be the goal for any project. An SPI *less than* 1 indicates that the project is behind schedule and that the project team is not utilizing time efficiently.

The CPI index shows the performance of the project with respect to cost. Keeping the CPI *at* 1 or *above* should also be the goal for any project. A CPI *less than* 1 indicates that the project is over budget and that the project team is not utilizing project resources efficiently.

The SPI (time) index is the same as SPI except that SPI (time) is measured in units of time, not cost. Therefore, in calculations, SPI (time) gives a more realistic picture of performance than SPI, which uses cost.

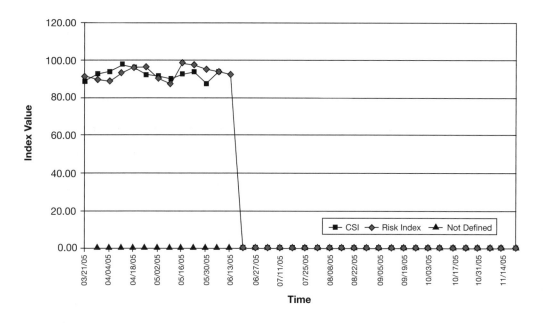

Figure 8.9. Other indexes graph.

THE OTHER INDEXES GRAPH

Another indexes graph plots the values of additional indexes which are set up in the EVM template; the risk index, the customer satisfaction index (CSI), etc. (Figure 8.9). (Remember that the template allows tracking of three other indexes in addition to the regular indexes.) Note: Tracking additional indexes and relating the data to the project are dependent on the index being tracked, which is beyond the scope of this book. This type of tracking should be managed by the person who is using these indexes.

9

ADDITIONAL SCHEDULE MANAGEMENT TECHNIQUES

DRILLING DOWN TO CHECK TASKS AT RISK

When you begin tracking a project with MPP and monitoring it using the EVM template, tracking and monitoring are actually done at the *project* level. However, depending on the project's status (or for every reporting period), you can drill down to the EVM values and check the EVM parameters at the task level to understand which tasks and/or resources are contributing to the project variances you are experiencing to try to maximize the positive variances and minimize the negative variances.

In Figure 9.1, the project has a negative schedule variance (SV) and a positive cost variance (CV). Therefore, at the project level (Task 1), the project is performing well with the budget, but not doing so well with the schedule. By drilling down to the task level, you can see SV and CV at this level and take corrective and/or preventive action.

MPP is problematic in that it does not give the performance measures plotted over time which can be seen at the project level in the EVM template. Additionally, not all performance measures are given, e.g., the time-based schedule performance measures, that are available in the EVM template.

Steps:

➡ Open the EVM report template.

	Task Name	% Compl	BCWS	BCWP	ACWP	SV	CV	EAC	BAC	VAC
1	⊟ Sample Software Project	16%	$261.40	$120.00	$114.00	($141.40)	$6.00	$664.62	$699.60	$34.98
2	⊟ Team Meeting	11%	$1.40	$1.00	$1.00	($0.40)	$0.00	$2.60	$2.60	$0.00
3	Team Meeting 1	100%	$1.00	$1.00	$1.00	$0.00	$0.00	$1.00	$1.00	$0.00
4	Team Meeting 2	0%	$0.20	$0.00	$0.00	($0.20)	$0.00	$0.20	$0.20	$0.00
5	Team Meeting 3	0%	$0.20	$0.00	$0.00	($0.20)	$0.00	$0.20	$0.20	$0.00
6	Team Meeting 4	0%	$0.00	$0.00	$0.00	$0.00	$0.00	$0.20	$0.20	$0.00
7	Team Meeting 5	0%	$0.00	$0.00	$0.00	$0.00	$0.00	$0.20	$0.20	$0.00
8	Team Meeting 6	0%	$0.00	$0.00	$0.00	$0.00	$0.00	$0.20	$0.20	$0.00
9	Team Meeting 7	0%	$0.00	$0.00	$0.00	$0.00	$0.00	$0.20	$0.20	$0.00
10	Team Meeting 8	0%	$0.00	$0.00	$0.00	$0.00	$0.00	$0.20	$0.20	$0.00
11	Team Meeting 9	0%	$0.00	$0.00	$0.00	$0.00	$0.00	$0.20	$0.20	$0.00
12	⊟ Initiation	100%	$31.00	$31.00	$29.00	$0.00	$2.00	$29.00	$31.00	$2.00
13	Project Kick Off Meeting	100%	$8.00	$8.00	$8.00	$0.00	$0.00	$8.00	$8.00	$0.00
14	⊟ Project Charter	100%	$23.00	$23.00	$21.00	$0.00	$2.00	$21.00	$23.00	$2.00
15	Prepare Project Charter	100%	$20.00	$20.00	$18.00	$0.00	$2.00	$18.00	$20.00	$2.00
16	Review Project Charter	100%	$2.00	$2.00	$2.00	$0.00	$0.00	$2.00	$2.00	$0.00
17	Sign Off Project Charter	100%	$1.00	$1.00	$1.00	$0.00	$0.00	$1.00	$1.00	$0.00
18	⊟ Planning	100%	$66.00	$66.00	$62.00	$0.00	$4.00	$62.00	$66.00	$4.00
19	⊟ Estimation	100%	$21.00	$21.00	$25.00	$0.00	($4.00)	$25.00	$21.00	($4.00)
20	Prepare Estimates	100%	$18.00	$18.00	$20.00	$0.00	($2.00)	$20.00	$18.00	($2.00)
21	Review Estimates	100%	$2.00	$2.00	$4.00	$0.00	($2.00)	$4.00	$2.00	($2.00)
22	Sign Off Estimates	100%	$1.00	$1.00	$1.00	$0.00	$0.00	$1.00	$1.00	$0.00
23	⊟ Project Plan	100%	$45.00	$45.00	$37.00	$0.00	$8.00	$37.00	$45.00	$8.00
24	Prepare Project Plan	100%	$40.00	$40.00	$32.00	$0.00	$8.00	$32.00	$40.00	$8.00
25	Review Project Plan	100%	$4.00	$4.00	$4.00	$0.00	$0.00	$4.00	$4.00	$0.00
26	Sign Off Project Plan	100%	$1.00	$1.00	$1.00	$0.00	$0.00	$1.00	$1.00	$0.00
27	⊟ Requirements	32%	$44.00	$22.00	$22.00	($22.00)	$0.00	$69.00	$69.00	$0.00
28	⊟ SRS Module 1	81%	$27.00	$22.00	$22.00	($5.00)	$0.00	$27.00	$27.00	$0.00

Figure 9.1. Drill down view of EVM values for EVM parameters at task level.

➢ Navigate to the main menu tab as shown at the bottom left corner of the screen (see Figure 6.1).

➢ Click on the **Summary** button to go to the **Summary** screen.

➢ The **Summary** screen shows the various performance measures at the project level. A particular performance measure—e.g., cost variance (CV)—can then be identified. Then drill down to see the tasks that are affecting the CV performance measure.

➢ Go to MPP.

➢ In the menu, go to the **View** menu and from the **Tables** submenu choose the **More Tables** submenu item to view the **Tables** dialog box.

➢ In the **Tables** dialog box, navigate to and select **Earned Value** and then click **Apply**.

➢ Click **OK** to see the **Earned Value** table.

	🛈	% Compl	Priority	Task Name	Cost	Work	Duration	Start	Finish
1		16%	800	⊟ Sample Software Project	$693.60	700 hrs	47.88 days	Mon 10/2/06	Wed 12/6/06
2	↻	11%	1000	⊞ Team Meeting	$2.60	9 hrs	40.13 days	Mon 10/2/06	Mon 11/27/06
12	✓	100%	800	⊞ Initiation	$29.00	29 hrs	2.88 days	Mon 10/2/06	Wed 10/4/06
18	✓	100%	700	⊞ Planning	$62.00	62 hrs	6.88 days	Wed 10/4/06	Fri 10/13/06
27		32%	600	⊟ Requirements	$69.00	69 hrs	17.5 days	Mon 10/2/06	Wed 10/25/06
28		81%	590	⊞ SRS Module 1	$27.00	27 hrs	3.38 days	Mon 10/2/06	Thu 10/5/06
32		0%	580	⊞ SRS Module 2	$27.00	27 hrs	3.38 days	Wed 10/18/06	Tue 10/24/06
36		0%	570	⊞ SRS Final	$15.00	15 hrs	1.88 days	Mon 10/23/06	Wed 10/25/06
40		0%	500	⊟ Design	$119.00	119 hrs	13.63 days	Wed 10/25/06	Mon 11/13/06
41		0%	490	⊞ Design Module 1	$47.00	47 hrs	5.88 days	Wed 10/25/06	Wed 11/1/06
45		0%	480	⊞ Design Module 2	$47.00	47 hrs	5.88 days	Wed 11/1/06	Thu 11/9/06
49		0%	470	⊞ Design Final	$25.00	25 hrs	3.13 days	Wed 11/8/06	Mon 11/13/06
53		0%	400	⊟ Development	$256.00	256 hrs	28.25 days	Mon 10/2/06	Thu 11/9/06
54		0%	390	⊞ Develop Module 1	$112.00	112 hrs	14 days	Mon 10/2/06	Fri 10/20/06
58		0%	380	⊞ Develop Module 2	$112.00	112 hrs	14 days	Fri 10/20/06	Thu 11/9/06
62		0%	370	⊞ Develop Final	$32.00	32 hrs	4.25 days	Fri 11/3/06	Thu 11/9/06
66		0%	300	⊟ Testing	$156.00	156 hrs	19.5 days	Thu 11/9/06	Wed 12/6/06
67		0%	290	⊞ Develop Module 1	$52.00	52 hrs	6.5 days	Thu 11/9/06	Fri 11/17/06
71		0%	280	⊞ Develop Module 2	$52.00	52 hrs	6.5 days	Fri 11/17/06	Tue 11/28/06
75		0%	270	⊞ Develop Final	$52.00	52 hrs	6.5 days	Tue 11/28/06	Wed 12/6/06

Figure 9.2. Drill down view showing priorities of SRS Module 1 and SRS Module 2.

➢ Get the cost variance (CV) from the top-level task (Task 1).

➢ Expand/collapse the WBS to drill down to the lowest task level to see tasks at risk.

RESEQUENCING TASKS IN A SCHEDULE

When asked "How many times have you had to change the sequence of tasks in a schedule?" no doubt your answer will be "many times." Using the conventional way of sequencing tasks, many predecessors must be changed to adjust the schedule. If a project has many tasks, and priorities are often changing, this process becomes quite tedious.

Yet, because of the way we have set up our project plan, priorities need only to be realigned at the summary task level to resequence the tasks in the project plan. As discussed earlier, after resequencing, perform resource leveling and rebaseline the schedule (discussed later in this chapter).

Let's look at the example in Figure 9.2. Assume that due to project constraints we need to resequence the SRS Module 1 and SRS Module 2 tasks. Right now, SRS Module 1 has a higher priority than SRS Module 2, meaning SRS Module 1 will be done before SRS Module 2. Suppose, however, due to project constraints, we need to have SRS Module 2 start *before* SRS Module 1 is completed. If this is the case, all we need to do is to reverse the priorities of these modules and then perform resource leveling once again, which will change the priorities. If the same resources are working on both tasks, MPP will automatically reschedule SRS Module 2 to finish before SRS Module 1. Note: Resequencing tasks which have different resources will yield a different result because priority-based resequencing only works for the same set of resources.

PUTTING A SCHEDULE ON HOLD

Schedules are put on hold for various reasons. For example, an entire schedule might be put on hold due to an impending issue that will affect the project, e.g., a stay resulting from a government regulation. At times, some resources might be put on hold (unrelated to regular vacation time) because these resources need to be diverted to other projects, but will resume work on their original project after a certain period of time.

A simple method to put a schedule on hold is to mark the effected days on the **Project Calendar** or **Resource Calendar** as nonworking days. Using this method, however, does not provide a record to allow tracking of the reasons the schedule or a particular resource was put on hold. Let's discuss two different methods of putting a schedule on hold which will help to keep track of the project's schedule and costs.

An Entire Schedule

To put an entire schedule on hold, add a task in MPP and set its priority at 1000. Also assign all of the resources in the project to this task at a 100% level or at the maximum units as specified in the **Resource Sheet**. Set the dates and the duration for this task. Then perform resource leveling. The project then is put on hold for the period specified for this task.

You will also have a record of why the schedule is on hold in MPP. If the hold is due to valid reasons and approval to delay the project has been obtained from project stakeholders, the schedule can be rebaselined. (Rebaselining a schedule will be discussed later in this chapter.)

Selective Resources

To put selective resources on hold, repeat the instructions to put an entire project on hold, but designate *only* those resources that are to be put on hold, not all of the resources. This process will facilitate project management by keeping track of which resources were put on hold and for what period of time. As with the schedule, if putting the resources on hold has been approved by project stakeholders, the project can be rebaselined.

UPDATING RESOURCE LEAVE/VACATION TIME

Updating resource leave and vacation plans in the project plan at the beginning provides an "edge" for schedule management because leave and vacation time will not be considered in calculating the schedule. At the beginning of a project, update resource ad hoc leave (e.g., personal, sick, etc.) as is done for planned vacation. (Note: To enter ad hoc leave, see Chapter 5 for instructions in the *Setup Resource Calendar* section.) If there is agreement with project stakeholders concerning ad hoc leave, perform resource leveling and then rebaseline the project. Otherwise, the baseline must be left as it is.

To avoid the effect of ad hoc leave on a project, as part of the original project plan, also set aside the ad hoc leave that resources are *allowed* to take. Making an allowance for ad hoc leave will provide lead time as well as protection from ad hoc leave interruptions. Once an allowance has been made for ad hoc leave, this leave must be managed by permitting only the amount of leave allotted to each person to be taken during the entire duration of the project. Managing resource leave and vacation is human resource intensive and key to the success of any project.

MANAGING SCOPE CREEP

Scope creep is a common occurrence in projects. It happens in almost all projects undertaken. Scope creep often occurs because the requirements and expectations of project stakeholders are not clearly stated and therefore are misunderstood in the initial planning stages. Scope creep can also be due to other factors which affect a project—unexpected internal events, external entities, suppliers, etc. It is well known that scope creep in projects cannot be controlled or eliminated by any technique or methodology—yet scope creep needs to be managed and managed *efficiently*.

Small values for the schedule and cost variance parameters are generally due to the estimation process. Small variances are expected to balance out at the project level; therefore, they are not of serious concern. Large schedule and cost variances, however, are indicators of potential scope creep.

To manage scope creep, first *know when* scope creep is likely to happen and then *recognize when* it does happen and take action. If a project manager knows that there is a scope creep and that it is affecting the project, he must take the necessary corrective/preventive steps to stop the creep from further affecting the project.

When scope creep exists that will affect a project (either the schedule or the costs), this situation can be identified by analyzing the schedule variance and/or cost variance for the tasks. The task(s) that is (are) causing scope creep can then be pinpointed. By performing root cause analysis on certain tasks—those which have large schedule and/or cost variances—potential scope creep can be identified and forwarded to project stakeholders to obtain agreement about possible revision of the schedule and/or the costs. Once agreement has been obtained, revise the schedule to avoid a schedule delay for the entire project. (Note: In this case, the actual cause of the delay would not be due to the inefficiency of resources.)

WHEN SHOULD A SCHEDULE BE REBASELINED?

A schedule can need rebaselining as a result of any change made to the schedule during the course of a project. Yet, many project managers do not rebaseline their projects when rebaselining needs to be done, which causes their projects to show huge, unrealistic variances at the end as well as during the project.

Whenever the estimates change for any task or additional tasks are added to the schedule or any change is made in the schedule (which has prior approval from all project stakeholders), the schedule must be rebaselined to reflect the correct schedule and cost details. By not rebaselining the schedule, EVM data will show huge, unrealistic variances which distort or camouflage the actual status (picture) of the project.

Rebaselining a Schedule

Suppose the project has started and you have already been tracking changes. Now, due to some of these changes, and with the prior approval of project stakeholders, the schedule has been changed. You now want to rebaseline the schedule.

Important: Take special care when overwriting an existing baseline for already completed tasks. At this point in the project, some tasks are likely to be 100% complete and variances might have been recorded for these tasks. You do not want to lose this information when rebaselining the schedule. If the *entire* schedule is rebaselined, however, the existing variances for tasks which are 100% complete will not be retained—that data will be lost. Instead select only the specific uncompleted tasks that need to be rebaselined.

To rebaseline specific tasks, expand MPP and select all tasks to be rebaselined, along with their summary tasks, and rebaseline using the option **Tools > Tracking > Save baseline**. In the dialog box, select the option **Selected tasks** instead of **Entire Project**. Also choose the two check boxes that indicate that you want to roll up the values to the summary tasks. This process keeps the old variances and still rebaselines uncompleted tasks. Remember: Select all of the summary tasks up to the project level to rebaseline a schedule.

Rebaselining the EVM Report Template

After rebaselining the schedule, it is important to rebaseline the EVM template to reflect the latest baseline. To do this, from MPP, update the **Baseline cost** field in the EVM data sheet of the EVM template. (For details about getting the baseline cost from MPP, refer to the *Preparing the Template for a New Project* section in Chapter 6.)

APPENDIX A:
EVM FOR PRODUCTION SUPPORT

INTRODUCTION

Compared to project management, production support is an entirely different "ball game." In project management, the focus is on time management and controlling costs, while in production support, the primary focus is on keeping the number of open calls/tickets low and meeting service level agreements. When discussing service level agreements, the most commonly used parameters are initial response time, restoration time, and final resolution time. These parameters are also used to measure the performance of teams and companies. Yet there is no *standard method* to analyze team performance with respect to these parameters or to notify a team that corrective and/or preventive action needs to be taken while a project is progressing.

To facilitate a common platform for comparison in development and maintenance projects, the author has developed a method using the EVM technique to measure and monitor team performance on production support issues. Traditional EVM typically involves monitoring schedule and cost variances using the *absolute cost* of a project. The author's method, however, is designed to focus on the *number of open* tickets and the *defined* service level agreement rather than cost/effort. The measure used in his method, therefore, is the number of open tickets. (Note: Hours instead of tickets may also be used. By using hours and the hourly rate for a resource, the technique can be extended to produce an absolute dollar value as well.)

In the author's method, the EVM concept is applied to calculate planned value, earned value, and actual value (which represent cost/effort) using the number of tickets/calls and the service level agreements; therefore, the terms planned tickets, earned tickets, and actual tickets are used (to represent tickets, not cost/effort units).

The author's technique facilitates status/progress tracking of production support engagements. The technique allows ease in tracking and also presents the status/progress of a production support engagement to project stakeholders in a readable, understandable format so that necessary corrective/preventive action may be taken to enable a production support engagement to function more smoothly.

METHODOLOGY

Let's now look at this new method which can be used to apply the EVM technique to production support engagements. We will start with information that is generally available for a production support engagement and how we can use this information and translate it into an EVM technique devised by the author.

First, maintain a log of all production support calls/tickets in a tracking system such as Microsoft® Office Excel. The following main attributes should be logged:

- Ticket number
- Brief description
- Severity
- Log time—when the ticket or call was received (logged in)
- Response time—when the initial response was made by the production support team
- Restoration time—when a solution to the problem was found and work was started (if required) (i.e., when the production support team has found a solution to the problem and/or has possibly given the customer a workaround for the problem while continuing to work on solving the problem; in some cases, a workaround is not available)
- Resolution time—when the problem has been resolved and fixes have been moved into production
- Status time—when the status is collected (i.e., the date and time when the status is collected to apply the EVM technique)

The parameters for these attributes can be easily extracted by any call tracking tool. A tracking tool is also used to maintain the basic attributes.

Table A.1. Service Level Agreement

Severity	Initial Response	Restoration Time	Resolution Time
1	2 hr	6 hr	8 hr
2	2 hr	16 hr	24 hr
3	16 hr	40 hr	56 hr
4	20 hr	48 hr	64 hr

In addition to the basic attributes, service levels are defined for each production service engagement. For our example, service levels are defined in Table A.1. From these attributes, the following parameters can be calculated:

- Initial response time in hours
- Restoration time in hours
- Resolution time in hours

Additionally, the % completion for each of these parameters (initial response, restoration, and resolution time) can be recorded:

- % completion initial response
- % completion restoration
- % completion final resolution

Using the attributes from our list above, the following can be calculated:

Parameter—Initial Response
- Planned tickets
- Earned tickets
- Actual tickets

Parameter—Restoration Time
- Planned tickets
- Earned tickets
- Actual tickets

Parameter—Resolution Time
- Planned tickets
- Earned tickets
- Actual tickets

We now need to sum up the values for the attributes (each one has been calculated at the individual ticket level) to get planned tickets (PT), earned tickets (ET), and actual tickets

(AT) for each parameter at the engagement level. Using these sums and standard EVM formulas, we can calculate:

- Schedule variance
- Cost variance
- Schedule variance %
- Cost variance %
- Schedule performance indicator
- Cost performance indicator

which will tell us how well we are performing production support calls.

Parameter—Initial Response

- *Schedule variance:* For an initial response, how much ahead/behind of the planned schedule are we (planned schedule being the defined service levels)?
- *Cost variance:* For an initial response, how much over/under budget are we (budget being the defined service levels)?
- *Schedule performance indicator:* How efficiently do we utilize time for initial responses?
- *Cost performance indicator:* How effectively do we use resources for initial responses?

Parameter—Restoration Time

- *Schedule variance:* In finding a solution, how much ahead/behind of the planned schedule are we (planned schedule being the defined service levels)?
- *Cost variance:* In finding a solution, how much over/under budget are we (budget being the defined service levels)?
- *Schedule performance indicator:* How efficiently do we utilize time in finding a solution?
- *Cost performance indicator:* How effectively do we use resources for restoration?

Parameter—Resolution Time

- *Schedule variance:* In resolving a problem, how much ahead/behind of the planned schedule are we (planned schedule being the defined service levels)?
- *Cost variance:* In resolving a problem, how much over/under budget are we (budget being the defined service levels)?
- *Schedule performance indicator:* How efficiently is time used to resolve a problem?
- *Cost performance indicator:* How effectively are resources used to resolve a problem?

FORMULAS

The following formulas are to be calculated at the individual ticket/call level:

- Initial response time in hours = response time – log time
- Restoration time in hours = restoration time – log time
- Resolution time in hours = resolution time – log time

Parameter: Initial Response
- Planned tickets: if (status date – log time) > service level, then 1; otherwise (status date – log time)/service level
- Earned tickets: 1 × % completion initial response
- Actual tickets: response hours/service level

Parameter: Restoration Time
- Planned tickets: if (status date – log time) > service level, then 1; otherwise (status date – log time)/service level
- Earned tickets: 1 × % completion restoration
- Actual tickets: restoration hours/service level

Parameter: Resolution Time
- Planned tickets: if (status date – log time) > service level, then 1; otherwise (status date – log time)/service level
- Earned tickets: 1 × % completion final resolution
- Actual tickets: resolution hours/service level

Parameter: All
- Schedule variance = ET – PT
- Cost variance = ET – AT
- Schedule variance % = (ET – PT)/ET
- Cost variance % = (ET – AT)/ET
- Schedule performance indicator = ET/PT
- Cost performance indicator = ET/AT

EXAMPLES

The figures in this section illustrate a summary sheet (Figure A.1), a data sheet (Figure A.2), an earned value graph (Figure A.3), a variance graph (Figure A.4), and schedule and cost performance indexes (Figure A.5).

Weekly EVM Report - XYZ Project

	Status Date	2-Jan		
	Legend		Performance measure is out of control. Needs attention	
			Performance measure is out of control. Controllable.	
			Performance measure is in control.	
			Help on Abbreviations	

Initial Response

Week	Performance Parameter	Performance Measure	Value	Performance Measure Outcome	Reasons	Corrective Action
2-Jan	Schedule/Time	SV %	0%			
2-Jan	Schedule/Time	SPI	1.00			
2-Jan	Cost/Effort	CV %	-10%			
2-Jan	Cost/Effort	CPI	0.91			

Restoration

Week	Performance Parameter	Performance Measure	Value	Performance Measure Outcome	Reasons	Corrective Action
2-Jan	Schedule/Time	SV %	20%			
2-Jan	Schedule/Time	SPI	1.25			
2-Jan	Cost/Effort	CV %	77%			
2-Jan	Cost/Effort	CPI	4.40			

Problem Resolution

Week	Performance Parameter	Performance Measure	Value	Performance Measure Outcome	Reasons	Corrective Action
2-Jan	Schedule/Time	SV %	-5%			
2-Jan	Schedule/Time	SPI	0.95			
2-Jan	Cost/Effort	CV %	51%			
2-Jan	Cost/Effort	CPI	2.06			

Figure A.1. Summary sheet.

		26-Dec	2-Jan	9-Jan	16-Jan	23-Jan	30-Jan	6-Feb	13-Feb	20-Feb	27-Feb	6-Mar	13-Mar	20-Mar	27-Mar	3-Apr	10-Apr	17-Apr
Initial Response	PT	0	14															
	ET	0	14															
	AT	0	15.4266															
Restoration	PT	0	11.2															
	ET	0	14															
	AT	0	3.17916															
Problem Resolution	PT	0	10.5215															
	ET	0	10															
	AT	0	4.8601															
Initial Response	SPI	1.00	1.00															
	CPI	1.00	0.91															
	SV	0	0															
	CV	0	-1.42662															
	SV %	0%	0%															
	CV %	0%	-10%															
Restoration	SPI	1.00	1.25															
	CPI	1.00	4.40															
	SV	0	2.8															
	CV	0	10.8208															
	SV %	0%	20%															
	CV %	0%	77%															
Problem Resolution	SPI	1.00	0.95															
	CPI	1.00	2.06															
	SV	0	-0.52147															
	CV	0	5.1399															
	SV %	0%	-5%															
	CV %	0%	51%															

Figure A.2. Data sheet.

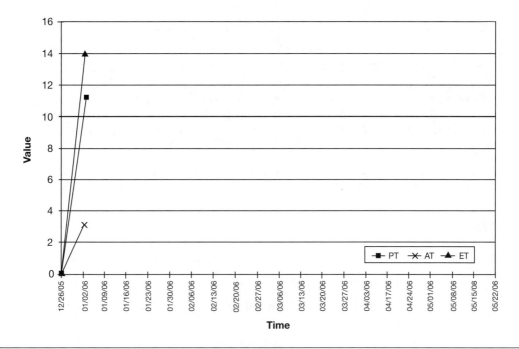

Figure A.3. Earned value graph.

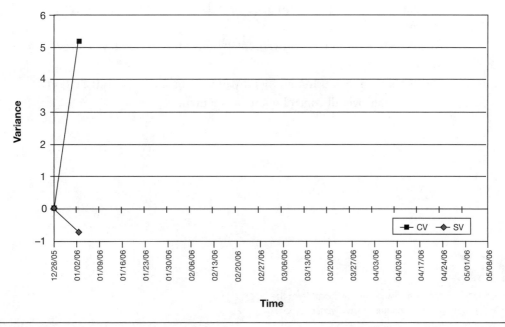

Figure A.4. Variance graph—restoration time.

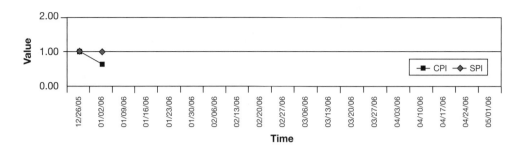

Figure A.5. Schedule and cost performance indexes.

SUMMARY

Multiple benefits are obtained from using EVM to monitor production support engagements. The following are a few of these benefits:

- Tracks team performance on an ongoing basis and facilitates better team performance
- Provides a single platform for comparing production support engagements and development projects
- Tracks performance of individual performance parameters (initial response, restoration, and resolution)
- Facilitates checking performance trends and taking corrective/preventive action
- Facilitates continuous improvement by altering service levels based on performance
- Shows value to the customer, thereby increasing customer satisfaction
- Allows better overall control of an engagement

APPENDIX B:
SCHEDULE MANAGEMENT—
AN END-TO-END EXAMPLE

Most of us have shelves of books that are supposed to teach us about different techniques. Yet, quite often, when we try to implement a technique that has been discussed in one of these books, we suddenly find ourselves having big problems. Obviously, we must have missed some of the finer details when reading the book. So we end up thinking that implementing a solution from a book is impossible. To avoid this situation, *Appendix B* is included and contains an example of a complete end-to-end tracking of a project using MPP and the EVM template tool supplied with this book. This appendix will describe several evolving scenarios to get the most out of MPP and the EVM template.

A typical software development project is used as the example to demonstrate the schedule management practices which have been outlined in this book. This project is the same one that has been used to illustrate the discussions in the chapters; therefore, readers are already familiar with details of the project. Let's now see how to go about planning, executing, monitoring, and closing a schedule.

PLANNING

Our project is a typical software development project. The scope of the project is to build software for a particular application. In our project, we are building software to cater to project management needs in our own organization. The software must provide functionality that will enable project managers to perform their duties with ease and, at the same time, allow senior management in the organization to get the information they need to monitor projects on a periodic basis and to see if there are concerns that need to be addressed. Let's assume that the scope of the project—what needs to be achieved through implementation of the software—has been defined by the PMO (Project Management Office) in our organization. Therefore, the scope is ready and we can pass the scope on to the software development team so they can begin:

SCOPE STATEMENT

The project management software is proposed to be developed to cater to the growing requirements of a complete enterprise-wide solution for the project management needs of the organization. The planning module involves creating the planning documents and storing them with version control. In this module, the users should be able to create the project plan and the subsidiary plans from scratch or from already available templates. All of the planning documents should be available for review and allow changes to be made at the project manager level and above; the planning documents should be available for viewing only by project team members. The schedule module involves managing the schedule of the project and roll up into master plans at the levels above master plan (e.g., program, portfolio, and business). In the schedule module, users should be able to create/modify a schedule using a WBS decomposed to the activity level. Users should be able to sequence tasks, assign resources to tasks, assign priorities to tasks, perform automated resource leveling, identify milestones, baseline the schedule, create multiple baselines, track progress of the schedule, and report progress at any level desired by the user. Progress of individual projects should roll up into the master plans at the levels above master plan. In addition to the functional specifications, the project management software should have the following features: Web-based, rich graphical user interface (dashboards for every user), predefined user roles and user-defined roles, dynamic workflows, and support generation of graphs and charts.

Typically the first thing that a software development team does is to estimate the amount of effort needed to complete the project based on the scope of the project as defined by the customer (which in our case is the PMO). In our example, we will use the bottom-up estimation technique which is the most commonly used estimation technique for all projects in various domains. (Note: As discussed earlier, several estimation techniques are available; however, we will not delve into these estimation techniques.)

Let's take another look at the scope statement to better understand the scope of the project and the deliverables to be obtained from the project. From the scope statement, it is clear that the proposed software will have three modules, namely, a planning module, a

	❶	Task Name	Duration	Start	Finish	Predecessors	Resource Names
1		⊟ **PM Software**	**1 day?**	**Mon 8/18/03**	**Mon 8/18/03**		
2		⊟ **Requirements**	**1 day?**	**Mon 8/18/03**	**Mon 8/18/03**		
3		Prepare Requirements	1 day?	Mon 8/18/03	Mon 8/18/03		
4		Review Requirements	1 day?	Mon 8/18/03	Mon 8/18/03		
5		Incorporate Review comments	1 day?	Mon 8/18/03	Mon 8/18/03		
6		User Review	1 day?	Mon 8/18/03	Mon 8/18/03		
7		User Review Comments Incorporation	1 day?	Mon 8/18/03	Mon 8/18/03		
8		Final Approval	1 day?	Mon 8/18/03	Mon 8/18/03		
9		⊟ **High Level Design**	**1 day?**	**Mon 8/18/03**	**Mon 8/18/03**		
10		Prepare High Level Design	1 day?	Mon 8/18/03	Mon 8/18/03		
11		Review HLD	1 day?	Mon 8/18/03	Mon 8/18/03		
12		Incorporate Review Comments	1 day?	Mon 8/18/03	Mon 8/18/03		
13		User Review	1 day?	Mon 8/18/03	Mon 8/18/03		
14		User Review Comments Incorporation	1 day?	Mon 8/18/03	Mon 8/18/03		
15		Final Approval	1 day?	Mon 8/18/03	Mon 8/18/03		
16		⊟ **Planning Module**	**1 day?**	**Mon 8/18/03**	**Mon 8/18/03**		
17		Prepare Low Level Design	1 day?	Mon 8/18/03	Mon 8/18/03		
18		LLD Review	1 day?	Mon 8/18/03	Mon 8/18/03		
19		LLD Review Comments Incorporation	1 day?	Mon 8/18/03	Mon 8/18/03		
20		Unit Test Plan Preparation	1 day?	Mon 8/18/03	Mon 8/18/03		
21		UTP Review	1 day?	Mon 8/18/03	Mon 8/18/03		
22		UTP Review Comments Incorporation	1 day?	Mon 8/18/03	Mon 8/18/03		
23		Coding	1 day?	Mon 8/18/03	Mon 8/18/03		
24		Unit Testing	1 day?	Mon 8/18/03	Mon 8/18/03		
25		Code Review	1 day?	Mon 8/18/03	Mon 8/18/03		
26		Code Review Comments Incorporation	1 day?	Mon 8/18/03	Mon 8/18/03		
27		Move to Integration Testing	1 day?	Mon 8/18/03	Mon 8/18/03		
28		⊞ **Schedule Module**	**1 day?**	**Mon 8/18/03**	**Mon 8/18/03**		
40		⊞ **Administration Module**	**1 day?**	**Mon 8/18/03**	**Mon 8/18/03**		

Figure B.1. Initial WBS.

schedule module, and an administration module. Additionally, we can also see that there are to be some nonfunctional specifications—web-based, rich graphical user interface with dashboards, user roles, etc. Let's now prepare a WBS using MPP software.

First, in Figure B.1, look at the initial WBS which has been derived from the scope statement. Notice that the scope statement has been decomposed into a WBS to the lowest activity level possible (see under Tasks 2, 9, and 16). (Notice also that the **Start** and **Finish** dates have been populated by MPP.) Once the WBS has been decomposed, circulate the WBS to appropriate experts in each area. Ask them to assign estimates to the lowest-level activities. For example, send the WBS to a business analyst to assign estimates for the **Requirements** section. Similarly, send the WBS to a technical lead or an architect to assign the estimates for **High Level Design** and the remaining activities.

	⊕	Task Name	Work	Duration	Start	Finish	Predecessors	Resource Names
1		⊟ **PM Software**	**2,662 hrs**	**1 day**	**Mon 8/18/03**	**Mon 8/18/03**		
2		⊟ **Requirements**	**113 hrs**	**1 day**	**Mon 8/18/03**	**Mon 8/18/03**		
3		Prepare Requirements	80 hrs	1 day	Mon 8/18/03	Mon 8/18/03		
4		Review Requirements	8 hrs	1 day	Mon 8/18/03	Mon 8/18/03		
5		Incorporate Review comments	8 hrs	1 day	Mon 8/18/03	Mon 8/18/03		
6		User Review	8 hrs	1 day	Mon 8/18/03	Mon 8/18/03		
7		User Review Comments Incorporation	8 hrs	1 day	Mon 8/18/03	Mon 8/18/03		
8		Final Approval	1 hr	1 day	Mon 8/18/03	Mon 8/18/03		
9		⊞ **High Level Design**	**113 hrs**	**1 day**	**Mon 8/18/03**	**Mon 8/18/03**		
16		⊟ **Planning Module**	**316 hrs**	**1 day**	**Mon 8/18/03**	**Mon 8/18/03**		
17		Prepare Low Level Design	40 hrs	1 day	Mon 8/18/03	Mon 8/18/03		
18		LLD Review	8 hrs	1 day	Mon 8/18/03	Mon 8/18/03		
19		LLD Review Comments Incorporation	8 hrs	1 day	Mon 8/18/03	Mon 8/18/03		
20		Unit Test Plan Preparation	40 hrs	1 day	Mon 8/18/03	Mon 8/18/03		
21		UTP Review	8 hrs	1 day	Mon 8/18/03	Mon 8/18/03		
22		UTP Review Comments Incorporation	8 hrs	1 day	Mon 8/18/03	Mon 8/18/03		
23		Coding	120 hrs	1 day	Mon 8/18/03	Mon 8/18/03		
24		Unit Testing	40 hrs	1 day	Mon 8/18/03	Mon 8/18/03		
25		Code Review	24 hrs	1 day	Mon 8/18/03	Mon 8/18/03		
26		Code Review Comments Incorporation	16 hrs	1 day	Mon 8/18/03	Mon 8/18/03		
27		Move to Integration Testing	4 hrs	1 day	Mon 8/18/03	Mon 8/18/03		
28		⊞ **Schedule Module**	**596 hrs**	**1 day**	**Mon 8/18/03**	**Mon 8/18/03**		
40		⊞ **Administration Module**	**316 hrs**	**1 day**	**Mon 8/18/03**	**Mon 8/18/03**		
52		⊞ **Integration Testing**	**432 hrs**	**1 day**	**Mon 8/18/03**	**Mon 8/18/03**		
59		⊞ **User Acceptance Testing**	**432 hrs**	**1 day**	**Mon 8/18/03**	**Mon 8/18/03**		
66		⊞ **Pilot Implementation**	**256 hrs**	**1 day**	**Mon 8/18/03**	**Mon 8/18/03**		
72		⊞ **Production Rollout**	**88 hrs**	**1 day**	**Mon 8/18/03**	**Mon 8/18/03**		

Figure B.2. WBS with estimates.

Once the estimates for the various sections of the schedule have been received from the different experts, consolidate these estimates into your schedule to come up with a final estimate for the project. Notice at this point that the only information we have about the project is from the scope statement. Because we have relatively little information at this time, ensure that a contingency is included in the estimate to handle revisions of the estimates based on completion of the requirements and design phases. Once completed, these phases will provide a clearer picture of the project. Depending on your confidence level, set aside a contingency of 10 to 25% for future revisions.

Let's now look at how the estimates appear in the schedule for the various activities. After collecting input from all of the area experts in the various areas of the project, we now have the effort estimates as shown in the **Work** column of Figure B.2. Notice that the estimates have been incorporated into the schedule, but the tasks have not been sequenced. So we must now sequence the tasks in the schedule following the technique discussed in Chapter 5. The tasks will be sequenced at the summary level using the **Priority** field and at the lowest level using the **Predecessor** field.

	Priority	Task Name	Work	Duration	Start	Finish	Predecessors	'8 W T F S	Mar 2, '08 S M T W T F S	Mar 9, '08 S M T W T
1	800	⊟ PM Software	2,662 hrs	45 days	Mon 3/3/08	Fri 5/2/08				
2	700	⊟ Requirements	113 hrs	6 days	Mon 3/3/08	Mon 3/10/08				
3	700	Prepare Requirements	80 hrs	1 day	Mon 3/3/08	Mon 3/3/08				
4	700	Review Requirements	8 hrs	1 day	Tue 3/4/08	Tue 3/4/08	3			
5	700	Incorporate Review comments	8 hrs	1 day	Wed 3/5/08	Wed 3/5/08	4			
6	700	User Review	8 hrs	1 day	Thu 3/6/08	Thu 3/6/08	5			
7	700	User Review Comments Incorporation	8 hrs	1 day	Fri 3/7/08	Fri 3/7/08	6			
8	700	Final Approval	1 hr	1 day	Mon 3/10/08	Mon 3/10/08	7			
9	600	⊞ High Level Design	113 hrs	6 days	Tue 3/11/08	Tue 3/18/08	2			
16	500	⊞ Planning Module	316 hrs	11 days	Wed 3/19/08	Wed 4/2/08	9			
28	500	⊞ Schedule Module	596 hrs	11 days	Wed 3/19/08	Wed 4/2/08	9			
40	500	⊞ Administration Module	316 hrs	11 days	Wed 3/19/08	Wed 4/2/08	9			
52	400	⊞ Integration Testing	432 hrs	6 days	Thu 4/3/08	Thu 4/10/08	16,28,40			
59	300	⊞ User Acceptance Testing	432 hrs	6 days	Fri 4/11/08	Fri 4/18/08	52			
66	200	⊞ Pilot Implementation	256 hrs	5 days	Mon 4/21/08	Fri 4/25/08	59			
72	100	⊞ Production Rollout	88 hrs	5 days	Mon 4/28/08	Fri 5/2/08	66			

Figure B.3. WBS after sequencing.

Notice also that there are some tasks at the lowest level which need to be completed sequentially (e.g., in the **Planning Module**); therefore, we will use the finish-to-start relationship for these tasks to sequence them. Also there are some tasks at the summary level which need to be completed before other summary-level tasks should be started (e.g., **Requirements** before **High Level Design**). For these tasks we will use the **Predecessor** field to sequence the tasks rather than the **Priority** field setting.

Figure B.3 displays how the sequencing of tasks appears in the schedule. Notice that the tasks are now sequenced so let's review how that was done. Overall, at the project level, we have set the priority at 800; we have started setting priorities for the summary-level tasks from 700 to 100. Notice that for the summary task **Requirements** that we have set a priority of 700; we have also set the same priority for all of the lower-level tasks in **Requirements**. We have also set a finish-to-start relationship for the lower-level tasks (which can be seen in the predecessor tasks). There are two advantages to this method of sequencing—one is that significant time is saved in sequencing the tasks and the other is that lower-level tasks, which are generally performed one after the other, are tightly coupled.

Notice also that we have set the predecessors for summary-level tasks below the **Requirements** summary task because there is a dependency between the **Requirements** task and the rest of the tasks. In this project we have determined that only after **Requirements** is completed can we move on to **High Level Design** and then to **Coding** of the individual modules. So although we have set a priority, we need to only set the predecessor at the summary level because the **Priority** field setting will not work if tasks are performed by two different resources. For example, in our project, we know that

Requirements is being done by business analysts and **High Level Design** is done by technical leads or architects.

Yet notice that we have set the same priority (500) and predecessor (9) for the development of the individual modules (Tasks 16, 28, and 40). This is because these modules are similar tasks which can be performed by resources with the same skill sets—but these tasks are still dependent on the completion of **Requirements** and **High Level Design**; therefore we have the predecessor setting. These tasks can also be done in any order depending on the availability of resources.

Continuing with our discussion of sequencing, notice the **Integration Testing** task. This task has a predecessor of three tasks (Tasks 16, 28, and 40) because the **Integration Testing** task can only be performed after all of the individual modules (i.e., Tasks 16, 28, and 40) have been completed. The **Integration Testing** task is also generally done by a different set of resources.

Now, notice in the **Duration** column that 45 days is the duration for the project; however, effort remains the same at 2662 hours. The next step is to identify the resource requirements and add these resources to the schedule. For this schedule, to complete the tasks, we need the following resources: project manager, business analyst, architect, developer, technical leader, tester, and user. Let's discuss how we can vary the number of resources for each of these skill categories and optimize the schedule and costs. Let's assume the following rates for the different resources:

- Project manager—$100/hour
- Business analyst—$80/hour
- Architect—$120/hour
- Developer—$50/hour
- Technical leader—$70/hour
- Tester—$50/hour
- User—$120/hour

Using these resource rates and keeping in mind the project's schedule and budget constraints, let's determine the optimal mix of resources needed for the project. Let's put these resources at the 100% level in MPP (shown in Figure B.4).

Before we assign the resources to the tasks, let's add some of the common tasks that we often forget to the schedule, e.g., team and status meetings. Project team members spend some finite amount of time on these tasks; if not accounted for in the schedule, this time will impact the schedule—most often negatively. Team and status meetings are generally

	ⓘ	Resource Name	Type	Material Label	Initials	Group	Max. Units	Std. Rate	Ovt. Rate	Cost/Use	Accrue At	Base Calendar	Code
1		Project Manager	Work		P		100%	$100.00/hr	$0.00/hr	$0.00	Prorated	Standard	
2		Business Analyst	Work		B		100%	$80.00/hr	$0.00/hr	$0.00	Prorated	Standard	
3		Architect	Work		A		100%	$120.00/hr	$0.00/hr	$0.00	Prorated	Standard	
4		Developer	Work		D		100%	$50.00/hr	$0.00/hr	$0.00	Prorated	Standard	
5		Technical Leader	Work		T		100%	$70.00/hr	$0.00/hr	$0.00	Prorated	Standard	
6		Tester	Work		T		100%	$50.00/hr	$0.00/hr	$0.00	Prorated	Standard	
7		User	Work		U		100%	$120.00/hr	$0.00/hr	$0.00	Prorated	Standard	

Figure B.4. Initial resource list.

	ⓘ	Priority	Task Name	Work	Duration	Start	Finish	Predecessors
1		800	⊟ PM Software	2,662 hrs	45 days	Mon 3/3/08	Fri 5/2/08	
2	↻	1000	⊟ **Weekly Team Meeting**	0 hrs	40.13 days	Mon 3/3/08	Mon 4/28/08	
3	▦	1000	Weekly Team Meeting 1	0 hrs	1 hr	Mon 3/3/08	Mon 3/3/08	
4	▦	1000	Weekly Team Meeting 2	0 hrs	1 hr	Mon 3/10/08	Mon 3/10/08	
5	▦	1000	Weekly Team Meeting 3	0 hrs	1 hr	Mon 3/17/08	Mon 3/17/08	
6	▦	1000	Weekly Team Meeting 4	0 hrs	1 hr	Mon 3/24/08	Mon 3/24/08	
7	▦	1000	Weekly Team Meeting 5	0 hrs	1 hr	Mon 3/31/08	Mon 3/31/08	
8	▦	1000	Weekly Team Meeting 6	0 hrs	1 hr	Mon 4/7/08	Mon 4/7/08	
9	▦	1000	Weekly Team Meeting 7	0 hrs	1 hr	Mon 4/14/08	Mon 4/14/08	
10	▦	1000	Weekly Team Meeting 8	0 hrs	1 hr	Mon 4/21/08	Mon 4/21/08	
11	▦	1000	Weekly Team Meeting 9	0 hrs	1 hr	Mon 4/28/08	Mon 4/28/08	
12	↻	1000	⊞ **Weekly Status Meeting**	0 hrs	40.13 days	Tue 3/4/08	Tue 4/29/08	
22		700	⊞ **Requirements**	113 hrs	6 days	Mon 3/3/08	Mon 3/10/08	
29		600	⊞ **High Level Design**	113 hrs	6 days	Tue 3/11/08	Tue 3/18/08	22
36		500	⊞ **Planning Module**	316 hrs	11 days	Wed 3/19/08	Wed 4/2/08	29
48		500	⊞ **Schedule Module**	596 hrs	11 days	Wed 3/19/08	Wed 4/2/08	29
60		500	⊞ **Administration Module**	316 hrs	11 days	Wed 3/19/08	Wed 4/2/08	29
72		400	⊞ **Integration Testing**	432 hrs	6 days	Thu 4/3/08	Thu 4/10/08	36,48,60
79		300	⊞ **User Acceptance Testing**	432 hrs	6 days	Fri 4/11/08	Fri 4/18/08	72
86		200	⊞ **Pilot Implementation**	256 hrs	5 days	Mon 4/21/08	Fri 4/25/08	79
92		100	⊞ **Production Rollout**	88 hrs	5 days	Mon 4/28/08	Fri 5/2/08	86

Figure B.5. Recurring tasks.

recurring activities; therefore, we need to create recurring tasks for these activities. Now look at the schedule after adding these activities (shown in Figure B.5).

Next look at the schedule after we assign the resources at a 100% level, which means that for **Requirements** *one* of each resource (project manager, business analyst, and user) is working on the project (shown in Figure B.6). Notice that the resources have been assigned to the tasks and resource leveling has been completed. With this loading of resources, we now have a schedule duration of a little over 340 days (340.08), which is

	% Work Complete	Priority	Task Name	Cost	Work	Duration	Start	Finish	Pred	Resource Names
1	0%	800	⊟ PM Software	$203,210.00	2,974 hrs	340.08 days	Mon 3/3/08	Mon 6/22/09		
2	0%	1000	⊞ Weekly Team Meeting	$4,230.00	54 hrs	40.13 days	Mon 3/3/08	Mon 4/28/08		
12	0%	1000	⊞ Weekly Status Meeting	$1,980.00	18 hrs	40.13 days	Tue 3/4/08	Tue 4/29/08		
22	0%	700	⊞ Requirements	$9,560.00	113 hrs	14.25 days	Mon 4/28/08	Fri 5/16/08		
29	0%	600	⊞ High Level Design	$8,760.00	113 hrs	14.5 days	Fri 5/16/08	Thu 6/5/08	22	
36	0%	500	⊟ Planning Module	$16,600.00	316 hrs	67 days	Thu 6/12/08	Mon 9/15/08	29	
37	0%	500	Prepare Low Level Design	$2,000.00	40 hrs	5 days	Thu 6/12/08	Thu 6/19/08		Developer - 1
38	0%	500	LLD Review	$560.00	8 hrs	1 day	Thu 6/19/08	Fri 6/20/08	37	Technical Leader
39	0%	500	LLD Review Comments Incorporation	$400.00	8 hrs	1 day	Fri 6/27/08	Mon 6/30/08	38	Developer - 1
40	0%	500	Unit Test Plan Preparation	$2,000.00	40 hrs	5 days	Tue 7/1/08	Tue 7/8/08	39	Developer - 1
41	0%	500	UTP Review	$560.00	8 hrs	1 day	Tue 7/8/08	Wed 7/9/08	40	Technical Leader
42	0%	500	UTP Review Comments Incorporation	$400.00	8 hrs	1 day	Tue 7/29/08	Wed 7/30/08	41	Developer - 1
43	0%	500	Coding	$6,000.00	120 hrs	15 days	Wed 8/6/08	Wed 8/27/08	42	Developer - 1
44	0%	500	Unit Testing	$2,000.00	40 hrs	5 days	Mon 9/1/08	Mon 9/8/08	43	Developer - 1
45	0%	500	Code Review	$1,680.00	24 hrs	3 days	Mon 9/8/08	Thu 9/11/08	44	Technical Leader
46	0%	500	Code Review Comments Incorporation	$800.00	16 hrs	2 days	Thu 9/11/08	Mon 9/15/08	45	Developer - 1
47	0%	500	Move to Integration Testing	$200.00	4 hrs	0.5 days	Mon 9/15/08	Mon 9/15/08	46	Developer - 1
48	0%	480	⊞ Schedule Module	$31,400.00	596 hrs	71 days	Mon 9/15/08	Tue 12/23/08	29	
64	0%	500	⊞ Administration Module	$16,600.00	316 hrs	61.5 days	Thu 6/5/08	Mon 9/1/08	29	
76	0%	400	⊞ Integration Testing	$22,320.00	432 hrs	182.75 days	Mon 4/28/08	Wed 1/7/09		
85	0%	300	⊞ User Acceptance Testing	$45,600.00	432 hrs	44.2 days	Wed 1/7/09	Wed 3/11/09	76	
94	0%	200	⊞ Pilot Implementation	$26,240.00	256 hrs	32 days	Wed 3/11/09	Fri 4/24/09	85	
100	0%	100	⊞ Production Rollout	$7,920.00	88 hrs	11 days	Fri 4/24/09	Mon 5/11/09	94	
106	0%	80	Contingency Buffer	$12,000.00	240 hrs	30 days	Mon 5/11/09	Mon 6/22/09	100	Developer - 1

Figure B.6. Initial resource assignment.

much higher than the initial duration of 45 days that we had before the resources were assigned (see Figure B.5). This situation occurs because initially duration is *not* calculated; therefore duration appears as 1 day—even for a 160-hour effort task; whereas when we assign one resource to the task, duration is calculated as 20 days because resources generally have an 8-hour workday. Also notice that cost is $203,210. Now, to optimize the schedule, we must add resources to improve the current status of the duration and cost.

Remember that we originally assigned only one of each resource to the project. We can see that the schedule is being unduly extended because there is only one developer and three modules that he needs to finish. If we add two more developers, however, taking the developer count to three, then we have a very high possibility of reducing the duration of the project. Let's see how adding two developers will affect the schedule (shown in Figure B.7).

Notice that two new developers have been added to the schedule. Now we have three developers instead of the one developer who was originally assigned to the project. Also notice that the duration of the project has been significantly reduced from 340 days to a little over 277 days (277.21). The cost, however, remains the same because the schedule assumes that resources are being brought in when they are needed and then moved out of the project when their work is completed. (Note: Cost will change if resources need to be

	ⓘ	Priority	Task Name	Cost	Work	Duration	Start	Finish	Predecessors	Resource Names
1		800	⊟ PM Software	$203,290.00	2,734 hrs	277.21 days	Mon 3/3/08	Wed 3/25/09		
2	⟳	1000	⊞ Weekly Team Meeting	$4,230.00	54 hrs	40.13 days	Mon 3/3/08	Mon 4/28/08		
12	⟳	1000	⊞ Weekly Status Meeting	$1,980.00	18 hrs	40.13 days	Tue 3/4/08	Tue 4/29/08		
22		700	⊞ Requirements	$9,560.00	113 hrs	14.13 days	Mon 4/28/08	Fri 5/16/08		
29		600	⊞ High Level Design	$8,760.00	113 hrs	14.13 days	Fri 5/16/08	Thu 6/5/08	22	
36		500	⊞ Planning Module	$16,600.00	316 hrs	39.5 days	Thu 6/5/08	Wed 7/30/08	29	
48		500	⊟ Schedule Module	$31,400.00	596 hrs	74.5 days	Thu 6/5/08	Wed 9/17/08	29	
49		500	Prepare Low Level Design	$4,000.00	80 hrs	10 days	Thu 6/5/08	Thu 6/19/08		Developer - 2
50		500	LLD Review	$1,120.00	16 hrs	2 days	Thu 6/19/08	Mon 6/23/08	49	Technical Leader
51		500	LLD Review Comments Incorporation	$400.00	8 hrs	1 day	Mon 6/23/08	Tue 6/24/08	50	Developer - 2
52		500	Unit Test Plan Preparation	$4,000.00	80 hrs	10 days	Tue 6/24/08	Tue 7/8/08	51	Developer - 2
53		500	UTP Review	$1,120.00	16 hrs	2 days	Tue 7/8/08	Thu 7/10/08	52	Technical Leader
54		500	UTP Review Comments Incorporation	$400.00	8 hrs	1 day	Thu 7/10/08	Fri 7/11/08	53	Developer - 2
55		500	Coding	$12,000.00	240 hrs	30 days	Fri 7/11/08	Fri 8/22/08	54	Developer - 2
56		500	Unit Testing	$4,000.00	80 hrs	10 days	Fri 8/22/08	Fri 9/5/08	55	Developer - 2
57		500	Code Review	$3,360.00	48 hrs	6 days	Fri 9/5/08	Mon 9/15/08	56	Technical Leader
58		500	Code Review Comments Incorporation	$800.00	16 hrs	2 days	Mon 9/15/08	Wed 9/17/08	57	Developer - 2
59		500	Move to Integration Testing	$200.00	4 hrs	0.5 days	Wed 9/17/08	Wed 9/17/08	58	Developer - 2
60		500	⊞ Administration Module	$16,600.00	316 hrs	42.5 days	Thu 6/5/08	Mon 8/4/08	29	
72		400	⊞ Integration Testing	$25,280.00	432 hrs	47.33 days	Wed 9/17/08	Mon 11/24/08	36,48,60	
79		300	⊞ User Acceptance Testing	$42,720.00	432 hrs	47.33 days	Mon 11/24/08	Wed 1/28/09	72	
86		200	⊞ Pilot Implementation	$26,240.00	256 hrs	28.67 days	Wed 1/28/09	Tue 3/10/09	79	
92		100	⊞ Production Rollout	$7,920.00	88 hrs	11 days	Tue 3/10/09	Wed 3/25/09	86	

Figure B.7. Developers added.

kept on the project in spite of not having enough work for them. We will discuss this shortly.)

Let's now see how duration of the project can be further reduced. Notice in Figure B.7 that **Integration Testing** and **User Acceptance Testing** appear to be taking too long. We should try to reduce the duration of these tasks. Remember that for **Integration Testing** we originally assumed that we would have one tester; however, if we increase the number of testers to five, we can significantly reduce duration.

Another option would be for the testers to write the *Integration Test Plan* instead of the business analyst as originally planned, which would reduce cost as well as duration. Similarly, the same option could be used for **User Acceptance Testing**. Instead of the business analyst, additional users could write the *User Acceptance Plan*, but this will increase costs because users are billed to the project at a higher rate ($120/hour) than a business analyst ($80/hour). We could also use the same option for **Pilot Implementation** by increasing the number of users on the pilot run to further reduce duration. Let's implement all of these changes to **Requirements** to see how the schedule is affected. The changes are reflected in Figure B.8.

Notice that the schedule duration has come down drastically to 194.01 days from 277 days. For this project, we seem to have the maximum number of resources that could be

	Priority	Task Name	Cost	Work	Duration	Start	Finish	Predecessors	Resource Names
1	800	⊟ PM Software	$203,210.00	2,734 hrs	194.01 days	Mon 3/3/08	Fri 11/28/08		
2	1000	⊞ Weekly Team Meeting	$4,230.00	54 hrs	40.13 days	Mon 3/3/08	Mon 4/28/08		
12	1000	⊞ Weekly Status Meeting	$1,980.00	18 hrs	40.13 days	Tue 3/4/08	Tue 4/29/08		
22	700	⊞ Requirements	$9,560.00	113 hrs	14.13 days	Mon 4/28/08	Fri 5/16/08		
29	600	⊞ High Level Design	$8,760.00	113 hrs	14.13 days	Fri 5/16/08	Thu 6/5/08	22	
36	500	⊞ Planning Module	$16,600.00	316 hrs	39.5 days	Thu 6/5/08	Wed 7/30/08	29	
48	500	⊞ Schedule Module	$31,400.00	596 hrs	74.5 days	Thu 6/5/08	Wed 9/17/08	29	
60	500	⊞ Administration Module	$16,600.00	316 hrs	42.5 days	Thu 6/5/08	Mon 8/4/08	29	
72	400	⊟ Integration Testing	$22,320.00	432 hrs	14.53 days	Wed 9/17/08	Wed 10/8/08	36,48,60	
73	400	Integration Test Plan Preparation	$4,000.00	80 hrs	2 days	Wed 9/17/08	Fri 9/19/08		Tester[500%]
74	400	Integration Test Plan Review	$1,280.00	16 hrs	2 days	Fri 9/19/08	Tue 9/23/08	73	Business Analyst
75	400	Integration Test Plan Review Comments Incorpo	$400.00	8 hrs	0.2 days	Tue 9/23/08	Wed 9/24/08	74	Tester[500%]
76	400	Integration Testing	$12,000.00	240 hrs	6 days	Wed 9/24/08	Thu 10/2/08	75	Tester[500%]
77	400	Integration Test Bug Fixing	$4,000.00	80 hrs	3.33 days	Thu 10/2/08	Tue 10/7/08	76	Developer - 1,Develo
78	400	Integration Test Sign Off	$640.00	8 hrs	1 day	Tue 10/7/08	Wed 10/8/08	77	Business Analyst
79	300	⊟ User Acceptance Testing	$45,600.00	432 hrs	13.73 days	Wed 10/8/08	Tue 10/28/08	72	
80	300	User Acceptance Test Plan Preparation	$9,600.00	80 hrs	2 days	Wed 10/8/08	Fri 10/10/08		User[500%]
81	300	User Acceptance Test Plan Review	$1,280.00	16 hrs	2 days	Fri 10/10/08	Tue 10/14/08	80	Business Analyst
82	300	User Acceptance Test Plan Review Comments	$960.00	8 hrs	0.2 days	Tue 10/14/08	Tue 10/14/08	81	User[500%]
83	300	User Acceptance Testing	$28,800.00	240 hrs	6 days	Tue 10/14/08	Wed 10/22/08	82	User[500%]
84	300	User Acceptance Test Bug Fixing	$4,000.00	80 hrs	3.33 days	Wed 10/22/08	Mon 10/27/08	83	Developer - 1,Develo
85	300	User Acceptance Test Sign Off	$960.00	8 hrs	0.2 days	Mon 10/27/08	Tue 10/28/08	84	User[500%]
86	200	⊟ Pilot Implementation	$26,240.00	256 hrs	11.87 days	Tue 10/28/08	Thu 11/13/08	79	
87	200	Pilot Planning	$2,400.00	24 hrs	3 days	Tue 10/28/08	Fri 10/31/08		Project Manager
88	200	Pilot Deployment	$1,680.00	24 hrs	3 days	Fri 10/31/08	Wed 11/5/08	87	Technical Leader
89	200	Pilot Run	$19,200.00	160 hrs	4 days	Wed 11/5/08	Tue 11/11/08	88	User[500%]
90	200	Pilot Run Bug Fixing	$2,000.00	40 hrs	1.67 days	Tue 11/11/08	Wed 11/12/08	89	Developer - 1,Develo
91	200	Pilot Run Sign Off	$960.00	8 hrs	0.2 days	Wed 11/12/08	Thu 11/13/08	90	User[500%]
92	100	⊞ Production Rollout	$7,920.00	88 hrs	11 days	Thu 11/13/08	Fri 11/28/08	86	

Figure B.8. Testers and users added.

added because there is little opportunity to further reduce the number of days by adding more resources; doing so would not make sense.

Now let's see if the resources are optimally loaded over the execution period of the project by going to the **Resource Usage** tab wherein we can collapse the right-hand-side table to a monthly view (shown in Figure B.9). Notice that the project resources are not loaded completely—only the developers are loaded completely and for only a specific period (remember that we also have testers and users). We can leverage resources who are not loaded fully and use them for other projects and/or switch them between projects (e.g., the architect and business analyst). Note: Resources such as the project manager and technical leader should be carried. The assigned tasks for a project manager and technical leader might consume very little time, but these resources have many unscheduled activities. Planning for unscheduled tasks is very difficult; however, a blanket 8 hours of work can be planned for the project manager and the technical leader throughout the project to keep costs consistent in MPP. Although a project manager could be shared with another project, a technical leader needs to be available full time to give technical assistance to the developers.

Figure B.9 shows that some resources do not begin significant work on the project until late May, which is because we have not leveled the resources using the split option.

		Resource Name	Work	Details	Qtr 2, 2008				Qtr 3, 2008			Qtr 4, 2008	
	❻				Mar	Apr	May	Jun	Jul	Aug	Sep	Oct	Nov
1		⊞ Project Manager	74 hrs	Work	9h	9h	8h					24h	24h
2		⊞ Business Analyst	169 hrs	Work	5h	27h	73h				16h	24h	24h
3		⊞ Architect	17 hrs	Work	5h	4h	6h	2h					
4		⊞ Developer - 1	351.67 hrs	Work	5h	4h		125h	151h			53.33h	13.33h
5		⊞ Developer - 2	582.67 hrs	Work				125h	168h	168h	55h	53.33h	13.33h
6		⊞ Developer - 3	342.67 hrs	Work				117h	144h	15h		53.33h	13.33h
7		⊞ Technical Leader	313 hrs	Work	5h	4h	80h	64h	64h		48h	6.87h	41.13h
8		⊞ Tester	337 hrs	Work	5h	4h					285h	43h	
9		⊞ User	547 hrs	Work	4h	5h	9h	9h				336h	184h

Figure B.9. Initial resource loading.

		Resource Name	Work	Details	Qtr 2, 2008				Qtr 3, 2008			Qtr 4, 2008	
	❻				Mar	Apr	May	Jun	Jul	Aug	Sep	Oct	Nov
1		⊞ Project Manager	74 hrs	Work	17h	9h				34.93h	13.07h		
2		⊞ Business Analyst	169 hrs	Work	101h	4h			40h		24h		
3		⊞ Architect	17 hrs	Work	5h	12h							
4		⊞ Developer - 1	530.67 hrs	Work	5h	92h	173h	114h	26.67h	40h	80h		
5		⊞ Developer - 2	464.67 hrs	Work		94h	160h	44h	46.67h	40h	80h		
6		⊞ Developer - 3	521.67 hrs	Work		88h	167h	120h	26.67h	40h	80h		
7		⊞ Technical Leader	313 hrs	Work	54h	90h	30h	91h		24h	24h		
8		⊞ Tester	337 hrs	Work	5h	4h			328h				
9		⊞ User	547 hrs	Work	13h	14h			158.67h	345.33h	16h		

Figure B.10. Resource loading after adjustment.

Because we added **Weekly Team Meeting** as a recurring task with a priority of 1000, and we did not specify resource leveling to split the remaining work on the task, all weekly team meetings have been scheduled ahead of the remaining project tasks. This situation needs to be corrected by performing resource leveling using the split option. Using the split option will ensure that the work is divided to accommodate the weekly team meetings, but that work is not pushed out until all weekly team meetings have been completed.

Now look at the developers. In Figure B.9, we see that the developers need to be brought into the project in June 2008. Notice that Developer 1 is completely free in August 2008 and Developer 3 is relatively free in August 2008, but Developer 2 is completely loaded or partially loaded through September 2008. This situation provides us a definite opportunity to reduce duration further. Therefore, to try to finish earlier, we need to realign the work of Developer 2 so that the work can be done by all three resources. Let's see how this can be achieved and how it affects the schedule.

In Figure B.10, the resources are now optimally loaded. As stated earlier, all project managers have different views about resource optimization in their projects; however, optimization can often be improved depending on the situation and the project require-

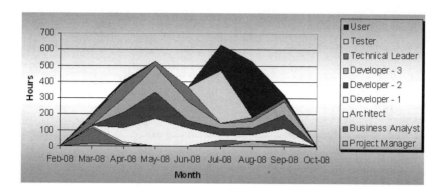

Figure B.11. Resource usage graph.

ments. Let's discuss how to bring resources with different skills into the project and how to release them from the project.

The graph in Figure B.11 illustrates when resources need to be brought into the project and how long the resources need to stay. This graph can be plotted using the data in Figure B.10.

Schedule approval. Now that the resources are loaded optimally and the schedule is optimized, the schedule can be presented to project stakeholders to obtain their concurrence on dates, duration, and cost of the project. Remember to include the costs associated with resources who are carried on the project even when they are not assigned work. Also remember to state the contingency buffer that is set aside for the project. Generally, a contingency of up to 10% is used; however, estimating the contingency needed based on identified risks for the project is ideal. For our example, we will use a 10% contingency buffer and add it to the schedule. Once approval is obtained from project stakeholders, baseline the project, communicate that you have done so to the stakeholders, and start the project.

Let's look at the project schedule with the 10% contingency added and the project baselined. Figure B.12 illustrates the view obtained when the table **Baseline** is applied. Use **View > Ta**b**le > More Tables > Baseline**. Our schedule is now baselined and ready to be tracked.

Now let's see how this baselined schedule is translated into the EVM report template and check out the performance measurement baseline. From our discussion, remember that we need to apply baseline effort or cost in the EVM report template.

First, we need to decide about the reporting period that we will use for EVM reporting. Because a status meeting is held every week, we will use the reporting period of weeks. Go into the **Task Usage** view and collapse/expand the right-hand-side table to reflect the

	Task Name	Baseline Dur.	Baseline Start	Baseline Finish	Baseline Work	Baseline Cost
1	⊟ **PM Software**	**149.63 days**	**Mon 3/3/08**	**Fri 9/26/08**	**2,974 hrs**	**$203,210.00**
2	⊞ **Weekly Team Meeting**	**40.13 days**	**Mon 3/3/08**	**Mon 4/28/08**	**54 hrs**	**$4,230.00**
12	⊞ **Weekly Status Meeting**	**40.13 days**	**Tue 3/4/08**	**Tue 4/29/08**	**18 hrs**	**$1,980.00**
22	⊞ **Requirements**	**14.5 days**	**Mon 3/3/08**	**Fri 3/21/08**	**113 hrs**	**$9,560.00**
29	⊞ **High Level Design**	**14.5 days**	**Fri 3/21/08**	**Fri 4/11/08**	**113 hrs**	**$8,760.00**
36	⊞ **Planning Module**	**40.75 days**	**Fri 4/11/08**	**Fri 6/6/08**	**316 hrs**	**$16,600.00**
48	⊞ **Schedule Module**	**59.38 days**	**Fri 4/11/08**	**Thu 7/3/08**	**596 hrs**	**$31,400.00**
64	⊞ **Administration Module**	**43.75 days**	**Fri 4/11/08**	**Wed 6/11/08**	**316 hrs**	**$16,600.00**
76	⊞ **Integration Testing**	**14.53 days**	**Thu 7/3/08**	**Thu 7/24/08**	**432 hrs**	**$22,320.00**
83	⊞ **User Acceptance Testing**	**13.73 days**	**Thu 7/24/08**	**Tue 8/12/08**	**432 hrs**	**$45,600.00**
90	⊞ **Pilot Implementation**	**11.87 days**	**Tue 8/12/08**	**Thu 8/28/08**	**256 hrs**	**$26,240.00**
96	⊞ **Production Rollout**	**11 days**	**Thu 8/28/08**	**Fri 9/12/08**	**88 hrs**	**$7,920.00**
102	Contingency Buffer	10 days	Fri 9/12/08	Fri 9/26/08	240 hrs	$12,000.00

Figure B.12. Baselined schedule.

	❶	Task Name	Work	Details	Mar '08				Apr '08				May
					2	9	16	23	30	6	13	20	27
1		⊟ **PM Software**	**2,974 hrs**	Base. Cost	$3,810.00	$3,810.00	$4,220.00	$3,420.00	$3,470.00	$4,780.00	$6,480.00	$6,510.00	$6,690.00
2	⟳	⊞ **Weekly Team Meet**	**54 hrs**	Base. Cost	$470.00	$470.00	$470.00	$470.00	$470.00	$470.00	$470.00	$470.00	$470.00
12	⟳	⊞ **Weekly Status Mee**	**18 hrs**	Base. Cost	$220.00	$220.00	$220.00	$220.00	$220.00	$220.00	$220.00	$220.00	$220.00
22		⊞ **Requirements**	**113 hrs**	Base. Cost	$3,120.00	$3,120.00	$3,320.00						
29		⊞ **High Level Design**	**113 hrs**	Base. Cost			$210.00	$2,730.00	$2,780.00	$3,040.00			
36		⊞ **Planning Module**	**316 hrs**	Base. Cost						$350.00	$2,070.00	$1,640.00	$2,110.00
48		⊞ **Schedule Module**	**596 hrs**	Base. Cost						$350.00	$2,000.00	$2,140.00	$2,130.00
64		⊞ **Administration Mo**	**316 hrs**	Base. Cost						$350.00	$1,720.00	$2,040.00	$1,760.00
76		⊞ **Integration Testing**	**432 hrs**	Base. Cost									
83		⊞ **User Acceptance T**	**432 hrs**	Base. Cost									
90		⊞ **Pilot Implementati**	**256 hrs**	Base. Cost									
96		⊞ **Production Rollout**	**88 hrs**	Base. Cost									
102		⊞ Contingency Buffer	240 hrs	Base. Cost									

Figure B.13. Baseline cost by week.

baseline cost in weeks; copy that data into the EVM report template. Now take a look at how baseline cost by week appears in Figure B.13.

In Figure B.13 notice that the highlighted row (the top level row) contains the baseline cost data for the project. Upload this data into the EVM report template, which will prepare the EVM report template for use. When this data is populated in the EVM report template, we will *not* get the desired S-curve for BAC (budget at completion) because we did not follow the 8- to 80-hour rule when preparing our schedule and we have many hard dependencies among major tasks. Let's reduce the hard dependencies by adding a few additional tasks—by splitting existing tasks—to further reduce the schedule. For example, we have planned to do **Integration Testing** activities after all of the modules are completed. Instead we can split **Integration Testing** to start that activity earlier, performing the **Integration Testing** activity separately for each module.

	ⓘ	Task Name	Work	Duration	Start	Finish	Details	Qtr 2, 2008				Qtr 3, 2008		
								Mar	Apr	May	Jun	Jul	Aug	Sep
1		⊟ PM Software	2,974 hrs	########	Mon 3/3/08	Tue 9/2/08	Base. Cost	$21,900.00	$25,260.00	$27,760.00	$32,280.00	$73,010.00	$20,730.00	$2,270.00
2	↻	⊞ Weekly Team Meet	54 hrs	40.13 days	Mon 3/3/08	Mon 4/28/08	Base. Cost	$2,350.00	$1,880.00					
12	↻	Weekly Status Meeting	18 hrs	40.13 days	Tue 3/4/08	Tue 4/29/08	Base. Cost	$880.00	$1,100.00					
22		⊞ Requirements	113 hrs	14.5 days	Mon 3/3/08	Fri 3/21/08	Base. Cost	$9,560.00						
29		⊞ High Level Design	113 hrs	14.5 days	Fri 3/21/08	Fri 4/11/08	Base. Cost	$3,430.00	$5,330.00					
36		⊞ Planning Module	316 hrs	42.63 days	Fri 4/11/08	Tue 6/10/08	Base. Cost		$5,310.00	$8,610.00	$2,680.00			
48		⊞ Schedule Module	596 hrs	57.5 days	Fri 4/11/08	Tue 7/1/08	Base. Cost		$5,820.00	$10,070.00	$15,260.00	$250.00		
64		⊞ Administration Mo	316 hrs	39.63 days	Fri 4/11/08	Thu 6/5/08	Base. Cost		$5,820.00	$9,080.00	$1,700.00			
76		⊞ Integration Testing	432 hrs	88.5 days	Mon 3/3/08	Thu 7/3/08	Base. Cost	$5,680.00	$0.00	$0.00	$12,640.00	$4,000.00		
85		⊞ User Acceptance T	432 hrs	10.4 days	Thu 7/3/08	Fri 7/18/08	Base. Cost					$45,600.00		
94		⊞ Pilot Implementatic	256 hrs	11.87 days	Fri 7/18/08	Mon 8/4/08	Base. Cost					$23,160.00	$3,080.00	
100		⊞ Production Rollout	88 hrs	11 days	Mon 8/4/08	Tue 8/19/08	Base. Cost						$7,920.00	
106		⊞ Contingency Buffer	240 hrs	10 days	Tue 8/19/08	Tue 9/2/08	Base. Cost						$9,730.00	$2,270.00

Figure B.14. Baseline cost by month.

One might argue, however, that integration testing should be done only after the entire coding process has been completed. To accommodate this argument, we can always have a separate window of time for that as well.

Now let's look at schedule baseline cost (**Base. Cost**) by month after modifications to the schedule have been made (shown in Figure B.14). Reporting periods will be in months in this example. Notice that **Base. Cost** by month continues to grow until it reaches a peak (July 2008); then **Base. Cost** comes down. This situation is ideal—it should be the expected result after a schedule is prepared. This situation also yields a proper S-curve. Because we are using months (instead of days), the S-curve will be smaller.

Let's now prepare the EVM report template for use and then look at the details. The options that we have to set up in the EVM report template are shown in Figure B.15. These values must be input for the initial setup. Notice that we initially entered the **Project End Date** as 26-Sep-08. This date needs to be changed to 2-Sep-08 because this is our new end date after we have applied the 8- to 80-hour rule and have tried to further minimize the schedule to yield a more appropriate schedule. Notice that the **Setup Status** appears as **Setup Not Done !!!.** We now need to set up the template for use by going into the **Configuration** tab. Click on the **Configuration** button and make the entries in the fields shown in Figure B.16

Notice in Figure B.16 that the **Monthly** option should be chosen. The **No. of Reporting Periods** are calculated automatically to 7 because we have defined that we want one additional reporting period. Because our project will go into the month of September by only 2 days, we still need to add an additional reporting period and report the status at that time. Now by clicking the **Setup** button we have set up the template successfully—the **Setup Status** field reflects **Setup Successful !!!.**

Now we are ready to start loading data into this template. Go into the EVM **Data Sheet** from the main menu and input the monthly data in Figure B.14. Once this data has

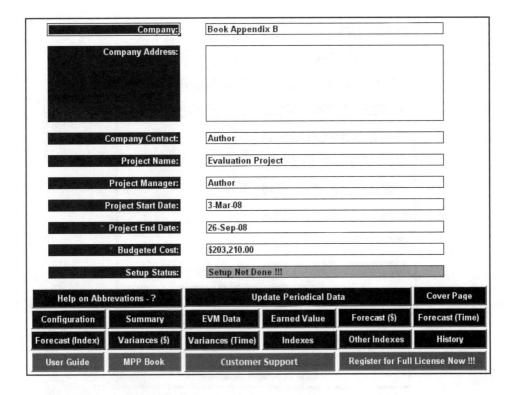

Figure B.15. EVM template—initial setup.

been input, the template is set up completely and we can start tracking the progress of our schedule. Let's now see how the data are populated in the template (shown in Figure B.17).

Once the data are loaded, we can look at a forecast ($) graph to see if we have an S-curve for BAC (the budget at completion). To see the forecast ($) graph, go to the main menu and click on the **Forecast ($)** button. The result is the curve shown in Figure B.18. Notice that the curve for BAC is a typical S-curve. EAC is tracked against this curve. We need to ensure that the EAC curve (currently at the bottom of the graph) is always below the BAC curve so that our project will progress smoothly.

Now that we have the schedule baselined and the EVM report template is set up, we are ready to execute the project—but we have forgotten to consider the vacation plans of resources and the holiday calendar. Both vacation time and holidays need to be incorporated into our plan. For this example, we will ignore this omission; however, always remember to include vacation and holiday time as part of your original schedule—before you present the schedule to project stakeholders.

Reporting Period :	Monthly
Project Start Date :	3-Mar-08
Project End Date :	2-Sep-08
No. of Reporting Periods :	7
Additional Reporting Periods :	1
Other Index 1 :	Risk Index
Other Index 2 :	CSI
Other Index 3 :	
EAC Calculation Method :	1
Setup Status :	Setup Successful !!!

Back to Main Page	Setup	Clear Setup

Additional Reporting Periods :	1

Add Additional Periods

Figure B.16. EVM template—configuration.

TRACKING

Our project has now gone on for 1 month. There have been no "hiccups" in the first month of execution. Everything is going smoothly.

So let's update the schedule with the status of the individual tasks. Once we complete updating, we will need to look at the status in the EVM template, which will tell us where we stand at the end of the project's first month. The updated schedule at the end of the first month is shown in Figure B.19.

Notice the updates to the schedule that have been made at the end of the first month. These updates have been made based on input that has been received from the project team about their effort on each of the activities. We can easily see that the project is 10% complete (**% Comp.**). From this view, it seems that most of the activities are on schedule and on budget.

Parameter	3-Apr-08	3-May-08	3-Jun-08	3-Jul-08
% Complete	0.00%	0.00%	0.00%	0.00%
Baseline Cost	$21,900.00	$25,260.00	$27,760.00	$32,280.00
EV	$0.00	$0.00	$0.00	$0.00
PV	$21,900.00	$47,160.00	$74,920.00	$107,200.00
AC	$0.00	$0.00	$0.00	$0.00
BAC	$21,900.00	$47,160.00	$74,920.00	$107,200.00
ETC	$0.00	$0.00	$0.00	$0.00
EAC	$0.00	$0.00	$0.00	$0.00
VAC	$21,900.00	$47,160.00	$74,920.00	$107,200.00
ET (Periods)	1	2	3	4
PT (Periods)	0.00	0.00	0.00	0.00
SPI ($)	$0.00	$0.00	$0.00	$0.00
CPI	1.00	1.00	1.00	1.00
TCPI	0.00	0.00	0.00	0.00
SV ($)	$0.00	$0.00	$0.00	$0.00
CV ($)	$0.00	$0.00	$0.00	$0.00
SV ($) %	0%	0%	0%	0%
CV ($) %	0%	0%	0%	0%
SV (Time)	0.00	0.00	0.00	0.00
SV (Time)%	0%	0%	0%	0%
SPI (Time)	0.00	0.00	0.00	0.00
Total Periods	0	0	0	0
EAC (Time)	0.00	0.00	0.00	0.00
TSPI (Time)	0.00	0.00	0.00	0.00
Risk Index	0.00	0.00	0.00	0.00
CSI	0.00	0.00	0.00	0.00
Not Defined	0.00	0.00	0.00	0.00

Figure B.17. EVM **Data Sheet**.

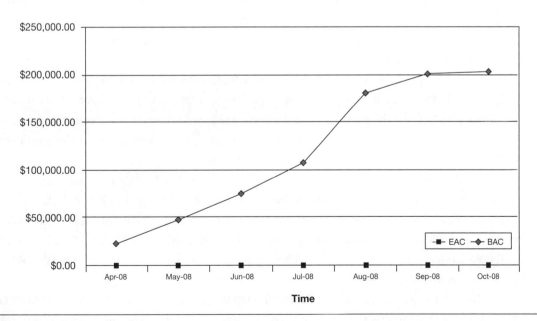

Figure B.18. Forecast ($)—S curve.

Let's see how the earned value (EV) looks from the schedule (shown in Figure B.20). This view is obtained when you apply the **Earned Value** table to a **Gantt Chart** view (or any other view). To get the **Earned Value** view, go to **View > Table > More Tables > Earned Value**. The **Earned Value** view shows the different earned value parameters and the associated values for each of these parameters.

Let's take a look at this in Figure B.20. Clearly, at the project level, the schedule variance (**SV**) is –$630 and cost variance (**CV**) is –$400. We can also see that the CV is due to the **Requirements** task, which has taken extra effort to complete, and that the SV is due to the **High Level Design** task not being up to speed on completion. We do not, however, know what the actual schedule variance will be in terms of months.

We can also see all of the earned value parameters in the EVM report template. From the view in Figure B.20, take the **BCWP** (**EV**) and **ACWP** (actual cost, **AC**) and the **% Comp**. and enter this into the EVM template, which gives the summary status of the project.

Let's look at how this data is shown in the EVM template (Figure B.21). Notice that we have the summary status of the project at the end of the first month. Clearly, the project is "yellow" for the schedule and cost parameters. (Note: Remember that in the EVM template, color coding comes up automatically. The color yellow represents a 0 to 10% variance. In Figure B.21 "yellow," or the performance measure, is out of control; but manageable is in light gray.) Reasons have been given for each "yellow" performance measure, along with the planned corrective action that is to be taken to correct each situation. Also given is the outcome of the performance measures. The outcome of each performance measure is recorded, reasons for the measure are provided, and planned corrective action is given on this sheet.

This view (and the tool) provides a clear insight into the amount of time that has not been used effectively in the project in terms of months (–0.05). We have a 0.05-month schedule variance, which tells us exactly how much we are behind schedule in terms of time. Note: A 0.05-month overrun at the beginning of a 6-month project is insignificant. We can easily make this time up by the end of the project.

Now let's see how the other EVM parameters look in the tool and discuss them. All of the EVM calculations are available in the EVM **Data Sheet** (shown in Figure B.22). These EVM calculations have been done automatically and then displayed. What does each measure indicate? The **% Complete**, **Baseline Cost**, **EV**, **AC**, and **ETC** are entered through the **Periodical Data** update screen. These inputs are provided by the tool; the rest of the data is automatically calculated.

Notice in Figure B.22 that **ET (Periods)** (elapsed time) is shown in decimal form rather than with linear numbers (1, 2, 3, etc.). This occurs because although theoretically 1 month

	Task Name	Baseline Start	Baseline Finish	Act. Start	Act. Finish	% Comp.	Act. Dur.	Rem. Dur.	Act. Cost	Work	Act. Work
1	☐ PM Software	Mon 3/3/08	Tue 9/2/08	Mon 3/3/08	NA	10%	13.52 days	119 days	$21,670.00	2,979 hrs	300 hrs
2	⊞ Weekly Team Meeting	Mon 3/3/08	Mon 4/28/08	Mon 3/3/08	NA	56%	22.29 days	17.83 days	$2,350.00	54 hrs	30 hrs
12	⊞ Weekly Status Meeting	Tue 3/4/08	Tue 4/29/08	Tue 3/4/08	NA	44%	17.83 days	22.29 days	$880.00	18 hrs	8 hrs
22	☐ Requirements	Mon 3/3/08	Fri 3/21/08	Mon 3/3/08	Mon 3/24/08	100%	15.13 days	0 days	$9,960.00	118 hrs	118 hrs
23	Prepare Requirements	Mon 3/3/08	Mon 3/17/08	Mon 3/3/08	Mon 3/17/08	100%	10.63 days	0 days	$6,800.00	85 hrs	85 hrs
24	Review Requirements	Mon 3/17/08	Tue 3/18/08	Tue 3/18/08	Wed 3/19/08	100%	1 day	0 days	$800.00	8 hrs	8 hrs
25	Incorporate Review comment	Tue 3/18/08	Wed 3/19/08	Wed 3/19/08	Thu 3/20/08	100%	1 day	0 days	$640.00	8 hrs	8 hrs
26	User Review	Wed 3/19/08	Thu 3/20/08	Thu 3/20/08	Fri 3/21/08	100%	1 day	0 days	$960.00	8 hrs	8 hrs
27	User Review Comments Inco	Thu 3/20/08	Fri 3/21/08	Fri 3/21/08	Mon 3/24/08	100%	1 day	0 days	$640.00	8 hrs	8 hrs
28	Final Approval	Fri 3/21/08	Fri 3/21/08	Mon 3/24/08	Mon 3/24/08	100%	0.13 days	0 days	$120.00	1 hr	1 hr
29	☐ High Level Design	Fri 3/21/08	Fri 4/11/08	Mon 3/24/08	NA	35%	5.13 days	9.37 days	$2,800.00	113 hrs	40 hrs
30	Prepare High Level Design	Fri 3/21/08	Fri 4/4/08	Mon 3/24/08	NA	50%	5 days	5 days	$2,800.00	80 hrs	40 hrs
31	Review HLD	Fri 4/4/08	Mon 4/7/08	NA	NA	0%	0 days	1 day	$0.00	8 hrs	0 hrs
32	Incorporate Review Commen	Tue 4/8/08	Tue 4/8/08	NA	NA	0%	0 days	1 day	$0.00	8 hrs	0 hrs
33	User Review	Wed 4/9/08	Wed 4/9/08	NA	NA	0%	0 days	1 day	$0.00	8 hrs	0 hrs
34	User Review Comments Inco	Thu 4/10/08	Thu 4/10/08	NA	NA	0%	0 days	1 day	$0.00	8 hrs	0 hrs
35	Final Approval	Fri 4/11/08	Fri 4/11/08	NA	NA	0%	0 days	0.13 days	$0.00	1 hr	0 hrs
36	⊞ Planning Module	Fri 4/11/08	Tue 6/10/08	NA	NA	0%	0 days	44.75 days	$0.00	316 hrs	0 hrs
48	⊞ Schedule Module	Fri 4/11/08	Tue 7/1/08	NA	NA	0%	0 days	57.5 days	$0.00	596 hrs	0 hrs
64	⊞ Administration Module	Fri 4/11/08	Thu 6/5/08	NA	NA	0%	0 days	39.63 days	$0.00	316 hrs	0 hrs
76	☐ Integration Testing	Mon 3/3/08	Thu 7/3/08	Mon 3/3/08	NA	29%	25.76 days	63.37 days	$5,680.00	432 hrs	104 hrs
77	Integration Test Plan Preparat	Mon 3/3/08	Wed 3/5/08	Mon 3/3/08	Wed 3/5/08	100%	2 days	0 days	$4,000.00	80 hrs	80 hrs
78	Integration Test Plan Review	Mon 3/17/08	Thu 3/20/08	Mon 3/17/08	Thu 3/20/08	100%	2 days	0 days	$1,280.00	16 hrs	16 hrs
79	Integration Test Plan Review	Thu 3/20/08	Thu 3/20/08	Thu 3/20/08	Thu 3/20/08	100%	0.2 days	0 days	$400.00	8 hrs	8 hrs
80	Integration Testing - Planning	Tue 6/10/08	Thu 6/12/08	NA	NA	0%	0 days	2 days	$0.00	80 hrs	0 hrs
81	Integration Testing - Schedule	Tue 7/1/08	Thu 7/3/08	NA	NA	0%	0 days	2 days	$0.00	80 hrs	0 hrs
82	Integration Testing - Administ	Thu 6/5/08	Mon 6/9/08	NA	NA	0%	0 days	2 days	$0.00	80 hrs	0 hrs
83	Integration Test Bug Fixing	Fri 6/20/08	Wed 6/25/08	NA	NA	0%	0 days	3.33 days	$0.00	80 hrs	0 hrs
84	Integration Test Sign Off	Wed 6/25/08	Thu 6/26/08	NA	NA	0%	0 days	1 day	$0.00	8 hrs	0 hrs
85	⊞ User Acceptance Testing	Thu 7/3/08	Fri 7/18/08	NA	NA	0%	0 days	10.4 days	$0.00	432 hrs	0 hrs

Figure B.19. Schedule updates for the first month.

has elapsed at the end of the first month, work on the project is not scheduled to be done in a linear manner. Instead project work follows an S-curve, which means that work on the project starts slowly, begins to peak during the middle, and then fades away. Therefore, the tool is configured to calculate **ET** based on the work scheduled on the project, which gives a more accurate schedule variance and a variance that will be closer to the traditional schedule variance based on cost. **SV (Time)** also shows the variance in units of time (months in this case).

Notice that we have a difference between **SV (Time) %** and **SV ($) %,** which ideally should be the same. The explanation for this difference is that **SV (Time)** is dependent on **% Complete**, whereas **SV ($) %** is dependent on **EV** and **PV**.

So what is the difference? In our project, **EV** is $21,270 and **PV** is $21,900 and the **% Complete** is 10% (from the MPP schedule). So **SV ($) %** is calculated as **SV** divided by **EV**, or 630 ÷ 21,270 = 0.0296 or 3%. However, **SV (Time) %** is calculated as **SV (Time)** divided by **PT**, or 0.05 ÷ 0.61 = 0.081 or 8%.

What is the "catch" here? The catch is that % complete as reported by MPP does not include decimals, but if we reverse calculate the % complete, which can be done by divid-

Task Name	BCWS	BCWP	ACWP	SV	CV	EAC	BAC	VAC
1 ⊟ PM Software	$21,900.00	$21,270.00	$21,670.00	($630.00)	($400.00)	$207,031.53	$203,210.00	($3,821.53)
2 ⊞ Weekly Team Meet	$2,350.00	$2,350.00	$2,350.00	$0.00	$0.00	$4,230.00	$4,230.00	$0.00
12 ⊞ Weekly Status Mee	$880.00	$880.00	$880.00	$0.00	$0.00	$1,980.00	$1,980.00	$0.00
22 ⊟ Requirements	$9,560.00	$9,560.00	$9,960.00	$0.00	($400.00)	$9,960.00	$9,560.00	($400.00)
23 Prepare Requirer	$6,400.00	$6,400.00	$6,800.00	$0.00	($400.00)	$6,800.00	$6,400.00	($400.00)
24 Review Requirer	$800.00	$800.00	$800.00	$0.00	$0.00	$800.00	$800.00	$0.00
25 Incorporate Revi	$640.00	$640.00	$640.00	$0.00	$0.00	$640.00	$640.00	$0.00
26 User Review	$960.00	$960.00	$960.00	$0.00	$0.00	$960.00	$960.00	$0.00
27 User Review Co	$640.00	$640.00	$640.00	$0.00	$0.00	$640.00	$640.00	$0.00
28 Final Approval	$120.00	$120.00	$120.00	$0.00	$0.00	$120.00	$120.00	$0.00
29 ⊟ High Level Design	$3,430.00	$2,800.00	$2,800.00	($630.00)	$0.00	$8,760.00	$8,760.00	$0.00
30 Prepare High Lev	$3,430.00	$2,800.00	$2,800.00	($630.00)	$0.00	$5,600.00	$5,600.00	$0.00
31 Review HLD	$0.00	$0.00	$0.00	$0.00	$0.00	$960.00	$960.00	$0.00
32 Incorporate Revi	$0.00	$0.00	$0.00	$0.00	$0.00	$560.00	$560.00	$0.00
33 User Review	$0.00	$0.00	$0.00	$0.00	$0.00	$960.00	$960.00	$0.00
34 User Review Co	$0.00	$0.00	$0.00	$0.00	$0.00	$560.00	$560.00	$0.00
35 Final Approval	$0.00	$0.00	$0.00	$0.00	$0.00	$120.00	$120.00	$0.00
36 ⊞ Planning Module	$0.00	$0.00	$0.00	$0.00	$0.00	$16,600.00	$16,600.00	$0.00
48 ⊞ Schedule Module	$0.00	$0.00	$0.00	$0.00	$0.00	$31,400.00	$31,400.00	$0.00
64 ⊞ Administration Mo	$0.00	$0.00	$0.00	$0.00	$0.00	$16,600.00	$16,600.00	$0.00
76 ⊟ Integration Testing	$5,680.00	$5,680.00	$5,680.00	$0.00	$0.00	$22,320.00	$22,320.00	$0.00
77 Integration Test F	$4,000.00	$4,000.00	$4,000.00	$0.00	$0.00	$4,000.00	$4,000.00	$0.00
78 Integration Test F	$1,280.00	$1,280.00	$1,280.00	$0.00	$0.00	$1,280.00	$1,280.00	$0.00
79 Integration Test F	$400.00	$400.00	$400.00	$0.00	$0.00	$400.00	$400.00	$0.00
80 Integration Testir	$0.00	$0.00	$0.00	$0.00	$0.00	$4,000.00	$4,000.00	$0.00
81 Integration Testir	$0.00	$0.00	$0.00	$0.00	$0.00	$4,000.00	$4,000.00	$0.00
82 Integration Testir	$0.00	$0.00	$0.00	$0.00	$0.00	$4,000.00	$4,000.00	$0.00
83 Integration Test E	$0.00	$0.00	$0.00	$0.00	$0.00	$4,000.00	$4,000.00	$0.00
84 Integration Test S	$0.00	$0.00	$0.00	$0.00	$0.00	$640.00	$640.00	$0.00
85 ⊞ User Acceptance T	$0.00	$0.00	$0.00	$0.00	$0.00	$45,600.00	$45,600.00	$0.00

Figure B.20. Earned value parameters.

ing **EV** by the total budget, we have 21,270 ÷ 203,210 = 0.1046 or 10.46%. However, we entered % complete in the tool as 10% and that accounts for the difference. If we now apply the same formula for calculating **SV (Time) %**, we will get a 3% variance, which is the same as the **SV ($) %**.

The % work complete is a more accurate measure, but even that measure will not yield exact results. Therefore, for calculation-oriented project managers, the author advises reverse calculating the % complete and then entering the result into the tool so that the correct **SV (Time) %** is obtained. Project managers who can tolerate minor variations can proceed with what is provided. This issue will not cause major problems—it will correct itself as the project progresses.

					Periodical Status Report		

		Project	Evaluation Project			Update Status Date	Create History
		Status Date	1-Apr-2008				
		Legend		Performance Measure is Out of Control. Needs Attention.		Clear History	
				Performance Measure is Out of Control. Manageable.			
				Performance Measure is In Control.			
				Help on Abbreviations			

S.No.	Week	Performance Parameter	Performance Measure	Value	Performance Measure Outcome	Reasons	Corrective Action
1	1-Apr-2008	Schedule/Time	BAC (t-wks)	6.09	Total budgeted time for the project is around 6 months.		
2	1-Apr-2008	Schedule/Time	SV(t-wks)	-0.05	There is a schedule variance for the project of 0.05 months.	There is a schedule variance due to HLD activity not being on time.

Expect to catch up by the next week. | To advise the resource to catch up with the work in the remaining time. |
| 3 | 1-Apr-2008 | Schedule/Time | SPI(t-wks) | 0.93 | The project team is currently utilizing the time available on the project at 93% efficiency compared to the optimal 100% efficiency levels. | | |
| 4 | 1-Apr-2008 | Schedule/Time | EAC(t-wks) | 6.56 | With the current schedule variance the project is estimated to be completed in 6.56 months compared to the 6.09 months originally budgeted. | | |
| 5 | 1-Apr-2008 | Cost/Effort | CV | -400.00 | There is a cost variance of $400. | Requirements preparation has taken more effort than estimated.

Expect to catch up in the remaining Requirements activities. | To push the resources working on Requirements to catch up with extra effort. |
6	1-Apr-2008	Cost/Effort	CPI	0.98	The project team is currently utilizing the money available on the project at 98% efficiency levels compared to the optimal 100% efficiency levels.		
7	1-Apr-2008	Cost/Effort	TCPI	1.00	The forecast efficiency level for the project team on cost is 100%		
8	1-Apr-2008	Cost/Effort	TSPI	1.01	The forecast efficiency level for the project team on time is 101%.		
9	1-Apr-2008	Effort	BAC	203,210.00	Total budgeted cost for the project is around $200,000		
10	1-Apr-2008	Cost/Effort	EAC(effort)	203,610.00	The project is estimated to cost $203,610 with the current variances.		
11	1-Apr-2008	Cost/Effort	VAC	-400.00	Variance at completion is at $400.		
12	1-Apr-2008	Schedule/Time	ETC	181,940.00	Estimate to complete the remaining work on the project is $181,940.		

Figure B.21. Summary status—first month.

Reminder: These two schedule variances are given because one provides the variance in terms of the schedule and the other provides the variance in terms of cost. The cost-based schedule variance will *nullify* itself at the end of the project, but the time-based schedule variance will not—it will show the actual schedule variance even at the end of the project.

Note: So far, we have not recorded any additional indexes, e.g., the risk index (RI) and the customer satisfaction index (CSI). We can do this and also report the status of these indexes using the tool. There is a provision for reporting trends on three additional indexes, but this is beyond the scope of EVM and is calculated separately.

We have now finished reporting for the first month and know that the project is slightly behind schedule and slightly over budget. We have identified the necessary corrective actions. During the course of the next month, we need to ensure that the corrective actions are implemented successfully so that variances are minimized. Two corrective actions have been identified for our project:

Parameter	1-Apr-08	1-May-08	1-Jun-08
% Complete	10.00%	0.00%	0.00%
Baseline Cost	$21,900.00	$25,260.00	$27,760.00
EV	$21,270.00	$21,270.00	$21,270.00
PV	$21,900.00	$47,160.00	$74,920.00
AC	$21,670.00	$21,670.00	$21,670.00
BAC	$21,900.00	$47,160.00	$74,920.00
ETC	$0.00	$0.00	$0.00
EAC	$22,300.00	$47,560.00	$75,320.00
VAC	-$400.00	-$400.00	-$400.00
ET (Periods)	0.66	1.41	2.25
PT (Periods)	0.61	0.00	0.00
SPI ($)	$0.97	$0.00	$0.00
CPI	0.98	0.98	0.98
TCPI	1.00	0.00	0.00
SV ($)	-$630.00	$0.00	$0.00
CV ($)	-$400.00	$0.00	$0.00
SV ($) %	-3%	0%	0%
CV ($) %	-2%	0%	0%
SV (Time)	-0.05	0.00	0.00
SV (Time)%	-8%	0%	0%
SPI (Time)	0.93	0.00	0.00
Total Periods	6.091603053	0	0
EAC (Time)	6.56	0.00	0.00
TSPI (Time)	1.01	0.00	0.00
Risk Index	0.00	0.00	0.00
CSI	0.00	0.00	0.00
Not Defined	0.00	0.00	0.00
	0.00	0.00	0.00
Back to Main Page	0.00	0.00	0.00

Figure B.22. EVM Data—first month.

- Finish the remaining **Requirements** tasks with a lower budget.

- Finish **High Level Design** activities on time.

With these corrective actions in mind, we have an informal chat with the resources who are working on these two tasks and let them know what is expected from them in order to get the project back on track. We also listen to their views about getting the project back on track. The resources agree to our plan and commit to completing their tasks as expected. So the corrective action plan is now implemented.

During the course of the next month, two special situations have occurred. First, the client requested a presentation of the proposed architecture of the project by the architect. The presentation is to take 2 days; however, the architect is not available for 2 days. Then there was a political emergency on April 9 in the country where the project is being executed. As a result, all commercial establishments had to be closed causing us to lose a workday. Let's see how these two situations can be incorporated into the MPP schedule and how the EVM template is impacted:

The architect. For the architect's new (additional) work time, we need to add another task (**Architect to Present Architecture to the Client**) to the schedule at the top level, assign a priority of 1000 to it, and assign the architect to the task. In this situation, we create a new task because the architect will be performing an additional task that was *not* in the original budget.

The political emergency. In this situation in which none of the resources are able to work for 1 day, we also add another task (**Political Emergency**) to the schedule, assign a priority of 1000 to it, and assign all of the resources to that task, but first we must identify all of the resources who have work planned for them on that particular day (April 9) and assign only those resources to the task.

In both of these situations, because we are carrying the costs of the resources on the project, we create additional tasks and assign resources to them. However, if the architect needs to work on another project, and this cost is *not* carried by the project for that period, we would simply make those days nonworking days in the architect's project calendar.

Let's look at how these situations are reflected in the schedule (shown in Figure B.23). Notice that two new tasks have been added at the beginning of the schedule (**Architect to Present Architecture to the Client** and **Political Emergency**). The architect has been assigned to the first new task because he is performing an additional task, but no resources have been added for the second new task; only a record has been made of this new task. We know from the schedule that on April 9, when the political emergency occurred that work has only been planned for the user who is in a different country; therefore, there is no impact to the schedule or costs. However, to keep track of events that occur during the project, we record these situations and store the information in the schedule.

If work had been planned, however, the scenario would be different. Having work planned is a perfect example of how the contingency buffer, which we have included in the schedule, could be used—*if* the contingency buffer has been built on risks which have been identified by the project manager. In our example, however, we added a 10% contingency buffer *irrespective* of the risks associated with the project. Note: A good practice is to identify the risks associated with a project and then determine the estimated impact of each of those risks in terms of hours and costs. Calculate the total hours and costs associated with these risks and include that sum as the contingency buffer.

	❶	% Complete	Priority	Task Name	Cost	Work	Duration	Start	Finish	Predecessors	Resource Names
1		10%	800	⊟ PM Software	$203,530.00	2,955 hrs	132.23 days	Mon 3/3/08	Wed 9/3/08		
2	📅	0%	1000	Architect to Present Architecture to the Client	$1,920.00	16 hrs	2 days	Mon 4/7/08	Tue 4/8/08		Architect
3	📅	0%	1000	Political Emergency	$0.00	0 hrs	1 day	Wed 4/9/08	Wed 4/9/08		
4	⟳	56%	1000	⊞ Weekly Team Meeting	$4,230.00	54 hrs	40.13 days	Mon 3/3/08	Mon 4/28/08		
14	⟳	44%	1000	⊞ Weekly Status Meeting	$1,980.00	18 hrs	40.13 days	Tue 3/4/08	Tue 4/29/08		
24	✓	100%	700	⊞ Requirements	$9,960.00	118 hrs	15.13 days	Mon 3/3/08	Mon 3/24/08		
31		35%	600	⊟ High Level Design	$8,760.00	113 hrs	16 days	Mon 3/24/08	Tue 4/15/08	24	
32		50%	600	Prepare High Level Design	$5,600.00	80 hrs	10 days	Mon 3/24/08	Mon 4/7/08		Technical Leader
33		0%	600	Review HLD	$960.00	8 hrs	1 day	Wed 4/9/08	Wed 4/9/08	32	Architect
34		0%	600	Incorporate Review Comments	$560.00	8 hrs	1 day	Thu 4/10/08	Thu 4/10/08	33	Technical Leader
35		0%	600	User Review	$960.00	8 hrs	1 day	Fri 4/11/08	Fri 4/11/08	34	User
36		0%	600	User Review Comments Incorporation	$560.00	8 hrs	1 day	Mon 4/14/08	Tue 4/15/08	35	Technical Leader
37		0%	600	Final Approval	$120.00	1 hr	0.13 days	Tue 4/15/08	Tue 4/15/08	36	User
38		0%	500	⊞ Planning Module	$16,600.00	316 hrs	42.5 days	Tue 4/15/08	Thu 6/12/08	31	
50		0%	480	⊞ Schedule Module	$31,400.00	596 hrs	57.38 days	Tue 4/15/08	Thu 7/3/08	31	
66		0%	500	⊞ Administration Module	$16,600.00	316 hrs	39.5 days	Tue 4/15/08	Mon 6/9/08	31	
78		29%	400	⊞ Integration Testing	$22,320.00	432 hrs	90.5 days	Mon 3/3/08	Mon 7/7/08		
87		0%	300	⊞ User Acceptance Testing	$45,600.00	432 hrs	10.4 days	Mon 7/7/08	Tue 7/22/08	78	
96		0%	200	⊞ Pilot Implementation	$26,240.00	256 hrs	11.87 days	Tue 7/22/08	Wed 8/6/08	87	
102		0%	100	⊞ Production Rollout	$7,920.00	88 hrs	11 days	Wed 8/6/08	Thu 8/21/08	96	
108		0%	80	Contingency Buffer	$10,000.00	200 hrs	8.33 days	Thu 8/21/08	Wed 9/3/08	102	Developer - 1 ,Deve

Figure B.23. WBS—second month.

Because of the inclusion of these two new tasks, overall we have incurred a delay of about a day and an extra cost of about $2,000 (for the architect to present to the client). We will now have to use the initially planned contingency buffer to reduce the duration and cost (see Figure B.23), but in this scenario we have set aside the contingency buffer only for the developers. Therefore, using the original contingency buffer will reduce the contingency for the developers by $2,000.

Notice in Figure B.23 that our schedule will now finish on 9/3/08. Costs are about the same as planned (see Figure B.18).

Costs: Remember from an earlier discussion that if particular resources move out of the project for a couple of days, and their costs are not assigned to the project, that we can go to the resource calendar for each resource and set these days up as nonworking days. By doing this, the project does not incur extra costs; instead the project schedule is delayed due to the nonavailability of these resources.

The two situations described above could be negotiated with the client. If the reasons for changing the schedule are justified, and the project stakeholders agree to do so, you can rebaseline the schedule and *not* adjust the contingency buffer. For the first situation, in which the architect has been requested to present the architecture of the proposed software to the client, this activity was not planned—it was requested by the client. Therefore, this schedule change stands a good chance of receiving approval from project stakeholders. If

	❶	% Compl	Priority	Task Name	Cost	Work	Duration	Start	Finish	Predecessors	Resource Names
1		10%	800	⊟ PM Software	$205,530.00	2,995 hrs	133.89 days	Mon 3/3/08	Thu 9/4/08		
2	▦	0%	1000	Architect to Present Architecture to the Client	$1,920.00	16 hrs	2 days	Mon 4/7/08	Tue 4/8/08		Architect
3	▦	0%	1000	Political Emergency	$0.00	0 hrs	1 day	Wed 4/9/08	Wed 4/9/08		
4	↻	56%	1000	⊞ Weekly Team Meeting	$4,230.00	54 hrs	40.13 days	Mon 3/3/08	Mon 4/28/08		
14	↻	44%	1000	⊞ Weekly Status Meeting	$1,980.00	18 hrs	40.13 days	Tue 3/4/08	Tue 4/29/08		
24	✓	100%	700	⊞ Requirements	$9,960.00	118 hrs	15.13 days	Mon 3/3/08	Mon 3/24/08		
31		35%	600	⊞ High Level Design	$8,760.00	113 hrs	16 days	Mon 3/24/08	Tue 4/15/08	24	
38		0%	500	⊞ Planning Module	$16,600.00	316 hrs	42.5 days	Tue 4/15/08	Thu 6/12/08	31	
50		0%	480	⊞ Schedule Module	$31,400.00	596 hrs	57.38 days	Tue 4/15/08	Thu 7/3/08	31	
66		0%	500	⊞ Administration Module	$16,600.00	316 hrs	39.5 days	Tue 4/15/08	Mon 6/9/08	31	
78		29%	400	⊞ Integration Testing	$22,320.00	432 hrs	90.5 days	Mon 3/3/08	Mon 7/7/08		
87		0%	300	⊞ User Acceptance Testing	$45,600.00	432 hrs	10.4 days	Mon 7/7/08	Tue 7/22/08	78	
96		0%	200	⊞ Pilot Implementation	$26,240.00	256 hrs	11.87 days	Tue 7/22/08	Wed 8/6/08	87	
102		0%	100	⊞ Production Rollout	$7,920.00	88 hrs	11 days	Wed 8/6/08	Thu 8/21/08	96	
108		0%	80	Contingency Buffer	$12,000.00	240 hrs	10 days	Thu 8/21/08	Thu 9/4/08	102	Developer - 1 ,Deve

Figure B.24. Rebaselined WBS.

agreement is received, an adjustment does not need to made to the contingency buffer; instead this additional activity is added and the schedule is simply rebaselined with only the new task and the tasks which are not yet completed.

Let's assume that the additional task for the architect has been approved by the client and other project stakeholders. Notice how the rebaselining is reflected in the schedule (shown in Figure B.24). We now have a rebaselined WBS with the total budget increasing by about $2,000 to $205,530 (shown by increasing the Contingency Buffer back to $12,000). Now that the schedule is rebaselined, we need to incorporate the rebaselined cost into the EVM template so that the template can calculate the variances correctly.

To incorporate the rebaselined cost into the EVM template, we need to know what the differences are and try and incorporate them into the EVM template. Let's look at how baseline cost is reflected in the **Task Usage** tab (shown in Figure B.25). Notice that baseline costs have changed from the costs originally shown in Figure B.14. These changes are basically because we added additional activities, received approval for adding them, and rebaselined the schedule. Also notice that the **Base. Cost** for the month of March has *not* changed because we rebaselined *only* the activities that are yet to start—only these activities will be changed because of the addition of activities.

Important: Ensure that already-completed tasks remain intact by rebaselining *only* a selected set of tasks. Rebaselining a selected set of tasks is done by expanding the WBS completely and then selecting the tasks which have a value of 0% complete next to them. In certain situations, however, some tasks that are partially complete will have to be selected as well, e.g., when in-progress tasks are also involved in a change either directly or

	❶	Task Name		Work	Duration	Start	Finish	Details	Mar	Qtr 2, 2008 Apr	May	Jun	Qtr 3, 2008 Jul	Aug	Sep
1		⊟ PM Software		2,995 hrs	133.89 days	Mon 3/3/08	Thu 9/4/08	Base. Cost	$21,900.00	$24,480.00	$27,080.00	$34,840.00	$64,230.00	$27,930.00	$4,670.00
2	☷	⊞ Architect to Present A		16 hrs	2 days	Mon 4/7/08	Tue 4/8/08	Base. Cost		$1,920.00					
3	☷	Political Emergency		0 hrs	1 day	Wed 4/9/08	Wed 4/9/08	Base. Cost		$0.00					
4	↻	⊞ Weekly Team Meet		54 hrs	40.13 days	Mon 3/3/08	Mon 4/28/08	Base. Cost	$2,350.00	$1,880.00					
14	↻	⊞ Weekly Status Mee		18 hrs	40.13 days	Tue 3/4/08	Tue 4/29/08	Base. Cost	$880.00	$1,100.00					
24	✓	⊞ Requirements		118 hrs	15.13 days	Mon 3/3/08	Mon 3/24/08	Base. Cost	$9,560.00						
31		⊞ High Level Design		113 hrs	16 days	Mon 3/24/08	Tue 4/15/08	Base. Cost	$3,430.00	$5,330.00					
38		⊞ Planning Module		316 hrs	42.5 days	Tue 4/15/08	Thu 6/12/08	Base. Cost		$4,410.00	$8,960.00	$3,230.00			
50		⊞ Schedule Module		596 hrs	57.38 days	Tue 4/15/08	Thu 7/3/08	Base. Cost		$4,980.00	$9,160.00	$16,190.00	$1,070.00		
66		⊞ Administration Mo		316 hrs	39.5 days	Tue 4/15/08	Mon 6/9/08	Base. Cost		$4,860.00	$8,960.00	$2,780.00			
78		⊞ Integration Testing		432 hrs	90.5 days	Mon 3/3/08	Mon 7/7/08	Base. Cost	$5,680.00	$0.00	$0.00	$12,640.00	$4,000.00		
87		⊞ User Acceptance T		432 hrs	10.4 days	Mon 7/7/08	Tue 7/22/08	Base. Cost					$45,600.00		
96		⊞ Pilot Implementatic		256 hrs	11.87 days	Tue 7/22/08	Wed 8/6/08	Base. Cost					$13,560.00	$12,680.00	
102		⊞ Production Rollout		88 hrs	11 days	Wed 8/6/08	Thu 8/21/08	Base. Cost						$7,920.00	
108		⊞ Contingency Buffer		240 hrs	10 days	Thu 8/21/08	Thu 9/4/08	Base. Cost						$7,330.00	$4,670.00

Figure B.25. Rebaselined costs.

indirectly. Suppose the architect is already working on a task and that task is pushed out due to the addition of a new activity; then the architect's current task would have to rebaselined as well. In this scenario, however, if the task already has a schedule or cost variance, that variance will be nullified due to the rebaselining.

Let's look at how the rebaselined costs are reflected in the EVM template (shown in Figure B.26). Compare Figure B.26 with Figure B.22. Notice in Figure B.26 that the **Baseline Cost** field has been updated with the new values, which is very important; this update will now drive the calculation of the EVM performance measures. Also notice with this rebaselined schedule that the end date of the project has increased—in terms of months, the increase is 0.06 months (2 days ÷ 30 days for 1 month). Originally, the total number of months for the project was at 6.09, which has now increased to 6.15 months (6.09 + 0.06 = 6.15). To allow this increase in the schedule, one additional period needs to be added in the EVM template with 0.06 as the period value. So go into the configuration screen of the EVM template and add an additional period with a period value of 0.06. Remember: The template does not allow you to change the original project end date because all calculations are derived from that date.

Various project execution scenarios have been presented and we have discussed how to handle these scenarios in MPP and the EVM template. A few months have passed. Let's look at a few charts to see what the project status looks like now. These are charts in the EVM template that depict status information about the project. These charts can be used to interpret information and to identify areas that need to be addressed to keep the project on track from the perspective of schedule and cost.

Parameter	1-Apr-08	1-May-08	1-Jun-08	1-Jul-08	1-Aug-08
% Complete	10.00%	0.00%	0.00%	0.00%	0.00%
Baseline Cost	$21,900.00	$24,480.00	$27,080.00	$34,840.00	$64,230.00
EV	$21,270.00	$21,270.00	$21,270.00	$21,270.00	$21,270.00
PV	$21,900.00	$46,380.00	$73,460.00	$108,300.00	$172,530.00
AC	$21,670.00	$21,670.00	$21,670.00	$21,670.00	$21,670.00
BAC	$21,900.00	$46,380.00	$73,460.00	$108,300.00	$172,530.00
ETC	$0.00	$0.00	$0.00	$0.00	$0.00
EAC	$22,300.00	$46,780.00	$73,860.00	$108,700.00	$172,930.00
VAC	-$400.00	-$400.00	-$400.00	-$400.00	-$400.00
ET (Periods)	0.66	1.39	2.20	3.25	5.17
PT (Periods)	0.62	0.00	0.00	0.00	0.00
SPI ($)	$0.97	$0.00	$0.00	$0.00	$0.00
CPI	0.98	0.98	0.98	0.98	0.98
TCPI	1.00	0.00	0.00	0.00	0.00
SV ($)	-$630.00	$0.00	$0.00	$0.00	$0.00
CV ($)	-$400.00	$0.00	$0.00	$0.00	$0.00
SV ($) %	-3%	0%	0%	0%	0%
CV ($) %	-2%	0%	0%	0%	0%
SV (Time)	-0.04	0.00	0.00	0.00	0.00
SV (Time)%	-7%	0%	0%	0%	0%
SPI (Time)	0.94	0.00	0.00	0.00	0.00
Total Periods	6.091603053	0	0	0	0
EAC (Time)	6.56	0.00	0.00	0.00	0.00
TSPI (Time)	1.01	0.00	0.00	0.00	0.00
Risk Index	0.00	0.00	0.00	0.00	0.00
CSI	0.00	0.00	0.00	0.00	0.00
Not Defined	0.00	0.00	0.00	0.00	0.00
	0.00	0.00	0.00	0.00	0.00
Back to Main Page	0.00	0.00	0.00	0.00	0.00

Figure B.26. Rebaselined EVM data.

First look at the earned value graph in Figure B.27. Clearly three sets of data are plotted over time (earned value, planned value, and actual cost or EV, PV, and AC). Notice that all of these three values are close to each other for the first 3 months, which means our project is on target at the end of 3 months.

Now look at the forecast graph in Figure B.28. The lines on this graph clearly show that the BAC and EAC data are very close to each other. Again, this is a perfect scenario wherein we are as close as possible to the budget. Note: Because we are using an example, achieving this situation appears easy. In actual project execution, however, this outcome is generally *not* the case. Projects are bound to have positive and/or negative variances. As a result, the BAC and EAC lines will be apart by some distance. The gap between these two values indicates VAC (variance at completion).

Next look at Figure B.29 which shows the variances that have existed over the course of the last 3 months. Notice that the variances are on the negative side in part of the first month. From there on, variances move to the positive side. Cost remains on the positive side, which is a good situation, but notice that the schedule returns to the negative side at

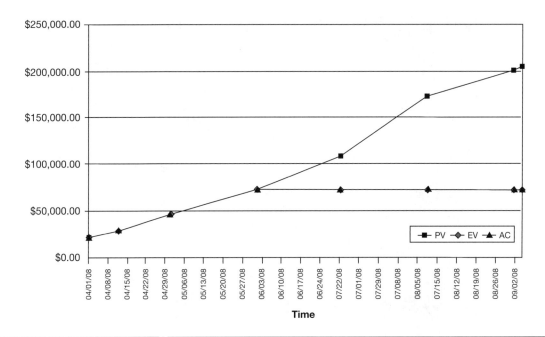

Figure B.27. Earned value ($) graph.

the end of the third month. This situation indicates we must monitor the schedule and try to bring it back to the positive side by evaluating different situations and working toward getting the schedule back on track. A variance graph is typically used to check on the trends of variances—particularly to optimize variances that benefit the project.

Now look at the forecast index graph shown in Figure B.30. This graph shows a forecast of the performance efficiency that will be needed by the project team for the remainder of the project. Note in our scenario that after 3 months that performance efficiency is slightly below the 100% level. Therefore, nothing special needs to be done, but we must ensure that the numbers continue to stay as close to 1 as possible.

We have now seen how some of the charts in the EVM template present information about the project's status. We have also discussed how this information can be interpreted to keep costs and the schedule for the project on track. Now let's see how the project's status looks at the end of the project.

FINISHING

Remember from our earlier discussion that at the end of the project we have a slight schedule variance, but the project is under budget. This situation is shown in the EVM template

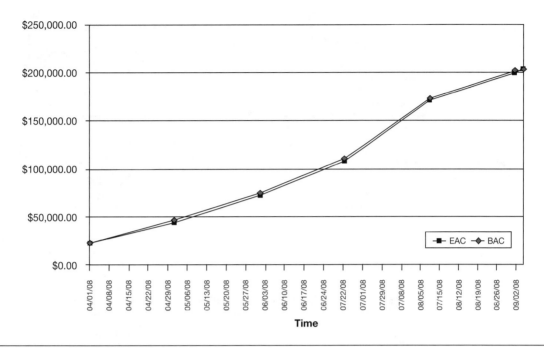

Figure B.28. Forecast ($) graph.

in Figure B.31. At the end of the project, the final data clearly show that there is a positive cost variance ($12,240) and a negative schedule variance (0.17). Notice that the schedule variance calculated using cost, **SV ($)**, is $0. This is because the time factor is used in calculating schedule variance, not a cost ($) value. Also notice in the time factor row, **SV (Time)**, that a schedule variance of 0.17 months occurred in the project because some activities were delayed due to a lack of availability of key project personnel.

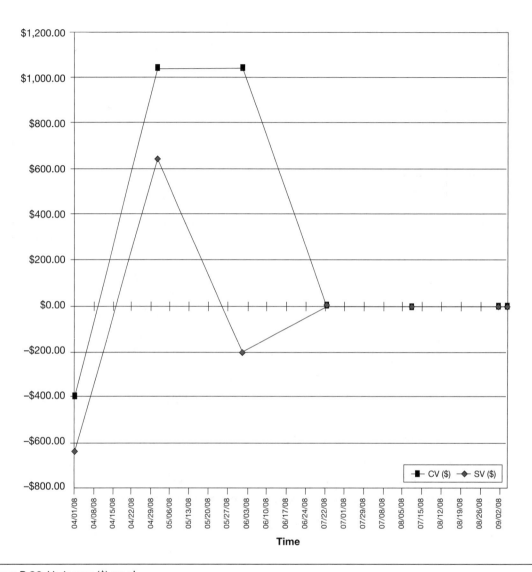

Figure B.29. Variances ($) graph.

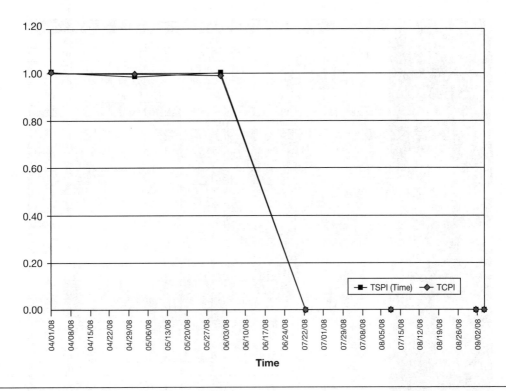

Figure B.30. Forecast index (time) graph.

Parameter	1-Apr-08	1-May-08	4-Sep-08	6-Sep-08	10-Sep-08
% Complete	10.00%	23.30%	93.21%	93.21%	100.00%
Baseline Cost	$21,900.00	$24,480.00	$2,000.00	$2,670.00	$0.00
EV	$21,270.00	$47,030.00	$205,130.00	$205,130.00	$205,130.00
PV	$21,900.00	$46,380.00	$202,460.00	$205,130.00	$205,130.00
AC	$21,670.00	$45,990.00	$192,890.00	$192,890.00	$192,890.00
BAC	$21,900.00	$46,380.00	$202,460.00	$205,130.00	$205,130.00
ETC	$0.00	$0.00	$0.00	$0.00	$0.00
EAC	$22,300.00	$45,340.00	$190,220.00	$192,890.00	$192,890.00
VAC	-$400.00	$1,040.00	$12,240.00	$12,240.00	$12,240.00
ET (Periods)	0.68	1.44	6.27	6.36	6.36
PT (Periods)	0.62	1.44	5.76	5.76	6.18
SPI ($)	$0.97	$1.01	$1.01	$1.00	$1.00
CPI	0.98	1.02	1.06	1.06	1.06
TCPI	1.00	0.99	0.00	0.00	0.00
SV ($)	-$630.00	$650.00	$2,670.00	$0.00	$0.00
CV ($)	-$400.00	$1,040.00	$12,240.00	$12,240.00	$12,240.00
SV ($) %	-3%	1%	1%	0%	0%
CV ($) %	-2%	2%	6%	6%	6%
SV (Time)	-0.06	0.00	-0.51	-0.59	-0.17
SV (Time)%	-10%	0%	-9%	-10%	-3%
SPI (Time)	0.91	1.00	0.92	0.91	0.97
Total Periods	6.13740458	6.13740458	6.13740458	6.13740458	6.13740458
EAC (Time)	6.98	6.34	6.92	7.01	6.54
TSPI (Time)	1.01	1.00	-2.73	-1.70	0.21
Risk Index	0.00	0.00	0.00	0.00	0.00
CSI	0.00	0.00	0.00	0.00	0.00
Not Defined	0.00	0.00	0.00	0.00	0.00
	0.00	0.00	0.09	0.05	0.17
Back to Main Page	0.00	0.00	3.00	2.09	4.71

Figure B.31. EVM data—project end.

APPENDIX C:
EVM TEMPLATE QUICK GUIDE

INTRODUCTION

The purpose of this appendix is to provide readers with a quick reference which may be used after reading the text. The appendix briefly covers the five key processes of the software that is supplied with this book. The appendix also indicates which chapters contain in-depth coverage of each process. The five key processes are as follows:

- Steps for setup of the EVM report template (see Chapter 6)
- Steps for setup of MPP prerequisites (see Chapters 2 and 5)
- Steps for EVM **Data Sheet** update (see Chapters 6 and 7)
- Steps for periodic updating of the EVM report template (see Chapter 7)
- Steps for periodic status/progress review (see Chapters 7 and 8)

Note: A free downloadable *EVM Report Template User Manual* is available from the Web Added Value™ Download Resource Center at www.jrosspub.com.

STEPS FOR SETUP OF THE EVM REPORT TEMPLATE

Project Details

1. Enter the project **Start Date** and **End Date**.

2. Enter the total **Budgeted Cost** of the project.

Configuration

1. Choose the **Reporting Period**. Options are **Weekly, Fortnightly, Monthly**, and **Bi-Monthly**.

2. Enter the number of **Additional Reporting Periods** needed over and above the reporting periods calculated.

3. Enter **Other Index 1** for tracking the first additional index that you might be using.

4. Enter **Other Index 2** for tracking the second additional index that you might be using.

5. Enter **Other Index 3** for tracking any other index that you might be using.

6. Choose the **EAC Calculation Method**. The options are **1**, variances are typical; **2,** past estimating assumptions are not valid; and **3**, variances will be present in the future.

7. Click the **Setup** button to set up the EVM report template.

8. You can choose to **Undo Setup** by clicking the **Clear Setup** button. Excel will give a prompt for deleting the sheets. *Important:* You **MUST** choose the option **Delete** on *all* of the prompts. Warning: Failing to choose **Delete** may corrupt sheets which are not deleted **beyond repair**.

MICROSOFT® OFFICE PROJECT PREREQUISITES AND RECOMMENDATIONS

There are two *mandatory* prerequisites for correct operation of the EVM template tool. Additionally, four *optional* prerequisites are recommended for improved utilization of the tool:

Mandatory Prerequisites

As part of MPP development, do the following:

1. Prepare a clear WBS (work breakdown structure) with the top-level activity being the *project* and the second-level activities being *phases* of the project (or some other type of task as required by the project). The WBS should appear as follows:

XYZ Project
    Requirements
        Requirements gathering
        Requirements review
        Requirements approval
    Design
        Coding
        Testing

2. Track the schedule using the **Duration** column. Track effort using the **Work** column.

Optional Recommended Prerequisites

Use of the following actions is recommended. Using these options should provide improved utilization of the tool:

1. MPP should be set up to have a default task type as **Fixed Work**. In the menu, use the **Tools** menu and the **Options** menu to select this setting.

2. Resources used on the project should be assigned standard and overtime rates as **1** if you want to track hours instead of cost. If you have the actual cost (**Act. Cost**) of resources, then you can apply the hourly rate of the resources. This can be done in the **Resource Sheet** of MPP.

3. When sequencing tasks, the *priority* of the tasks should be used rather than the *dependencies* of the tasks with **Predecessors/Successors**. Using **Predecessors/ Successors** is not recommended because you will spend far too much time adjusting the plan if there are substantial ongoing changes.

4. Resources should be leveled using the **Resource Leveling** feature in MPP. For details on resource leveling refer to MPP **Help**. Note: If resource leveling is not performed, you will not get an S-curve for BAC (budget at completion).

THE EVM DATA SHEET

1. Update the **PV** and the **BAC** rows with the data from the **Cumulative Baseline Cost** from MPP.
   a. Go to the **Task Usage Sheet** in MPP.
   b. In the **Task Usage Sheet**, click on the top-level task which represents the project (see the WBS example previously shown in *Mandatory Prerequisites*).
   c. On the right hand side of this sheet, right click and then select **Baseline Cost** and unselect all other items.
   d. Expand/collapse the work periods using the +/- magnifying glass icons to suit your project.
   e. Copy the values until the end of the project and paste them into column **C5** of the **EVM Data Sheet**.

STEPS FOR PERIODIC UPDATING OF THE EVM REPORT TEMPLATE

Data Entry

1. Enter the **Reporting Period Date**.

2. Ensure that the date is correct and available in the EVM report template in the **Period Availability** field.

3. Enter **% Complete** for the period from MPP.

4. Enter **Earned Value (BCWP)** from MPP.

5. Enter **Actual Cost (Act. Cost) (ACWP)** from MPP.

6. Enter **Estimate to Complete (ETC)** if you have chosen the **EAC Calculation Method** as **2**.

7. Choose the **EAC Calculation Method**.

8. Click on **Update Period Data** to update the periodical data.

STEPS FOR PERIODIC STATUS/PROGRESS REVIEW

Summary

1. Enter the project status date. **Status Date** should *only* be one of the planned reporting period dates. You cannot enter any other date.

2. Click on the **Update Status Date** button to get details for the status date.

3. Enter a description of the outcome of each performance measure in the **Performance Measure Outcome** column.

4. Enter the *reasons* for the outcome in the **Performance Measure Outcome** column.

5. Enter the *corrective actions* to be taken, if required, in the **Performance Measure Outcome** column.

6. You can save this periodical data to **History** by clicking on the **Create History** button.

7. You can choose to clear/wipe out the history record by clicking the **Clear History** button.

GLOSSARY

activities. Tasks that need to be performed to complete deliverables in a project. Generally, activities are tasks that are at the lowest level; beyond this level a task cannot be further split into multiple tasks. The 8- to 80-hour rule is used for creating activities. The 8- to 80-hour rule states that the most effective activity breakdown is when the effort for completing an activity (activities) is between 8 hours and 80 hours. (Note: In this book, activities are also referred to as tasks and lowest-level tasks.)

actual cost. The actual cost that has been spent on a particular task; also AC. Actual cost is generally derived by multiplying the number of actual hours that have been spent on a task by the resource rate. Actual cost can be greater than or less than planned value and earned value. The difference between earned value and actual cost will give cost variance. Actual cost is the basic element of the earned value management (EVM) technique.

actual cost of work performed (ACWP). The actual cost of work performed; an earlier term now known as actual cost (AC). (Note: Microsoft® Office Project used the term ACWP prior to the 2003 version. Older EVM books and other reference materials continue to use the term ACWP.)

actual tickets. The actual number of tickets that have been resolved in EVM for production support; the equivalent of actual cost in the customary project-based EVM technique. Actual tickets are calculated based on the hours that have been spent on each ticket and the SLA (service level agreement) for each ticket. Actual tickets are calculated for all performance parameters (e.g., initial response, restoration, and resolution).

actual time. The time version of actual cost wherein actual calendar time spent (passed) on a task or project is recorded; generally the calendar duration of a task from its start.

actual work. The effort version of actual cost wherein the actual effort spent on a task or project is recorded. Actual work multiplied by resource rate(s) provides actual cost. Actual work is generally used when resource cost details are not available and a $1/hour rate has been chosen for all resources. In general, actual work will be used to track progress of a schedule because this information is readily available for resources as a day-end status report.

assignments. The resource assignments to tasks (in this book). Resource assignments must be made to tasks to ensure that work (effort) and duration are calculated properly. Multiple resources can be assigned to the same task. In a project, resources can also be assigned to tasks at lower utilization levels than their total available utilization levels. When multiple resources are assigned or resources are assigned at lower levels than 100%, then duration should be adjusted accordingly.

baseline cost. The total budgeted cost for a task or an entire project. When a schedule is baselined—after approval has been received from the stakeholders of the project and cost has been arrived at by multiplying the effort in hours by the resource rates—the total cost will be the baseline cost. Baseline cost is fixed; it is changed only with approval from all project stakeholders. Baseline cost is an important element in that it is used to derive other performance measures in the EVM technique.

baseline work. The effort version of baseline cost; the total budgeted effort (generally in hours) for a particular task or an entire project. **Baseline work** is a Microsoft® Office Project field. Changes to baseline cost are actually affected by the **Baseline work** field because the value in the **Baseline work** field multiplied by the resource rate gives baseline cost. If resource rates change, baseline cost will automatically be adjusted based on the value in the **Baseline work** field.

bottom-up estimation. An estimation technique considered to be effective and accurate. The bottom-up estimation technique requires that the WBS (the work breakdown structure) be broken down to as granular a level as possible and that experts in the area assign estimates to the lowest-level tasks and roll up the estimates to an overall project level. Because estimation is done at a granular level and tasks are estimated and rolled up by experts, the chances of making an inaccurate estimate are much less. Although bottom-up estimating is the most accurate form of estimation, the technique is a time-consuming process.

budget at completion. Commonly known as the total budget allocated to a project; also BAC. BAC is generally obtained by rolling up baseline costs from the lowest task level to project level. Cumulative BAC is generally plotted over time and yields the well-known S-curve. BAC is generally compared with EAC (estimate at completion) to derive VAC (variance at completion). EAC is also accumulated and plotted over time in a line graph which yields an S-curve. The difference between the BAC and EAC S-curves at the end of a project is VAC (variance at completion).

budget at completion (time). Commonly known as the total budgeted time on a project; also BAC_t. BAC_t is the time version of BAC. In BAC_t, time or duration or the calendar time of a project is considered instead of costs. BAC_t generally represents the number of reporting periods in a project. Reporting periods could be weeks, months, etc., depending on project size.

budgeted cost for work performed (BCWP). Commonly known as earned value (EV). As the term suggests, BCWP represents the budgeted cost of work already completed at any given point in a project. BCWP is basically calculated as percent (%) complete multiplied by baseline cost. BCWP is the term used in Microsoft® Office Project 2003. See earned value for more details.

budgeted cost of work scheduled (BCWS). Commonly known as planned value (PV). As the term suggests, BCWS represents the budgeted cost of work scheduled at any given point in a project. The sum of scheduled work to a given date is the BCWS value. BCWS is the term used in Microsoft® Office Project 2003. See planned value for more details.

call tracking tool. A tool which allows tracking of production support calls or tickets. Available call tracking tools in the software industry include JIRA and Digital Workflow. Other industries may have their own tool sets. Call tracking tools allow users to log problems that are occurring. Built-in or customized workflow software then tracks these problems to closure and goes through the various stages and approvals required.

COCOMO. A popular estimation model (**co**nstructive **co**st **mo**del). Internet resources are available for details on COCOMO.

corrective action. An action performed to correct a problem situation which is occurring in a project; also a measure to correct a problem completely or to minimize the impact of the problem. Generally, corrective action is taken *after* a problem has occurred. Another aspect of a corrective action is to ensure that the problem *will not* recur (preventive). Therefore, corrective action addresses two things—to correct/minimize a problem which is currently occurring and to stop this problem from recurring going forward.

cost management. Judicial supervision of the costs of a project; involves keeping a record of costs incurred for a project; also involves keeping project costs from exceeding budgeted costs; a crucial aspect of project management. Projects can fail or exceed budget because of improper cost management. Different methods of managing project costs are available—the most commonly used and most effective method is the EVM technique.

cost overrun. A situation in which budgeted costs for a project have been exceeded; also the amount by which the budget has been exceeded. Cost overrun can be calculated at any time during a project or at the end of the project. A cost overrun that is identified during the course of a project can generally be reversed by taking an appropriate corrective action. Cost overruns that are calculated after a project ends cannot be corrected; at this stage, the project is final and irreversibly over budget.

cost performance indicator (CPI). Cost performance represented as an index which has a value of about 1, with 1 being the preferred value for the indicator. The cost performance indicator is calculated by dividing earned value for a project by actual project costs incurred. A value of 1 indicates that performance of project costs (the cost factor) is near ideal and that the project is on budget. A value above 1 indicates that performance of budgeted costs is proceeding smoothly and that the project is therefore under budget. A value below 1 indicates that performance of project costs is poor and that a project is over budget.

cost variance (CV). The variance between earned value and actual cost; can be negative or positive. Cost variance indicates the amount of a project's budget which has been overspent or underspent as of a given date or at the end of a project. A negative cost variance indicates that a project is over budget. A positive cost variance indicates that a project is under budget. A cost variance of zero indicates that a project is on budget (a rare situation in most projects).

cost variance %. Variance as a percentage of budgeted costs; the same as cost variance; can have negative or positive values. Cost variance % indicates how much a project is over or under budget as compared to the total budget.

cost/hr. To a company, the cost per hour of a resource to execute a project; different from the price of a resource which is charged to the company's client. In human resources, cost/hr generally factors in the salaries and the overhead costs of resources. In the case of machinery, cost/hr factors in the apportioned cost of the machinery and the running costs of the machinery.

Ctrl key. The control key on a computer keyboard. **Ctrl** is referenced in some tips for updating Microsoft® Office Project plan.

customer satisfaction index. An index which is calculated by using various customer service-related parameters; also CSI. See the EVM template that accompanies this book which allows tracking of three additional indexes apart from the regular EVM indexes.

deliverables-oriented WBS. A method of structuring a WBS (work breakdown structure). In a deliverables-oriented WBS, WBS levels are set up in such a way that project deliverables are in one level and the tasks needed to complete these deliverables are in a lower level. Because a WBS is an important part of a project schedule, the WBS must be well structured for optimum results. In a well-structured WBS, ideally the project is at the top level. The next level should be for phases in the project. The third level should be for deliverables from these phases. The last level should be for tasks required to complete the deliverables. When structuring a WBS, having a deliverables-oriented arrangement is particularly important to facilitate more effective tracking of a project.

drill down. The ability to switch from a macro view to a micro view with the click of a button; also known as the drill down feature. Drill down is the ability to see an exploded view from a high-level view with the click of a button. Different types of drill down features are provided by software. The most common form is the tree view in which the tree can be expanded to view details and then collapsed to view summary level information. Drill down is a feature in Microsoft® Office Project.

duration estimate. An estimate of the time factor; different from the effort factor. The time factor is related to workdays. The time factor indicates how long a project will last until it is finished. The effort factor is related to the number of man hours required to complete the work. For example, for 16 hours of work, with two people who have an 8-hour workday to complete the work, the effort estimate is 16 hours and the duration estimate is 8 hours or 1 workday.

earned tickets. The number of budgeted tickets that have been completed in the time utilized; also the equivalent of earned value in normal EVM for projects; used in a production support scenario. For example, if a SLA (service level agreement) is 4 hours for a severity 1 ticket and 50% of the work on the ticket has been completed, then earned tickets will be 0.5 because only 50% of the work has been completed. Important to remember: earned tickets for any particular ticket can never be more than 1.

earned value. The accumulated value of the work that has been completed on a project; also EV. Earned value is generally calculated as the total budgeted cost multiplied by the percent (%) complete on a particular task or the project. Earned value indicates what has been achieved in terms of monetary value at any given point in the course of a project. Obviously, at the end of a project, if the project has been completed successfully, the earned value will be equal to the total budgeted cost. Earned value cannot, however, at any point, exceed the total budgeted cost for a particular task or for the entire project. This criterion is a key element of the EVM technique because it is the element with which the other two elements (actual cost and planned value) are compared to derive schedule or cost variance. Because earned value depends on the % complete, using the weighted average method is necessary to compute the % complete when rolling it up to the project level. Microsoft® Office Project handles rolling up the % complete.

earned value graph. A line graph in the EVM reporting tool which is included with this book. An earned value graph has three parameters which are plotted over time—planned value, actual cost, and earned value. The earned value graph is important because it provides an overall picture of how a project has progressed over time. When using an earned value graph, a project manager has to ensure that the earned value line is always above the actual cost and planned value lines to ensure that the project is progressing smoothly.

earned value management. A cost management technique commonly used worldwide that combines triple constraints to give a project manager complete control over a project; a technique used to track the progress of a project and to periodically report the status; also EVM. EVM provides measures of a project which show schedule and cost performance and the associated performance values for all stakeholders. By using the EVM technique, a project manager and project stakeholders can effectively manage a project and reduce the risk of a project going over budget or falling behind schedule.

efficiency. In this book, the productivity of project team members. For example, when project team members are described as being efficient, efficient means that work that is planned to be completed in 8 hours is being completed in 8 hours or less.

effort estimate. An estimate of the effort factor for a project (different from a duration estimate). The effort factor indicates the number of man hours that are required for the project work to be completed. The time factor is related to the number of calendar days (workdays) that will be required for the project to be completed. For example, for 16 hours of work, with two people who have an 8-hour work day, the effort estimate is 16 hours and the duration estimate is 8 hours or 1 workday.

effort variance. Cost variance when measured in terms of effort; the variance obtained when $1 is used as the resource rate in place of the actual resource rate. Effort variance is calculated as the earned value in terms of effort minus actual cost in terms of effort. The basic difference between cost and effort variance is that cost variance is measured in dollars and effort variance is measured in hours. As a measure, using effort variance is less effective than using cost variance. Cost variance provides more accurate results because each project resource is charged at a different rate; therefore, a resource with a lower cost rate impacts overall cost variance with a smaller value than a resource with a higher cost rate.

elapsed time. The calendar time that has elapsed from the start of a project or a task; also ET. Elapsed time is generally represented in the units of the reporting periods being used for a project. For example, if project status is reported on a weekly basis, the elapsed time will be in the number of weeks. Important to remember: elapsed time cannot be recovered.

estimate at completion. A forecast of the cost at completion of a project using the current status of the project and the assumptions that have been made for the remainder of the project; also EAC. EAC can be calculated using three formulas for the three types of assumptions that can be made based on the current status of the project:

- The variances are typical at this stage of the project; they will not recur in the course of the project.
- Similar variances will exist throughout the project.
- Considering the current status of the project, the project manager has concluded that the earlier estimating assumptions are invalid and that new estimates must be used for the remainder of the project.

The difference between BAC (budget at completion) and EAC is VAC (variance at completion).

estimate at completion (time). A forecast of the time used at completion of the project using the current status of the project and the assumptions that have been made for the remainder of the project. EACT can be calculated using three formulas for the three types of assumptions that can be made based on the current status of the project:

- The variances are typical at this stage of the project; they will not recur in the course of the project.
- Similar variances will exist throughout the project.
- Considering the current status of the project, the project manager has concluded that the earlier estimating assumptions are invalid and that new estimates must be used for the remainder of the project.

The difference between BAC_t and EAC_t is VAC_t (the variance at completion time).

estimate to complete. A new estimate for the remainder of the project (once past estimates have been determined to be invalid because of specific reasons), which is used in calculation of EAC; an estimate generally taken during the course of a project. (Note: Sometimes remaining work on a project in terms of hours or dollars is also referred to as ETC.)

estimating assumptions. Assumptions made during the estimating process. By nature, assumptions can go either way—accurate or inaccurate. Compared to actual results, estimates are never completely accurate. Estimates cannot be accurate because of the assumptions that were made during the estimating process. When the assumptions hold up, then the estimates will be more or less accurate; yet when the assumptions do not hold up, the difference between the estimates and actual results will be significant. *Important:* Keep notes of all assumptions made in determining the estimates for a project to help in assessing negative situations that might develop during a project to enable appropriate actions.

EVM report template. The dashboard tool described in this book; uses the EVM technique and limited data entry to track progress and status of a project; an EVM report template tool which has been developed in Microsoft® Excel. The tool can be used for various types of projects and to report a project's status to project stakeholders. (Note: The CD included with this book contains a 6-month trial version of this software tool. The tool must be used with Microsoft® Office Project or some other scheduling software which supports EVM. System requirements are Windows NT/2000.XP/2003 and Server/Vista, Microsoft Excel 2003/Word 2003.)

finish-to-finish. A dependency that can be set between two tasks on a project which indicates that the two tasks which have this dependency must finish together irrespective of when they start.

finish-to-start. A dependency that can be set between two tasks on a project which indicates that the first task must be completed before the second one can be started. Finish-to-start is the most common task dependency used for all projects. It is the default dependency in most scheduling software (e.g., Microsoft® Office Project).

fixed overhead cost. Costs other than regular human resource and machinery expenses; generally includes office space, electricity, and other costs incurred by a company to execute a project. Fixed overhead costs are of particular importance if they are being used to track the progress and status of a project using the EVM technique because they impact the overall project budget. Fixed overhead costs are also an important factor to consider when executing an internal project. However, if executing a project for a customer, the rate/hour for resources generally includes this factor so it does not need to be tracked.

forecast graph. A graph in the EVM reporting tool that plots BAC (budget at completion) and EAC (estimate at completion) values over time. The BAC and EAC performance measures are calculated in either dollar values or effort in hours. A forecast graph displays a forecast of the project's cost based on the current status of the project. In a forecast graph, plots of the BAC and EAC values over time form an S-curve. *Important:* A project manager should ensure that EAC (the cost forecasting performance measure) is as close as possible to BAC (the cost budget).

forecast (index) graph. A graph in the EVM reporting tool that plots the "to-complete" forecasting indexes—TSPI (the to-complete *schedule* performance indicator) and TCPI (the to-complete *cost* performance indicator). These indexes are plotted over time. They provide an indication of the expected efficiency of a project team going forward to complete the project within budget and according to the allocated schedule. *Important:* A project manager should keep these indexes on track and maintain them at a level close to 1 or below 1. Note: In healthy project performance, the TSPI and TCPI indexes are close to or below 1.

forecast (time) graph. A graph in the EVM reporting tool that plots BAC_t (budget at completion/time) and EAC_t (estimate at completion/time) over time. BAC_t and EAC_t performance measures are calculated in number of reporting periods wherein reporting periods could be weeks, months, etc., depending on the project. The forecast (time) graph shows a forecast of project time based on the current status of the project. *Important:* A project manager should ensure that EAC_t (the time forecasting performance measure) is as close as possible to BAC_t (the time budget) forecasting. Mathematical prediction of the future performance and future state of a project. Generally, mathematical models are used to predict the future performance and state of a project. *Important:* So that project stakeholders will understand the likely impact of the current state of the project on the future performance or state of the project, use the current status of the project to forecast future performance. Forecasting helps project stakeholders to make appropriate decisions to correct the future state of a project.

function point analysis. A commonly used method of estimation in software development projects; involves estimating the function points of the functionality to be supported by the software and then arriving at effort estimates using industry standard or company standard productivity measures for the function points. Industry standard or company standard productivity measures are available in hours per function point which are then applied to the total function points to arrive at a final effort estimate for the project. (Visit www.ifpug.com for a detailed explanation of the procedure and the method of calculation.)

Gantt chart. The most commonly used pictorial depiction of a project schedule; shows planned activities over time, with the progress of each activity shown against a point in time; also shows dependencies between activities in a project.

hard dependencies. A form of dependency between tasks/activities in a project schedule known as "hard" because dependency is fixed and *cannot be changed.* For example, in a house construction project, painting activity cannot start until plastering is complete. However, the task of plastering can be split in the schedule to an each-wall level, resulting in a hard dependency between the plastering and painting tasks for each wall. By splitting tasks, the scheduled time will likely be reduced.

human resources. A type of resource involved in almost all projects; the most important resource in any project. Human resources are required to complete most projects and generally constitute 80% of the work on a project. The specific skills required for a project and the various people who have the skills required to complete the project are also involved in human resources.

index graph. A graph in the EVM report template. In an index graph, schedule and cost performance indexes are plotted over time. An index graph is important because it shows the current performance status of the schedule and cost indexes in a project and how the project has performed over time, giving an indication of the type of action required by project stakeholders to control variances in the project. *Important:* Project stakeholders should keep schedule and cost performance indexes as close to 1 as possible. Any value over 1 is considered to be healthy project performance.

IT department. Refers to a department that caters to IT needs in a business in which the core area of business is not IT, but instead is in other business domains. The challenges for a project manager in an IT department in a company that has a core area of business are quite different from a project manager in a company with a core business of IT. (Note: This book discusses how cost is a factor of contention for project managers from an IT department and price is a factor of contention for project managers from a pure IT services company.)

lag time. The time used to set dependencies between tasks/activities; the reverse of lead time. Lag time is generally used to delay a subsequent task by a specified time. For example, in traditional concrete construction, after laying a concrete slab for a roof, time must be allowed for the slab to cure before building of the next level can begin. Generally, a wait time of 21 days is required. In this case, the lag time is 21 days.

lead time. The time used to set dependencies between tasks/activities; the reverse of lag time. Lead time specifies how much earlier the second task should start before the first task is finished. Suppose the first task takes 10 days and the second task takes 20 days. Also suppose both of these tasks need to start one after the other. If a lead time of 5 days is specified for the second task, then the second task is started 5 days before the first task is completed. (Note: Lead time is not commonly used in most projects.)

lessons learned. The "story" to be told at the end of a project which contains the lessons that have been learned from execution of the project. *Important:* An organization or every individual project manager should have the ability to consolidate all of the lessons learned from project execution and then to use them to perform more efficiently in future projects. Using the lessons learned is a key factor in the continuous improvement of individuals as well as the organization as a whole. Lessons learned need to be shared with all project managers across an organization to overcome the hurdles encountered in past projects with ease and to avoid experiencing these same problems in current projects.

log time. In this book, it refers to the use of EVM for production support (see *Appendix A*); the time when an incident or ticket is logged; an important attribute in the calculation of the response, restoration, and resolution time of an incident. Log time is generally recorded in a date/time format because most SLAs (service level agreements) for different severity tickets are generally in hours. If the time part of this attribute is not recorded, then deriving the number of hours for response, restoration, and resolution will be impossible.

lowest-level activities. Activities at the lowest level in a WBS (work breakdown structure); activities that cannot be further broken down due to various reasons; end activities that must be performed by various resources on a project to complete deliverables of the project. Generally, hard dependencies are set between lowest-level activities; soft dependencies are set between the summary activities of lowest-level activities so that slack time for resources is minimized. Lowest-level activities should have effort estimates between 8 and 80 hours, meaning that lowest-level activities should not have effort estimates below or above the 8- to 80-hour mark.

machinery. A resource required to complete certain activities. Many projects require the use of machinery as one of the resources required to complete a certain set of activities. Machinery has a cost/hr or a rate/hr which impacts the project's budget. Although a significant amount of automated machinery is used for construction projects, some activities will need to be performed by human resources. Because the activities performed by human resources in a project are dependent on automated machine activities, include and track the performance and progress of activities performed by machinery.

macro-level management. A management style wherein a manager takes a high-level view of a project and manages it at a high level instead of becoming involved in the details of the project. Macro-level management helps a project manager or project stakeholders to have a big picture of a project and allows them to make decisions at higher levels. The macro-level management style also saves significant time for senior management. By avoiding involvement in project details, senior management can focus on the big picture. (Note: In this book, the macro-level management style is used with the EVM technique and Microsoft® Office Project, which allows project stakeholders to take a macro view of a project, and drill down to the micro level if needed.)

manage by exception. A management style wherein a manager manages a project by exception instead of going into the details of areas in which the project is progressing smoothly and without concerns. Managing by exception allows a manager to focus on project problem areas and to resolve these problems to facilitate having a successful project. In the managing by exception management style, a manager generally starts with a macro-level (or high-level) view of the project's status, chooses exceptions from this view, and drills down to resolve problems in these exception scenarios. Managing by exception is a very popular management style which saves significant time and energy for senior management. (Note: This book shows how the managing by exception management style can be used with the EVM report template and Microsoft® Office Project to save precious time.)

material resources. A type of resource used in many projects; the materials required to complete a deliverable of a project. Tracking material resources for a project is quite important. When discussing material, invariably the question of inventory arises. The material needed for a project must be in inventory so that a project team will be able to use that material to perform the activities that lead to a deliverable in the project. Tracking the material needed for a project will provide insight into the time lines of when material will be needed. Also the procurement process can kick off based on the time lines and the lead times required for procuring inventory.

micro-level management. A management style wherein a project manager becomes involved in project details at the task level. Some project managers prefer to be on top of all project tasks and to take a closer look at the details of each task, taking appropriate action to bring tasks back on track. The micro-level management style generally requires significant project management effort by a project manager. Yet, micro-level project management is often unnecessary—it is overkill. Instead, the micro-level management style should be used in exception scenarios. For example, a project manager only becomes involved in the details of an individual task in the event of an exception scenario such as a schedule or cost overrun. Throughout the course of a project, the technique of managing by exception is more effective than micro-level management.

Microsoft® Office Project. Software from Microsoft® Corporation used to prepare project schedules, track progress, and report the status of schedules; worldwide, the most commonly used project management software with millions of users; often abbreviated MPP. (Note: This book has been written to enable readers to use Microsoft Office Project effectively and to also be able to use Microsoft Office Project along with the EVM reporting dashboard tool provided with this book to track a project using the EVM technique. This book uses MPP throughout.)

Microsoft® Office Project plan. The general phrase used to describe a project schedule created using Microsoft® Office Project; often abbreviated as MPP; also the extension of a file name created by Microsoft® Office Project (.mpp) for a project schedule.

multiple baselines. The different baselines for a project schedule over the course of the project. During the course of the project, the schedule can undergo many changes. When the changes are significant enough and have been approved by all project stakeholders, a project manager rebaselines the project schedule. Many project managers prefer to keep a record of all of the baselines of a project's schedule over the course of the project to enable comparative reporting. Microsoft® Office Project allows users to store multiple baselines (up to ten). Multiple baselines also provide backup information for questions raised by project stakeholders at later stages of the project.

object point estimation. An estimation technique used in the software industry that is similar to function point estimation. However, in the object point estimation technique, estimates are based on the objects that need to be created within the software rather than the functions (which are used in function point estimation). The technique is generally used for software that needs to be developed on an object-oriented platform. (Note: The object point estimation technique is not commonly used and is not standardized.)

other indexes graph. A graph in the EVM report template dashboard; a graph that plots three additional indexes over time (different from the indexes used in the EVM technique). For example, the EVM report template allows users to track and report additional indexes, e.g., the risk, customer satisfaction, project health, and process compliance indexes. The EVM report template dashboard thus becomes a complete reporting tool for any project wherein project status and progress can be reported.

overallocation. A term used to describe a situation wherein resources for a project are allocated to project tasks at a higher level than the level at which these resources are available to the project. For example, suppose a project has an 8-hour workday and a resource has been allocated to a task which requires 16 hours to complete. If the resource has been allocated to complete this task in one working day, this situation represents an overallocation of the resource. A similar situation results when a resource is working at only 50% of the time on a project, but is allocated at 100% for a particular task. When resources are assigned to a project schedule, and the resources are not leveled properly, this situation can result in overallocations. To resolve these overallocations, use the resource leveling feature in Microsoft® Office Project to manually correct resource utilization. Only when all overallocations are resolved can an accurate, achievable schedule be established. Overallocations that are not resolved can be detrimental to a project because the schedule will indicate a completion date that is earlier than the date which is actually required for completion of the project.

percent (%) complete. The percentage of work completed on a particular task or an entire project; used for calculation of earned value; should be as accurate as possible, but can never be 100% accurate; is subject to interpretation. Different project managers can arrive at a different % complete on the same task. Methods such as weighted average, 50/50, etc. are used to assign the % complete. Microsoft® Office Project uses the weighted average for calculating the % complete on summary tasks based on entries made for lowest-level tasks.

performance measures. The various performance outcomes of the EVM technique; used to show the performance of a project in such aspects as schedule and cost. Performance measures can be used to present the current status of a project, to show progress made on a project, or to forecast the future performance of a project in lieu of the current performance of a project. Being able to show the various views of project performance is difficult, but quite possible using the EVM performance measures. (Note: Using the EVM reporting dashboard tool provided with this book enables easier reporting of the performance of a project.)

PERT estimation. A well-known estimation technique commonly used worldwide for most projects; an estimation derived from a three-point estimate wherein three different types of estimates are made and then a formula (the PERT formula) is applied to arrive at a final PERT estimate. The three types of estimates are *most likely* estimates, *pessimistic* estimates, and *optimistic* estimates. (Note: The PERT formula is discussed in the *Estimates* section of Chapter 2.)

planned tickets. The equivalent of PV (planned value) in production support EVM; represents the number of tickets planned to have been completed as of a particular date; the basic element of EVM for production support. Planned tickets are calculated for each of three parameters—initial response, restoration, and final resolution. Along with earned tickets, planned tickets are used to calculate schedule variance.

planned time. The time equivalent of earned value in the EVM technique; the time effectively utilized on a project; also PT. PT when compared to elapsed time shows how effectively the time portion of a project is being utilized. If PT is greater than or equal to elapsed time, then, so far, time on the project is being utilized effectively and no time has been lost—instead time has been gained. Similarly, if PT is less than elapsed time, time on the project has been lost.

planned value. The cost or value of work that was planned or scheduled to be completed as of a given date in a project; also PV. However PV does not represent the value that was actually completed which is represented by earned value. PV is always compared with earned value to derive schedule variance and other schedule performance measures (known as BCWS or budgeted cost of work scheduled in earlier terminology). PV is a basic element of the EVM technique and must be derived from the schedule. Microsoft® Office Project automatically provides PV if a schedule is properly prepared.

planning. Involves all of the ground work that needs to be completed to execute a project and to track progress of a project; primarily involves defining the scope of the project, deriving the WBS (work breakdown structure), estimating resources, estimating project effort, and deriving a schedule; also involves numerous tasks that must be completed before a project is started to ensure success in project endeavors.

PMI®. An acronym for Project Management Institute®, the premier institution for project management practitioners worldwide. PMI publishes standards for project management and brings project managers together from across the world and from different disciplines. (Note: Additional information about PMI may be found on the PMI website at www.pmi.org.)

point of no return. A situation in a project in which the project has already exceeded the planned total project duration or budget. After a project has crossed the total planned duration or the total planned budget, there is no way to get the project back on track. The only thing to be done at this point is to try to minimize schedule or cost variances.

Predecessor. A field in Microsoft® Office Project which is used to identify tasks that precede the current task; a field that may be used to specify the relationship between tasks. Four types of relationships can be defined using the **Predecessor** field—finish to finish, finish to start, start to start, and start to finish. By default, the **Predecessor** field assumes the finish-to-start relationship. Lead and lag times may also be specified using the **Predecessor** field. For example, to specify a finish-to-start relationship with a lag time of 10 days for the second task in relation to the first task, put 1FS+10 in the **Predecessor** field. The **Predecessor** field may also be used in a similar format for other relationships (1SS+10).

preventive action. Action that is taken to prevent problems from occurring or recurring in a project. For example, suppose in the course of a project that the project is behind schedule and that the cause(s) of this situation has been identified. The project manager would then take preventive action(s) to prevent the schedule from slipping further behind. Preventive action is generally used in conjunction with corrective action when a problem has already occurred.

Priority. A field in Microsoft® Office Project used to specify the priority of tasks in a schedule. Frequent changes to schedules are generally the "order of the day" in today's world. (Note: This book shows how to use the **Priority** field instead of the **Predecessor** field to specify the basic finish-to-start relationship with ease, saving precious time when creating a schedule, changing a schedule when changes are frequent, and updating a schedule. Resource leveling is used along with the **Priority** field to enable proper scheduling of the project. The default value for the **Priority** field in Microsoft® Office Project is 500. The **Priority** field accepts values from 0 to 1000, with 1000 being the highest priority and 0 being the lowest priority.)

production support. In the software environment, support provided to end users after software has "gone live" and is considered to be in production. The same term can be used in other disciplines. In production support engagements, a few resources constantly monitor problems faced by end users and respond to end user problems with solutions, either through a simple education session for an end user or by changing the software to fix an error or a feature that prevents the software from performing as intended (also known as a "bug"). Because production support activity does not have a definite end, it is not considered to be a project—instead production support is considered to be part of operations. (Note: *Appendix A* shows how to apply the EVM technique for production support engagements.)

production support calls/tickets. Engagements determined by requests for information and fixes from end users. These requests are raised by end users and are generally termed calls or tickets. They are tracked to closure by the production support team. Generally, requests are placed through a system such as Rational® ClearQuest or some other similar tool. A ticket is tracked from the time it is logged until closure, which is generally noted by an end user when the end user is satisfied with the response and the problem has been resolved. In some scenarios, requests for production support are actual telephone calls that are attended to by production support, leading to the term "calls." In most cases, however, it is the ticket that is logged into a support system.

project. An endeavor by a group of resources with a definite start and a definite end; generally performed to achieve an end goal which could include anything from building something to effecting a productivity improvement program. (For a more detailed description of a project, refer to PMBOK®, Project Management Body of Knowledge, published by PMI.)

project calendar. A calendar specific for a single project in which the project manager defines work times, weekdays, weekends, shifts, holidays, etc. only for that project. Setting up a project calendar in Microsoft® Office Project can ensure that no work is planned which is outside the working hours of the project and that holidays and weekends are taken into consideration when a schedule is generated. Keeping the established schedule updated is essential because of the effects of date slippage on the end date of the schedule. In addition to a project-level calendar which is applicable to all resources, a project manager can also have a resource-level calendar which will define the vacation plans of resources.

project deliverables. All tangible items that are to be delivered by executing a project. Because project deliverables are tangible items that are delivered by executing a project, having a schedule and a WBS (work breakdown structure) oriented to the project deliverables so that the deliverables can be tracked effectively and work can be done to ensure delivery on time and on budget is always advisable.

project end date. The estimated end date of a project which is derived from a schedule. At times, the end date for a project is imposed. In this case a project manager must work backward from the imposed date to ensure that the project is delivered on that date. Usually the project end date is provided by the project manager after all assumptions have been taken into consideration and a schedule has been prepared. This date will be baselined and will be the date against which the schedule is tracked.

project life cycle. The common phases of every project when put into a particular order. A project life cycle consists of initiation, planning, execution, monitoring, controlling, and closing. Project life cycle phases must be executed in the same order for each project. Each project life cycle phase has definite inputs and outputs as defined in PMBOK®. Only when defined outputs are completed and delivered can a phase be considered complete. Note: The monitoring and controlling phases are support phases which should be executed from project start to project end.

project manager. The person responsible for executing a project and producing the deliverables which have been identified in the scope of the project. The project manager is a critical resource for any project. Projects without a project manager often lack focus and direction and end up in failure. A project manager is appointed by the project sponsor when the project is initiated through an initiation note and is available for the entire duration of the project. After closing out a project, the project manager then moves on to other projects.

project start date. The start date for a project; generally the date when a project is initiated and a project manager is appointed. In importance, the project start date and the project end date are equal—the project start date is used to derive the project end date in most projects. Once a project is started, it is in the best interest of project stakeholders to ensure that they all work toward completing the project.

project team. The group of human resources responsible for working on a project to complete the stated objectives of the project and to produce the identified deliverables. A project team always consists of resources with different skills to ensure that the various types of project work are executed smoothly and by an experienced person in that field. For example, a house construction project could have architects, concrete workers, carpenters, painters, etc. These resource groups have different skills and perform different tasks which ensure that a house building project will be completed.

rate/hr. The rate at which a particular resource is charged to a client for 1 hour of work; common in time and material projects in which resources are charged to a project by the number of hours that they work on the project immaterial of how long the project will take. In this type of relationship, risk is generally taken by the client; therefore, it is the responsibility of the client's project manager to ensure that the hours being charged to the project are well utilized. Note: Even in fixed bid projects, the rate/hr can be defined at the resource level because this rate is the basis for the bid made by the company for the project. In a fixed bid project in which effort has been defined as a certain number of hours, the number of hours is generally fixed; therefore, any deviation from this number of hours is a risk to the vendor, which protects the client from risk. Rate per hour is generally defined in dollars per hour of work of a resource skill.

recurrence pattern. A frequency which can be specified for a recurring task in Microsoft® Office Project. A recurrence pattern can specify that a task must recur every day, weekly, monthly, or yearly; the day of the week, day of the month, etc. can also be specified. Microsoft® Office Project helps set up a recurrence pattern for a task and builds recurring tasks accordingly.

recurring tasks. Tasks that generally recur in a definite pattern throughout a project. For example, team meetings for a project might occur every week, probably every Monday of the week. These types of tasks can be set up using the recurring tasks feature of Microsoft® Office Project. Setting up recurring tasks in a project and tracking them by the specific amount of effort and time that goes into them is important.

reporting period. The period or frequency of planned reporting of project status and progress; used in setting up the EVM report template (which is set up according to the frequency chosen for reporting). EVM performance measures are calculated based on the reporting period chosen in the EVM report template. Different options available are weekly, fortnightly, monthly, or bimonthly. All graphs in the EVM report template that are plotted over time are based on the reporting periods that are set up in the template.

resequencing tasks. Changing the sequence of tasks, often because of unexpected events. More often than not, a project will undergo changes due to circumstances which are out of the control of the project team. Due to these circumstances, the project must be rescheduled and tasks must be resequenced. Resequencing means that a project manager changes the order of completion of a task(s). He wants a task that has been scheduled to be done after the completion of a few other tasks to be completed earlier. In this case, the sequence (or order) of tasks must be changed, i.e., resequenced. At times, resequencing of tasks is done to keep a project on track and/or to make use of slack time that is available in the project.

resolution time. The time taken to resolve tickets or incidents which have been reported by end users; a parameter in production support engagements; a particularly important metric which is tracked in a production support engagement when the SLA (service level agreement) defines resolution time (depends on the type of production support being provided).

resource calendar. A calendar which is set up for each resource in a project by Microsoft® Office Project. By using this calendar, work times, holidays, and vacation time can be specified for each resource even if the resources have different work times, holidays, and vacation times from the standard project calendar. When Microsoft® Office Project calculates a schedule, it takes into account the resource calendar over and above the project calendar to schedule the project. A resource calendar is usually used to define the vacation time of the resources because vacation time for these resources is different. Again, setting up a resource calendar correctly before calculating a schedule to obtain a realistic and achievable schedule is important.

resource costs. Costs associated with resources that work on a project. All resources working on a project have a cost associated with them. Each company has a definite cost for each resource such as salaries and overhead costs. Resource costs are particularly important when tracking an internal project that has an assigned budget which includes resource costs.

resource leave/vacation. Time taken off from work by a human resource. Human resources assigned to a project are likely to take time off from work for various reasons during the course of a project. This time off is known as resource leave or vacation plans. Resource leave/vacation plans must be tracked and planned for in advance to enable a project manager to arrive at a realistic schedule and to avoid planning any work for a particular resource during his/her vacation time. Resource leave/vacation time can be marked on the resource calendar in the Microsoft® Office Project. Note: Although resource leave can be planned for, it is always possible that some resources will become ill or need to take emergency leave. This unplanned leave cannot be planned for in advance; therefore, to ensure that the schedule is not affected, having a contingency plan for unplanned leave is always a good idea.

resource leveling. A technique or feature in Microsoft® Office Project that is used to level the work done by resources in an optimal way so that all resources are utilized to their maximum extent in the project to yield a realistic schedule. (Note: Often the resource leveling feature is not used by project managers because they think this feature pushes a schedule out to an unacceptable extent. This is incorrect. If the instructions in this book are followed, obtaining an optimal schedule that is realistic, achievable, and avoids problems due to overallocations in the later part of the project is ensured. Most importantly, significant time is saved by avoiding the need for manual leveling.)

resource usage. The current utilization of resources in a project; a defined view in Microsoft® Office Project which can be used to see how various resources are loaded with work over time; provides an idea of what work is being done on a project by what resource. The resource usage view provides a schedule by resource which shows the planned and actual work for a resource.

resources. Anything required to enable the completion of a project. Every project needs resources. These resources could be human, machinery, materials, etc. Almost all projects require some type of human resources. Although human resources are the most obvious resource used in a project, project management involves the effective management of all project resources to complete the project on time and on budget.

resources on hold. In resource leveraging, the time that resources are off a project to accommodate work on other projects. In some projects, many resources are used on a leveraged basis—these resources might spend only half of their time on a current project and perhaps be utilized for the remaining half of their time on other projects within the company. In resource leveling situations, some resources are likely to be off a project for short periods of time to allow for the accommodation of work pressures from other projects. During off periods, these resources should be put on hold in the current project. Microsoft® Office Project can then reschedule the project when these resources return. (Note: Achieving this type of rescheduling using Microsoft® Office Project is discussed in Chapter 9.)

response time. A parameter in production support engagements; the time taken to provide an initial response to an end user when a production support call/ticket is initiated; calculated by subtracting the date/time the response was given from the date/time the production support call was made or the ticket was initiated. In most production support engagements, SLAs (service level agreements) govern the response time parameter; therefore, response time is a very closely monitored metric. Response time for production support calls/tickets is also an important factor in customer satisfaction. For most consumer products, because customer satisfaction drives the growth of sales, customer satisfaction is an important index to track.

restoration time. A parameter in production support engagements; the time taken to restore a product to a usable state for an end user; a closely tracked metric in production support engagements. For example, in the software industry, suppose an end user calls to report that the software has stopped working. In this situation, the time taken by the production support team to restore the software to a usable state is known as restoration time. Restoration time is also a factor that affects customer satisfaction levels. More importantly, restoration time governs the losses which are incurred by a business in mission-critical applications.

risk index. Derived from the risks that are present in a project; generally derived using the probability of and the impact of each risk in a project. The risk index can be tracked with the EVM report template which provides for tracking of three types of indexes. Risk index is calculated at the overall project level and indicates the risk quotient of the project for senior management so they will be able to step in when needed.

schedule. A listing of all tasks to be performed in a project along with their time lines, dependencies, and the resources required to perform the tasks. Preparing a schedule for every project, regardless of size, is essential. A schedule consists of five basic elements—work breakdown structure, effort estimates, resources, resource costs, and task dependencies. When put together, these elements form a project schedule. A schedule is prepared, executed, monitored, and controlled so that a project can be completed on time and on budget.

schedule baseline. The "freezing" of a schedule. Once the initial schedule is prepared and presented to all project stakeholders, the schedule is approved by the project stakeholders. Once approved, the schedule is "frozen" to allow tracking of progress against the original schedule. This frozen schedule is known as the schedule baseline. To be able to apply the EVM technique to track schedule progress, it is mandatory that a schedule be baselined because actual results are compared to the baseline to show variances in time and cost.

schedule monitoring. The act of frequently checking (keeping an eye on) a schedule to observe any possible variances and then taking corrective or preventive action. Every project schedule should be prepared, baselined, tracked, monitored, and controlled. Close monitoring of a schedule is essential because doing so can reveal a potentially negative outcome(s) that could be controlled or even prevented. Close monitoring can also reveal a potentially positive outcome(s) that could be maximized to the benefit of the project. Monitoring a schedule involves checking the schedule progress with respect to the performance measures described in this book and then taking corrective and/or preventive action to ensure smooth completion and a positive outcome.

schedule on hold. The halting of work in a project due to circumstances which are beyond the control of the project team (a government order, acts of God, or any other event that is out of the control of the project team). When a project must be stopped for a short period of time, the schedule is put "on hold." (Note: You need to account for the work stoppage in Microsoft® Office Project to enable projection of revised dates in the schedule. Chapter 9 explains how a Microsoft® Office Project schedule can be put on hold so that the dates are revised and an accounting is made of the reasons for the hold.)

schedule overrun. The state of a project in which the planned schedule of work is not completed as planned or as scheduled; also, and more frequently, the amount of time by which a schedule has overshot the budgeted time. A schedule overrun can be calculated at any given point in a project using the EVM technique. Otherwise, arriving at a schedule overrun is difficult. Schedule overrun is calculated by using planned value (formerly budgeted cost of work scheduled, BCWS) and the earned value (formerly budgeted cost for work performed, BCWP) in the cost-based method and by using planned time and elapsed time in the time-based method. (Note: Schedule overruns at the beginning of a project are generally manageable and probably completely reversible by the end of the project. The impact of schedule overruns increases over time in a project.)

schedule performance indicator. An index indicating the performance of time on a project; derived using earned value (formerly budgeted cost of work scheduled, BCWP) and planned value (BCWS). The optimum value of this index is 1. Anything below 1 indicates that a project is behind schedule. Anything above 1 indicates that a project is ahead of schedule. The schedule performance indicator also indicates the efficiency of a project team in utilizing time in a project. Therefore, with a SPI of 1.1, a project team is 110% efficient in utilizing time in a project.

schedule performance indicator (time). The time equivalent of the SPI in which performance of a schedule from the aspect of time is shown; derived using planned time and elapsed time. The optimum value of this index is 1. Anything below 1 indicates that a project is behind schedule. Anything above 1 indicates that a project is ahead of schedule. The SPI also indicates the efficiency of a project team in utilizing time in a project. Therefore, with a SPI of 1.1, a project team is 110% efficient in utilizing time in the project.

schedule tracking. Updating a schedule with the actual progress made. Schedule tracking must be done periodically. In small projects, schedule tracking must be done almost daily. Schedule tracking uses data which is supplied by the resources on a project—the amount of effort that these resources have put into the particular task that they are working on and the % complete of the task so far. A simple daily status report template can be prepared and circulated to all resources. Resources fill in the report daily and return it at the end of the day so this information can be updated in the Microsoft® Office Project schedule. (Note: Track the schedule, which was prepared and then baselined, regularly to ensure that accurate information about a project's progress is available at all times during the course of a project.)

schedule variance. The variance of a schedule from the aspect of cost; indicates the cost of work not completed as originally scheduled on a given date; also known as schedule overrun. For example, originally, as of a particular date, the cost of work scheduled to have been completed is $1000. Yet the cost of work actually completed is $800. Therefore, schedule variance is $200. Schedule variance can be negative or positive. Negative indicates that a project is behind schedule; positive indicates that a project is ahead of schedule.

schedule variance %. The variance of a schedule in percent; indicates the percent of the schedule that has not been completed as planned. For example, for a 10% schedule variance in which the scheduled work so far in a project is valued at $1000, the schedule variance in dollars can be calculated by $1000 $\times$ 10% = $100. Schedule variance % provides a different view of schedule variance by indicating the % by which a schedule is out of balance. Schedule variance % can be negative or positive. Negative indicates that a schedule is behind; positive indicates that a schedule is ahead.

schedule variance % (time). The time equivalent of schedule variance %. The same things apply to the schedule variance % (time) performance measure as in schedule variance % except that schedule variance % (time) is calculated using the time factor. Results are provided in terms of time or reporting periods. Schedule variance % (time) can be negative or positive. Negative indicates that a schedule is behind; positive indicates that a schedule is ahead. For example, for a schedule variance % (time) of 10% and an elapsed time so far of 10 weeks, the schedule is behind/ahead of schedule, depending on the sign of the variance (+10% or –10%), by 10 weeks $\times$ 10% = 1 week.

schedule variance (time). The variance of a schedule from the aspect of time; indicates the number of reporting periods not utilized properly as originally scheduled as of a given date. For example, originally, as of a certain date, the number of reporting periods that have elapsed are 10 weeks and the amount of the work that has actually been completed is worth 9 weeks; therefore, the schedule variance is 1 week. Schedule variance can be negative or positive. Negative variance indicates that the schedule is behind; positive indicates that the schedule is ahead.

scope creep. A situation in which extra tasks/items have been added to a project's scope which were not planned for originally. The scope of a project is the *amount* of work that is to be done in the project. The scope of a project must be well defined. Generally the scope is recorded in a scope statement that *broadly* specifies the type of work to be done in a project and the outcome that must result from the project. More often than not, perhaps due to improper visualization or incomplete understanding at the beginning of the project, the scope is not well defined. As a result, project stakeholders, especially customers, request the inclusion of additional items throughout the project which were not planned for initially. These extra inclusions in a project's scope result in scope creep. Most projects worldwide and across various disciplines have scope creep in some form. A project manager must manage scope creep well so that customer needs are satisfied, but also manage the project in such a way that it stays on budget and on time.

scope statement. A statement broadly defining the amount of work to be done, the type of work to be done, and the expected outcome of a project. The scope or the amount of work that needs to be done in a project must be well defined in a scope statement. The scope statement forms the basis of all planning that a project manager does on a project. Proper visualization and a specific, well-defined scope statement by all project stakeholders are essential to avoid future scope creep and a failed project. Yet a scope statement is generally the first document written for a project and, more often than not, the scope statement is not well defined. A project team cannot hold a customer responsible for the scope statement because visualizing everything at the beginning of the project is impossible for the customer. A project manager and other project stakeholders must accept the potential for additional customer requests and work around situations that result in scope creep.

S-curve. A well-known S-shaped curve that shows BAC (budget at completion) and EAC (estimate at completion) performance measures plotted over time on a graph. The reason why BAC and EAC form an S-curve pattern is because work done in a project at the beginning is slow, picks up during the middle of the project, and flattens out at the end. This scenario is typical for all projects irrespective of discipline and geography. The difference at the end between the two S-curves showing BAC and EAC is generally called VAC (which is to be kept as low as possible). If the difference is negative, or the EAC curve is above the BAC curve, then there is a cost variance situation (an over-budget situation); if the EAC curve is below the BAC curve, then there is an under budget situation. Keeping the EAC curve below the BAC curve throughout a project is important to ensure an under- or on-budget situation at the end of the project.

sequencing tasks. Involves specifying the order in which the tasks in a project need to be performed to complete the project. Depending on the project and the discipline in which the project is being executed, the tasks in all projects will need to be sequenced in some particular order. For example, painting a wall cannot be completed until the wall is plastered. So plastering must be done first; then painting activity starts after plastering is completed. Sequencing, however, is more than just the ordering of one task after another. Sequencing also involves the use of multiple types of task sequencing—finish to start, finish to finish, start to finish, and start to start. (Note: Microsoft® Office Project allows finish-to-start, finish-to-finish, start-to-finish, and start-to-start sequencing. Using these relationships or sequences is explained in Chapter 2.)

service levels. Related to production support engagements in which a contract between a customer and a vendor includes certain agreed-upon service levels. For production support engagements, service levels are defined in terms of the time taken to provide the initial response to an issue, the restoration of service, and the final resolution of the service issue. Generally service levels are defined in the number of hours or minutes in which services need to be performed. (Note: Although production support engagements are ongoing operations in nature rather than projects, *Appendix A* discusses how to use the EVM technique for measuring and monitoring service levels.)

severity. Related to production support engagements in which incidents or calls or tickets initiated by end users are classified by severity (1, 2, 3, 4), depending on the type of problem and its impact on a business. The lower the severity number, the faster the response time should be by the production support team. Generally severity 1 calls or incidents indicate a complete breakdown of the system—the user is unable to use the product. Severity 1 incidents must be dealt with as quickly as possible.

slack time. The amount of time that a particular task can be delayed without delaying the project. Some tasks in every project have a certain amount of slack time that can be utilized to delay the task, if needed, without affecting the overall project end date. Other tasks have no slack time. Any delay in these tasks will definitely delay the project. Tasks which have no slack time are known as being on a critical path. The critical path method of tracking a project is the most popular. In the critical path tracking technique, critical path tasks are monitored closely and are not allowed to have date slippage, which almost certainly ensures that the project is delivered on time. *Important:* The critical path method does not address the cost aspect in a project; it only addresses the time aspect.

soft dependencies. A form of dependency between tasks in a project schedule which is not enforced using finish-to-start, start-to-finish, start-to-start, and finish-to-finish relationships (which are hard task dependencies); generally a dependency which arises due to resource loading. For example, if a resource is to work on two tasks, this resource cannot work on both tasks at the same time. The resource will almost certainly have to finish one task and then move on to the other task. This type of dependency is an unforced dependency which is known as a soft dependency. Soft dependencies are generally determined by resource availability. Every project is likely to have soft and hard dependencies.

stakeholders. The group of people who are directly or indirectly affected by project execution. Stakeholders generally include the customer, the vendor, the project team, and any other third parties who either contribute to the project or are dependent on the outcome of the project. Managing project stakeholder expectations is a key aspect of project management. The project manager assigned to a project is responsible for managing project stakeholder expectations. Keeping project stakeholders updated about the status and progress of a project, along with the risks and issues, will always help manage their expectations. Project stakeholders are also responsible for certain decisions which are made during the course of the project.

start-to-finish. A type of relationship that can be set up between tasks; also known as a task dependency. In start-to-finish dependency, the first task is set to start after the second task is finished (the reverse of finish-to-start dependency, which is the default). Start-to-finish dependency is rarely used in projects. Some complex situations, however, require use of this dependency.

start-to-start. A type of relationship that can be set up between tasks; also known as a task dependency. In start-to-start dependency, the first and the second tasks are set to start together. Start-to-start dependency is rarely used in projects. Some complex situations, however, require use of this dependency.

statement of work. A document written to describe the work that is to be performed on a project; a high-level picture of a project, providing the expectations of the customer and the vendor from the outcome of the project. A statement of work contains a high-level scope of the project and other details, such as expected deliverables, expected delivery dates, expected resources and their costs, quality expectations, and the total cost of the project in the case of a fixed bid project. Sometimes a statement of work is used in place of a scope statement. In this case, the statement of work also includes the scope statement along with the other details.

summary activities. Activities which are at the summary level; activities which generally represent phases or deliverables in a project; an activity that has lower-level activities which are to be completed in a specific order for the summary activity to be completed. (Summary activities are represented in boldface type in Microsoft® Office Project.) All details of summary activities are rolled up from lower-level activities, e.g., start date, end date, efforts, duration, etc. For a summary activity with four lower-level tasks, with each lower-level activity having an effort of 10 hours, the summary level efforts roll up to 40 hours. Although other details are rolled up, not all details are summed up. For example, the rolled up duration for a summary activity is the total duration required to complete all lower-level tasks, which can be different from the sum of the duration of all of these tasks because some tasks might be done in parallel.

task dependencies. Dependencies or relationships that one or more tasks have with other tasks which are defined as hard and soft. Hard dependencies generally *cannot* be changed—there are hard and fast rules which govern the execution or sequencing of these tasks in a project. Soft dependencies are generally dependent on resource availability and can be changed by increasing resource availability or resequencing tasks. Task dependency is a basic element of a schedule. Until task dependencies are set, a project schedule is incomplete.

task levels. The levels in a WBS (work breakdown structure). A WBS is generally set up in a hierarchical form that is similar to an organization chart. A WBS has different levels that define the different tasks involved in a project. Generally, a well-defined WBS has the project at the top-most level, followed by the phases in the next level, followed by deliverables in the next level, etc. (Note: These different levels can be defined in Microsoft® Office Project and expanded or collapsed to any level desired in a WBS created in Microsoft® Office Project. This feature is useful when monitoring a schedule because it provides a quick view of a project; how phases in the project or how deliverables within the phases are progressing.)

task relationship. Same as task dependency. Task dependencies are also referred to as task relationships.

task usage. A view in Microsoft® Office Project in which tasks, including the resources, scheduled and actual costs, and effort assigned to each task over time, may be viewed. This view is useful in updating the actual effort on tasks, particularly when tasks have multiple resources assigned at different utilization levels. (Note: If you choose to update the actual effort from the normal tracking Gantt view, Microsoft® Office Project will evenly spread the actual effort across all resources, but often there will be different effort levels from different resources on tasks.)

tasks. Work or jobs which must be performed to complete a portion of a project; also referred to as activities; an integral part of a WBS (work breakdown structure) and a project schedule. Tasks are independent activities that can be performed by resources, either human or machinery.

team meetings. Meetings held on a periodic basis by project team members to discuss the various issues in a project and to develop solutions for problems; meetings used as a mechanism to communicate project status to a project team and to facilitate bonding between the team members who would otherwise be working on the project in their individual work spaces; meetings used by project managers to motivate team members and to increase the discipline with which activities in the project are being performed.

to-complete cost performance indicator. A forecasting performance measure which provides a forecast of the CPI (cost performance indicator) that is required to complete a project on budget; also TCPI. By using the TCPI performance measure, the levels of effort required to be used in the next reporting period can be determined, to bring the project back on track if it is slipping into an over-budget situation or to maximize performance if the project is progressing well and under budget. For example, a TCPI of 0.9 indicates that a project is well under budget currently and that the project team needs to perform at 90% efficiency to keep the project on budget or to work more efficiently to maximize CPI.

to-complete schedule performance indicator. A forecasting performance measure which provides a forecast of the SPI (schedule performance indicator) that is required to complete a project on schedule; also TSPI. By using the TSPI performance measure, the level of effort required for the next reporting period can be determined, to bring the project back on track if the schedule is slipping or maximize performance if the project is well ahead of schedule. For example, a TSPI of 0.9 indicates that a project is well ahead of schedule currently and that the project team needs to perform at 90% efficiency to keep the project on schedule or to work more efficiently to maximize SPI.

to-complete schedule performance indicator (time). The time equivalent of TSPI, which indicates the performance levels required going forward in a project to be on schedule; also TSPI (time). TSPI (time) is a forecasting performance measure which provides a forecast of SPI (Time) that is needed to complete a project on schedule. By using the TSPI (time) performance measure, the levels of efficiency required in the next reporting period can be determined, to bring a project back on track if the schedule is slipping or to maximize performance if a project is well ahead of schedule. For example, a TSPI (time) of 0.9 indicates that a project is well ahead of schedule currently and that the project team needs to perform at 90% efficiency to keep the project on schedule or to work more efficiently to maximize SPI (time).

trend analysis. An analysis of the trends generated by graphs in which a particular performance measure has been plotted over time. In these graphs, trends can be upward or downward. Depending on the performance measure, preventive and/or corrective action must be taken to prevent a trend from moving to the negative side of a performance measure; stern actions must be taken to reverse a trend. In CPI/SPI, a downward trend must be controlled, an upward trend maintained. The reverse is true in TCPI/TSPI.

utilization. The percentage of time utilized on a project based on the total available time of resources; generally refers to resources and the amount of time that the resources are used on a project; can be calculated for different periods, such as daily, weekly, monthly, or annually as required. For example, resources generally work in shifts of 8 hours each. If a resource is utilized on a project for 6 hours a day, resource utilization would be $6 \div 8 = 75\%$. The optimum resource utilization level is 100%. (Note: Having said this, all project resources can never be utilized at their optimum levels throughout a project. Slack time is likely to occur for most resources. If certain resources are utilized at an optimum level of 100% of their available time, the tasks of those resources are generally critical. A project manager must monitor the tasks of these resources more closely.)

variance at completion. The projected variance expected at the end of a project based on the current status of the project; also VAC. VAC is calculated using EAC (estimate at completion) and BAC (budget at completion). VAC is the difference between BAC and EAC. A negative variance should be minimized and a positive variance should be maximized. (Note: Because VAC is based on EAC, VAC can only be a projection because EAC is a projected performance measure which depends on current circumstances in a project. Additionally, EAC calculation involves making assumptions as does VAC.)

variance at completion (time). The projected variance expected at the end of a project based on the current status of the project; also VAC_t. VAC_t is calculated using EAC_t and BAC_t. VAC_t is the difference between BAC_t and EAC_t. A negative variance should be minimized and a positive variance should be maximized. (Note: VAC_t is the time equivalent of VAC and is shown in terms of the number of reporting periods. Because VAC_t is based on EAC_t, VAC_t can only be a projection because EAC_t is a projected performance measure which depends on current circumstances in a project. Additionally, EAC_t calculation involves making assumptions as does VAC_t.)

variances graph. A graph available in the EVM report template that plots schedule and cost variances over time; an important graph/view to monitor for upward trends in the schedule and cost variance performance measures, which indicates that preventive and corrective actions need to be taken. A project manager should ensure that trend lines are always near zero on the Y axis. (Note: Most projects will have variances graph spikes that should be monitored so a negative trend can be reversed. An upward trend in the schedule and cost variance performance measures generally occurs when a project team becomes a bit relaxed. Having an upward trend indicates that a project manager needs to "charge up" the team at the next team meeting so the negative trend can be reversed.)

variances (time) graph. A graph available in the EVM report template that plots SV_t (schedule variance time) over time; a graph that can be used to monitor SV_t trends which could possibly negatively affect a project. A project manager should ensure that a trend line is always near zero on the Y axis. (Note: Most projects will have spikes in the variances (time) graph which should be monitored so a negative trend can be reversed. An upward trend in the SV_t performance measure generally occurs when the project team becomes a bit relaxed. An upward trend indicates that a project manager needs to "charge up" the team during the next team meeting to reverse the negative trend.)

vendor. Any company or group that sells services or products to other businesses; sometimes referred to as sellers. Customers are a company or group that pays for products or services. Every project has a customer/vendor relationship. In some situations, the vendor is the company or the group that executes the project to the benefit of the customer. In this case, the customer is the company or group that pays for execution of a project and benefits from the project execution. In the services industry, vendors provide project execution services and customers seek these project execution services. Even in organizations that execute projects internally, the group within the company that is executing the project is the internal vendor and the group that is seeking the services is the internal customer. In every project, having a customer/vendor relationship that benefits all project stakeholders is always a good practice.

WBS. Work breakdown structure; the basic element of a schedule; a structure which includes all tasks to be performed to complete project deliverables; similar to an organization chart because of its hierarchical organization nature; created from a scope statement; also WBS. For a project to be successful, a WBS must be well defined and all encompassing. To create a WBS, generally the scope statement or the statement of work is broken down into phases, activities, and deliverables. These groupings of phases, the deliverables within the phases, and the activities to be performed for each deliverable then become part of the WBS. Because a WBS is created from the scope statement, the WBS becomes the scope of the project because all activities needed for execution of the project have been included in the WBS. A WBS can be created using Microsoft® Office Project.

WBS templates. A form used to facilitate following a standard or to reduce the time required to prepare a WBS. A WBS is generally similar for the projects executed in a single domain, but WBS templates can be created for each domain, technology, or type of project. Having WBS templates available is essential in all companies for all types of projects being executed by the company. These templates should be reused for new projects. All lessons learned through the execution of projects should be incorporated into WBS templates so that the same mistakes are not repeated by other project managers.

INDEX

A

AC. *See* Actual cost

Actual cost (AC), 19, 24–26
    calculation of, 25
    earned value and, 25, 26
    red and green tasks in, 25
    WBS and, 28

Actual cost of work performed
    (ACWP), 19, 22, 24, 124,
    126

Actual tickets (AT), 150

ACWP. *See* Actual cost of work
    performed

Additional time, schedule
    adjustments, 122

Ad hoc leave time, 143

Adjustments while tracking
    schedule, 122–123

Assigning estimates, 84–87
    Column Definition dialog box,
    85
    Duration column, 85, 86
    steps for, 87
    Work column, 85, 86–87

Assigning priorities, summary
    tasks, 96–98
    lowest-level tasks, 98
    project levels expanded, 97
    steps for, 98

Assigning resources. *See* Resource
    assignment

Assumptions, scenarios and, 68

AT. *See* Actual tickets

B

BAC. *See* Budget at completion

Baselining of schedule, 106–108
    in end-to-end example, 167–168
    Save Baseline option, 106, 107
    steps for, 107–108

BCWP. *See* Budgeted cost of work
    performed

BCWS. *See* Budgeted cost of work
    scheduled

Bottom-up estimation, 12

Budget at completion (BAC)
    calculation of, 52
    cumulative planned value and,
    52
    EAC curve in relation to, 70,
    169
    populated graph, 115, 116
    schedule variance percent and,
    32
    total reporting periods and, 42

Budget at completion (time), 52
    calculation of, 53

Budgeted cost of work performed
    (BCWP), 19, 21, 124, 126

Budgeted cost of work scheduled
    (BCWS), 19, 20, 22

C

Calendar **Options** screen, 78–79

Call tracking. *See* Production
    support

Change, as "order of the day," 63–64

Change Working Time screen, 89

COCOMO (constructive cost
    model), 12

Colored attribute indicators. *See*
    Red/yellow/green indicators

Configuration sheet, 3

Contingency buffer, 63, 166, 178,
    179

Copying resources to tasks, 92, 93

Corrective actions
    early indications of problems
    and, 66
    point of no return and, 47–48,
    49
    schedule/cost variance and, 61
    schedule variance percent and,
    31–32
    SPI and, 34
    variance minimization and,
    176–178
    yellow indicators and, 172

Cost and schedule indexes, 5

Cost-based schedule variance, 171

Cost/effort variance (CV), 43–44,
    139
    calculation of, 44
    formula for, 43

Cost performance indicator (CPI),
    46–48, 134, 137
    calculation of, 47
    constant throughout project, 49,
    50
    formula for, 46
    resource efficiency levels and,
    46–47

Costs of corrections, 66